Bukavu Journal of Economics and Social Sciences

Revue de la faculté de sciences économiques et de gestion

Revue de la faculté de sciences économiques et de gestion

Publiée par l'Université catholique de Bukavu
Revue semestrielle

Conception graphique : Serge Lauret.

5-7 rue de l'École-Polytechnique
75005 Paris
ISBN : 978-2-343-11226-8
EAN : 9782343112268

UNIVERSITÉ CATHOLIQUE DE BUKAVU

Adoption des technologies et bien-être

En collaboration avec la collection « Comptes rendus »

L'HARMATTAN

Présentation **des auteurs**

Raouf Boucekkine, PhD – est professeur des universités (classe exceptionnelle) à l'Université d'Aix-Marseille, et membre senior de l'Institut Universitaire de France. Il est actuellement directeur général de l'Institut d'Etudes Avancées d'Aix-Marseille. Ses thèmes de recherche sont principalement la théorie de la croissance et du développement et la macroéconomie dynamique. Il est éditeur associé de nombreuses revues internationales de premier plan comme Journal of Mathematical Economics, Journal of Economic Dynamics and Control ou Macroeconomic Dynamics.

Bruno de Oliveira Cruz, PhD – holds a B. A. and a Master in economics from the University of Brasilia, and a Master of Arts and PhD from Université Catholique de Louvain. He has worked on. He has been researcher at IPEA since 1996, working in themes on investment and technological adoption, innovation and growth, regional and urban economics. In 2007, he was awarded the best paper in the 4th Urban Research Seminar at the World Bank, in the same year; he was nominated Deputy-director of Regional and Urban Studies at IPEA. Now, he is a Director for Economic and Social Research at CODEPLAN (Brasília, Federal District, Brazil).

Célestin Bucekuderhwa Bashige, PhD – est professeur associé à la faculté des Sciences Economiques et de Gestion et chercheur au Laboratoire d'Economie Appliquée au Développement (LEAD) de l'Université Catholique de Bukavu.

Ses thèmes de recherche embrassent l'économie rurale, la sécurité alimentaire, l'entrepreneuriat, la microéconomie du développement, l'accès aux services publics, l'intégration régionale et le commerce transfrontalier. Il est consultant dans plusieurs institutions et organismes internationaux comme la Banque Mondiale, le PNUD, l'EDF-RD, etc.

Eddy Balemba Kanyurhi, PhD – est professeur associé à la faculté des Sciences Economiques et de gestion de l'Université Catholique de Bukavu (UCB) et chercheur au Laboratoire d'Economie Appliquée au Développement (LEAD). Il détient un doctorat en Sciences Economiques et Gestion de la Warocqué School of Business and Economics de l'Université de Mons (Belgique). Ses recherches portent sur la microfinance, le marketing bancaire et l'entrepreneuriat. Il a récemment publié des articles dans les revues International Journal of Bank Marketing, African Journal of Marketing Management et Bukavu Journal of Economics and Social Sciences. Il mène aussi des consultances pour le compte du Programme des Nations Unies pour le Développement (PNUD), Adam Smith International, EDF-RD, etc.

Deogratias Bugandwa Mungu Akonkwa, PhD – Docteur en Sciences Economiques et de Gestion (Université Libre de Bruxelles) et détenteur d'un Diplôme d'Etudes Approfondies en Gestion (Université Catholique de Louvain), Deogratias Bugandwa Mungu Akonkwa est professeur des cours

de Méthodologies quantitatives en Economie et en Sciences Sociales à l'Université Catholique de Bukavu, à l'Université de Goma et à l'Institut Supérieur d'Informatique et de Gestion (Goma). Actuellement, il assure en même temps les fonctions de Directeur Général Adjoint chargé des Opérations & Finances de la Centrale des Mutuelles d'Epargne et de Crédit du Congo (MECRECO/COOCEC). Ses principaux domaines de recherche sont la Gouvernance des Institutions d'enseignement supérieur, la Gestion de la Qualité, le Marketing Stratégique et la recherche marketing.

Godelive Batano Kusimwa – est assistante à la faculté des Sciences économiques et de gestion de l'Université Catholique de Bukavu (UCB). Elle détient une licence en Economie rurale. Elle participe aux études du Laboratoire d'Economie Appliquée au Développement (LEAD) et du Centre d'Expertise et de Gestion Minière (CEGEMI). Ses recherches portent sur la pauvreté et les inégalités.

Jean-Baptiste Ntagoma Kushinganine, PhD – est professeur à la Faculté des Sciences Economiques et de Gestion de l'Université Catholique de Bukavu (UCB) et chercheur au Laboratoire d'Economie Appliquée au Développement (LEAD). Il est titulaire d'un doctorat en Sciences économiques de l'Université Catholique de Louvain. Ses travaux de recherche embrassent les thèmes suivants : l'intégration régionale, la décentralisation, les finances publiques, la macroéconomie de l'environnement, la politique économique. II a conduit plusieurs projets de recherche dans divers domaines, notamment en économie de l'environnement, économie de développement et sur le commerce transfrontalier. Il a été vice-recteur aux Affaires académiques de l'Université Catholique de Bukavu et consultant dans plusieurs institutions des Nations-Unies, notamment la Banque mondiale et la Commission Economique pour l'Afrique. Il est actuellement membre du Comité National de la Recherche Scientifique, du Comité national LMD en RDC et Conseiller Principal en

charge des Stratégies et Prospectives Economiques au Cabinet du Premier Ministre de la RDC.

Christian Kamala Kaghoma, PhD – Kamala Kaghoma has a Ph.D in Economics from Université de Yaoundé II-Soa with majors in Econometrics and Environmental economics. He is currently a Professeur Associé and the Dean of the faculty of Economics and Management of the Université Catholique de Bukavu (UCB) where he has been teaching for more than a decade. Kamala's main areas of research include Public Economics, Environmental Economics, Human resources Economics, Applied Macroeconomics, Welfare Economics, Applied econometrics, Development microeconomics and research methodology. His work focuses on child welfare related to water and sanitation access, poverty dynamics, social mobility and intergenerational (multidimensional) welfare transmission with emphasis on African countries. He is currently working on youth employment, entrepreneurship and internal migration in the Democra/c Republic of the Congo (DRC), his country. Mr. Kamala Kaghoma has conducted several field researches and surveys in DRC and has a broad consultancy experience in Africa.

Nene Morisho Mwana Biningo, PhD – holds a PhD in Institutional Economics from the University of Bayreuth in Germany. He also holds two masters degrees in Macroeconomics and Management of Development Projects (Development Studies). He is an Associate Professor at the Catholic University of Bukavu (UCB) where he teaches Macroeconomics and Public Finances. His fields of interest are Cross border trade, Regional Economic Integration and Institutions and growth.

Martin Doevenspeck, PhD – Professor of Geographical Conflict Research at the University of Bayreuth, Germany. His research focuses on violent conflict and the political geography of climate change and risk in West and Central Africa.

Table des matières

93,87
41,85
62,45
13,65
26,45
27,98
13,65
26,45
27,98
36,46
20,24
52,45
46,47
41,85
8,65 %
4,65 %
3,98 %
8,46 %
7,24 %
9,45 %
6,47 %
5,87 %

• • •

Technological progress and investment

A non-technical survey

Raouf BOUCEKKINE et Bruno de Oliveira CRUZ*

RÉSUMÉ/ABSTRACT

This paper presents a non-technical overview of the recent investment literature with a special emphasis on the connection between technological progress and the investment decision. First of all, we acknowledge that some dramatic advances have been made in the 1990s in understanding and modelling non-convex capital adjustment schemes and irreversibility. Nonetheless, this new literature has not always satisfactorily accounted for the investment-specific (or embodied) nature of technical progress. We argue that the recent technological trends towards more embodiment have had a heavy impact on the way the investment decision is taken and is to be taken. This is turn should imply the reconsideration of many empirical results, and a more careful modelling strategy taking into account the price variables and scrupulously choosing the most appropriate level of (dis)aggregation.

Keywords: Investment, Technological progress, Non-convex adjustment, irreversibility, Embodiment.

Journal of Economic Literature: E22, E32, O40.

1. Introduction

"Economic Theory can give reasonably good account of how the level of investment influences effective demand and employment. If only we knew more about the determinants of investment! But unfortunately, our knowledge in this direction is still very meager. One might well ask, what is wrong with the theory of investment? Or perhaps, what is wrong

* Bruno Cruz acknowledges the financial support of CAPES Foudation (Brazil) for this research.

with the subject matter itself! For one thing, this variable - the pivot of modern macroeconomics- has apparently lived a somewhat nomadic life among the various chapters of economic theory. Perhaps it has not stayed long enough in any one place. Perhaps it has been ill-treated" (Haavelmo, T. (1960) A Study in the Theory of Investment, pp.3)

With this astonishing paragraph, Haavelmo (1960) begins his famous book A Study in the Theory estment Theory in the early 1960s. Many surveys on the subject have appeared since then (for instance, Jorgenson, 1963; Chirinko, 1993); theory has made an incredible step towards a more comprehensible understanding of this important variable. Yet in 2000, Caballero, one of the most important researchers in the field, opened his talk "Aggregate Investment: Lessons from the Previous Millennium" with the following statement:

"But while we all may agree on the importance of investment for a nation's economic health, our understanding of its determinants, both at the microeconomic as well as the macroeconomic level, has remained limited. The empirical investment literature has been nearly merciless in evaluating investment theories." (Caballero, R. 2000 American Economic Association Session. In Memoriam: Robert Eisner, pp 1-2).

This pessimistic view about the evolution of our knowledge about investment might be influenced by the fact that researchers have been quite unsuccessful in empirically forecasting this component of aggregate demand. One can observe that heuristic models, such as accelerator models, have shown to be empirically better adjusted than models based on micro-foundations. The apparent superiority of heuristic models should not lead us to forget about price variables and Tobin's "q" when talking about investment. First of all, the superiority of estimated accelerator models, for example, does not mean that decision is made and how this decision is oriented by economic policy; there is not a theory behind the accelerator, it's just a technique that apparently works in some circumstances and that has its own problems (see Oliner, Rudebusch and Sichel, 1995, for example). Second, the bad empirical performances of optimal control-based investment models can be also partially attributed to the way they are tested in practice. For example, the way the rate of capital depreciation is traditionally treated in econometric applications is highly questionable, especially during the 1990s, as it does not accurately capture the pace at which capital goods actually become obsolete.

It seems therefore overwhelmingly clear that the traditional user cost and Tobin's q models are too much "stylized" to serve as universal and unquestionable models of both microeconomic and aggregate investment. There is an urgent need to profoundly study and document how the investment decision is effectively taken in real life over a wide variety of microeconomic cases. In particular, a much closer inspection into how the capital adjustment processes actually take place is required, especially in connection with the pace of technological progress. This calls for two major focuses:

a. In the traditional optimal control theory developed (see for instance Chirinko (1993)), the capital adjustment issue is settled by setting a convex adjustment function, usually a quadratic function for tractability. But is adjustment gradual in real life? The answer is definitely no. It is now known that investment at the firm level is lumpy and infrequent (Doms and Dunne, 1998), and that these two characteristics are unlikely to completely disappear in the aggregate (Cooper, Haltiwanger and Power, 1999). Doms and Dunne worked on the investment patterns of 12 000 plants in US manufacturing over the interval 1972-1989. For each firm, they constructed a series of the proportion of the total equipment investment of the firm. It turns out that the largest investment period accounts on average for more than 25 percent of the 17 year of investment. Moreover, more than half of the firms exhibit a capital growth of about 50 percent in a single year. Also, the second largest investment spike often comes next to the largest investment, which suggest that the two biggest spikes correspond to a single investment episode. Finally, Doms and Dunne studied the correlation between aggregate investment (summing up the investments done by all the establishments of their sample) and an index of microeconomic investments and showed that it is actually very high.

b. Recent empirical studies confirm that the Information and Communication Technologies (ICT hereafter) burst in the 1990s has considerably distorted the investment behavior at all levels: The associated dramatic decrease in the relative price of capital during the 1990s has rehabilitated price variables as a major determinant of investment decisions (see for instance Tevlin and Whelan, 2003). This has led some authors like Whelan (2002) to advocate another empirical appraisal of the investment decision, based on a two-sector accounting benchmark model in order to reflect the pace of the relative price of capital and the very fast depreciation of an increasingly large fraction of the capital stock. At the same time, another complementary view of investment emerged, resurgence of the vintage capital theory of the sixties: investment and technological innovations are not “separated”, investment is the unique vehicle of innovations decisions, as Greenwood and Jovanovic (2001) observe:

"In reality, advances in technology tend to be embodied in the latest vintages of capital. This means that new capital is better than old capital, not just because machines suffer wear and tear as they age, but also because new capital is better than the old capital was when the latter was new. It also means that there can be no technological progress without investment" (pp. 179-180, Italics ours).

In this paper, we carefully review the state of art of the literature investment regarding these two fundamental aspects. We start by a non-technical discussion of the "new" investment theories which have recently introduced non-convex adjustment costs and irreversibility in the heart of investment theory (Section II). We first notice that these theories have considerably improved our understanding of how the investment decision is taken both at the plant and the aggregate levels. However, we also observe that, with some very few exceptions, the modelling of technological progress in such theories is not markedly different from traditional "exogenous" modeling in the neoclassical model; the whole action inherent in these theories come from non-convex adjustment and other ingredients like irreversibility. Nonetheless as outlined just above, there are plenty of microeconomic and macroeconomic studies pointing at a significant change in the composition of technological progress after the 60s, and showing that embodiment should be seriously accounted for, especially in the computer era. We therefore end the survey with a detailed non-technical exposition on modelling embodiment both at the micro and macro level, and on the methodological consequences of the information technologies boom in the 1990s (Section III).

2. Characterization of microeconomic adjustment

As we have mentioned in the introduction, there is a compelling evidence that investment patterns at least at the plant level are far from gradual, which goes at odds with the optimal control investment model with convex adjustment costs. How could the economic theory deal with this clear inconsistency problem? We shall briefly review the recent stream of economic literature devoted to this fundamental issue. We start with the basic non-convex adjustment costs story, more sophisticated concepts will be treated along the way.

2.1. Non-convex capital adjustment costs

This issue is very comprehensively treated by Caballero (1999), among others. Following this author, assume that a given firm has an optimal capital stock, K^*, which depends on the interest rate and on any profitability (exogenous) variable (possibly technological innovations). The crucial thing is the specification of the adjustment costs. If one aims at generating infrequent and lumpy investment patterns at the optimum, he should care about the functional form to assign to these costs. The traditional simple convex form is inadequate. In order to generate infrequent investment, the adjustment costs function should be chosen such that it increases sharply around the point of no adjustment.

As mentioned by Caballero, a cost proportional to the size of the needed adjustment is enough. Now, this specification gives infrequency, but not lumpiness. To get the latter characteristic, there must be an advantage in bunching investment, and this can be achieved if for example adjustment requires a fixed cost. For a positive investment *I*, the associated adjustment cost is consequently: $c_f + c_v I$ where c_f and c_v are two positive constants. A similar adjustment costs function has to be set in case of disinvestment (when $I < 0$), including a positive fixed cost of disinvestment. We are in a typical situation where the adjustment technology exhibits **increasing returns**. For the relative importance of adjustment costs to be constant over time, the latter term is usually multiplied by K^*.

How does the optimization model perform with this modified adjustment costs function? And how does the obtained demand for capital goods look like, in particular in relation with technical innovations? The main properties of the optimization problems are stated in Caballero (1999), section 3. The following points can be highlighted:

1. In such a model, there is room for inaction. This a crucial departure from the standard models with quadratic adjustment costs. In such models, capital accumulation and investment paths are smooth in time, so there is no infrequent or lumpy investment episode. In the alternative model, things are very different. The intuitive reasoning behind is the following[1]. Call $K\frac{K}{K^*}$, a measure of capital imbalance. Assume that the actual capital imbalance is near the point which maximizes the value of the firm (roughly speaking the discounted sum of the present and (expected) future profits of the firm). Then, the firm may not have any incentive to pursue the adjustment because of the incurred adjustment costs. This is specially true for small adjustments because of the fixed costs. Hence, the firm may perfectly choose to be inactive in such a case. Indeed, it is possible to prove rigorously that there exists a non-empty range of inaction in the space of *Z*. More concretely, there exists a target point *L* such that there is no investment for $Z > L$, and a target point *U* such that there is no disinvestment for $Z < U$. Which ultimately means that there exists a range of inaction (*L*, *U*). Infrequency and lumpiness can therefore be generated within this alternative framework.

2. Is the q-theory robust to such a "realistic" specification of adjustment costs? Recall that in the basic optimization setting, we get the following relationship between investment and (marginal) q : $q=1+C'(I)$, when the unit price of capital is equal to 1 ($s = 1$). In the quadratic case, *ie.* when $C(I)=bI^2$, where $b > 0$, we get a linear relationship between q and *I*. In the general convex case, we get an implicit monotonic functional

1. The reader interested in the exact mathematical solution can _nd all the technicalities in Caballero (1999). The technique makes use of dynamic programming in continuous time with the associated optimality principle.

relation between q and $I : I = \varphi(q)$. To each value of q corresponds a single investment amount. Is this functional relationship preserved in the case of adjustment costs with increasing returns? The answer is no as demonstrated by Caballero and Leahy (1996). In effect, the relationship between marginal q and Z, the capital imbalance, is not functional over the Z space in that the same value of q is associated with different investment values. And in the region of the Z space where this relationship is functional, it is highly nonlinear. So in the very best case, the q-theory only holds "locally" but the induced functional relationship between q and I is by no way linear.

This suggests two main points. First of all, the q-theory is typically a non-robust theory. Indeed, there exists a huge literature on this particular point. Many authors have studied the implications of different specifications of the adjustment costs departing from the initial quadratic formulation. Some have removed the fixed costs; others have added a strictly convex term to the adjustment functions. In some contributions, the monotonic relationship between q and investment is recovered but at the cost of less realistic generated investment patterns, notably in terms of lumpiness (as in the very well-known Abel and Eberly's 1994 paper). Because of these robustness problems, the failures registered in its econometric implementation are not surprising at all. Second, a more favorable to the q-theory, these failures may be simply due to the use of linear regressions, as the "true" relationship between q and capital is probably highly nonlinear.

3. How do technological innovations enter this new investment set-up? Actually, these new microeconomically founded adjustment theories enrich in a considerable way the discussion on the effects of technological innovations (or any other external shock) on the demand for equipment. In the standard optimal control theory, there is no range for inaction. In the case of a technological improvement (raising the productivity of capital goods for example), q increases since it is a measure of the value to the firm of an additional unit of (new) equipment. As q goes up, investment is systematically stimulated, because q is monotonically related to I via the investment equation, $q = 1 + C'(I)$, under the strict convexity of the adjustment costs function. When a range of inaction (optimally) arises, a technical innovation does not necessarily trigger an investment boom[1].

Let us have a closer look at this specific point. A careful reading of Caballero and Engel (1999) allows to notice that technological progress, purely disembodied in this theory, exclusively operates through the optimal capital stock, K^*, thus through the imbalance ratio Z. Indeed, neither the threshold, L nor the threshold U

1. This may be true even in the absence of fixed costs. See Abel and Eberly (1994).

depends on technological progress: In Caballero and Engel (1999), both are function of the fraction of profits foregone due to capital stock adjustment, which is ultimately assumed to be randomly distributed[1]. Thus, a technological improvement has essentially the virtue of raising the optimal capital stock, K^*, which for given K, lowers the capital imbalance Z since $Z = \frac{K}{K^*}$. Suppose that initially Z is in the range of inaction *(L,U)*. A small technological shock is unlikely to lower Z at a value below the threshold L. For investment to occur, *ie.* for Z to be shifted below L, the magnitude of the technological improvement should be big enough. This is one the reasons why technological diffusion is not instantaneous. Investment involves some non-negligible adjustment costs which makes it optimal sometimes to not act, to not invest. In such a case, the institutions have a role to play, and economic policy crucially matters. For example, when the technological improvement is not enough big to encourage investment, a further decrease in the interest rate (or any other component of the user cost of capital) may help the diffusion (by increasing $K^{\square}$ and then by lowering even more the capital imbalance Z).

Uncertainty and irreversibility are other factors that call for inaction and delayed adoption of innovative tools, as it is explained in the next sub-section.

1. See page 8 of the article by Caballero and Engel (1999).

2. 2. *Irreversibility and uncertainty*

The literature relating investment and uncertainty has generated two different conclusions. In the one hand, the presence of constant returns to scale and symmetric adjustment costs have led to the conclusion that uncertainty increases the value of investment (see for instance Hartman, 1972, and Abel, 1983 and 1985)). In this set-up, the marginal value of capital is a convex function of the stochastic process: Jensen's inequality thus implies a higher demand for investment. On the order hand, the introduction of irreversibility gives rise to another different mechanism (Dixit and Pindyck, 1994, and Pindyck, 1988). Irreversibility of investment amounts to saying that undertaking investment projects results in some unrecoverable initial costs, the so-called sunk costs. Uncertainty on future benefits and costs of investment projects makes the resulting investment problem trickier. If we assume with Dixit and Pindyck that if the investment project is not undertaken today, the firms retain the option of undertaking the project tomorrow, there is a clear value of waiting: the firms have always the possibility to postpone investment tomorrow in order to learn more about present and future project payoffs. This value of waiting, this option of waiting, is the main characteristic of the above mentioned theories, and it has some crucial implications in terms of investment patterns (lumpiness, infrequency, as observed in micro data) and economic policy. We shall summarize the related stream of literature in the few following points.

1. As argued in Chirinko (1996), \...In the traditional optimal control model *àla* Jorgenson, investment is reversible because well-functioning secondary markets exist or the rate at which firms wish to reduce the capital stock is less than the rate of depreciation, *ie.* gross investment is always positive. Moreover, in the traditional approach, there is no room for flexible timing in investment: Either the firms invest *(I>o)* or they don't, and in the latter case, it is implicitly assumed that the investment opportunity lost will never be recovered. The optimal investment rule giving the optimal capital stock is basically: Investment is undertaken if and only if the (expected) marginal profitability of capital, *MPK*, is bigger than a user cost of capital, which includes the interest rate (the discounting rate), the depreciation rate of capital, and the (expected) rate of change of the acquisition price of capital. This is exactly what may happen if the firm, initially at equilibrium, is affected by a positive technical innovation; the curve is likely to be shifted upward, so that investment takes place. In Dixit-Pyndick's models, the rule is not that simple. There is an option of waiting. Even if a technical innovation unambiguously shifts upward *MPK*, uncertainty, irreversibility plus time flexibility may induce the firm to wait, and not react to the innovation by investing, that is the threshold value of expected *MPK* above which the firm invests, is a priori significantly bigger than the typical user cost or discounting rate threshold values encountered in the traditional theory. To these typical terms, one has to add the value of waiting, which is in general a function of a measure of uncertainty, typically the variance of a stochastic price or technological variables, and of the actual levels of the latter variables, including the capital depreciation rate[1].

It follows that investment patterns are potentially less smooth when one has to account for irreversibility under uncertainty. As in the models with non-convex adjustment costs seen above, there is room for inaction: provided the flexibility of the investment decision timing, the firms can decide to not act for a while since there is a value of waiting, which generates the infrequency characteristic.

What are the theoretical implications of this approach as to investment patterns? As we have just said, irreversibility plus uncertainty and time flexibility implies that equipment purchases occur only in spurts. To be precise, investment occurs if the (expected) profitability of marginal investment is enough high to compensate the cost of capital and the value of waiting. This is likely to happen in very good times (for example, when the demand for

1. The reader interested in the exact formula of the value of waiting can find the necessary material in Pindyck (1988).

the goods produced by the firms is very high using historical standards, as in Pindyck, 1988). But this is unlikely to happen for any good draw in the distribution of the stochastic environment. Typically the firms increase their productive capacity only periodically. These models usually have marginal increment, and are unable to generate lumpiness.

There is a much more important new direction in the irreversibility literature with respect to the traditional non-convex adjustment costs models: The role of the rate of utilization of capital. Allow the firms to choose this rate in presence of uncertainty, irreversibility and time flexibility, and forget about capital depreciation. The typical outcome is the following. In good times, there is little doubt that the optimal decision should be to fully utilize the productive capacity. In very good times, as we have just mentioned above, the firms additionally increase their capital stock. What happens in bad times? This crucial question is addressed in Dixit and Pindyck (1994), and before by Pindyck (1988) in a basic formal setting. In bad times, since investment is irreversible and capital depreciation is assumed to be zero, the capital stock held does not move. This inertia in the capital stock is coupled with a non-constant optimal utilization rate. An adverse shock need not reduce this rate systematically. For the rate of utilization to fall, the adverse (demand and/or technological) shock should be of a very large magnitude. For moderate negative shocks, full utilization (and zero investment) is optimal. The rate of capacity utilization plays therefore a central role in shaping investment patterns when irreversibility and uncertainty matters, and this should be of interest for practitioners seeking for the best investment decision in such a context. Typical wisdom from this approach is that firms must reuse all the units, that's increase their rate of capacity utilization if possible, before investing. Certainly, this behavior is not always corroborated by the empirical evidence. In certain cases, firms do invest even if they have not reached full capacity, which goes at odds with one of the main implications of the 1988 Pindyck's seminal work. This kind of behavior is highlighted in several micro-econometric studies (see for example Licandro *et al.* (2005) on Spanish data among many other firm level studies). Cruz and Pommeret (2010) show that accounting for investment-specific technological progress (via vintage capital modelling) is enough to explain this striking finding. Indeed, if investment is the exclusive vehicle of technological innovations and if a decisive technological upgrading is taking place, the decision to invest (often coupled with replacement of old and less productive equipment) is likely to be less intimately related to the rate of utilization control.

We shall insist on the necessity to account for this feature of technological progress (that's embodiment) in Section III, especially in connection with the ICT burst.

The q-theory is generally non-robust to extensions of the basic model incorporating non-convex adjustment costs. When the benchmark model is extended to include uncertainty, irreversibility and flexibility in timing, then this non-robustness is much less clear, as it is brilliantly explained by Dixit and Pindyck in their book[1]. True, there is no monotonic relationship between q and investment over the whole space of capital imbalance *Z*. But, in contrast to the model with non-convex adjustment costs where non-monotonicity may show up locally in the -space, the picture is simpler here: The *Z* space is divided in three regions where investment is respectively rising, falling or constant with increases in q. In other terms, there exist three distinct regimes but none shows up a non-monotonic relationship between q and investment. This leads many theorists, following Dixit and Pindyck, to argue that accounting for irreversibility and uncertainty does not only preserve the basic q-theory but it also allows to remedy the empirical failures of this theory. That is the usual tests do not consider the possible existence of a multiple regime *(q,I)* relationship. Their failure may come from this omission. While this claim is so far unproven, as correctly pointed out by Chirinko (1996), it gives an early idea about the complexity of the empirical debate surrounding the concepts of irreversibility, uncertainty and non-convex adjustment costs. The next sub-section addresses very briefly this issue, among others.

1. The reader can find a complete proof of these claims in the quoted book. These properties are mathematically quite intuitive: The presence of a fixed cost has a much more damaging effect on the concavity of the value functions of the firms, arising in the considered dynamic programming problems.

2.3. *Some remarks on the "new" investment theories*

Some crucial issues remain to be addressed. First of all, if it is widely admitted that non-convex adjustment costs and/or irreversibility are much more consistent with observed investment behavior at the plant level that the Jorgenson neoclassical model, it is crucial to study whether aggregation will not "kill" them. In other terms, it is important to assert neatly that non-convex adjustment costs and/or irreversibility have a first-order impact in explaining aggregate investment patterns. Second, it is important to examine if these new theories are not leaving in the dark, some crucial aspects of the investment decision; we shall argue in this respect that embodied technical progress, and more generally the vintage composition of the capital stock, are important but still insufficiently dealt with in these new theories.

1. With either non-convex adjustment costs or irreversibility, the investment patterns seem to be consistent with the empirical characteristics of micro adjustment as documented by Doms and Dunne (1998), namely infrequency and lumpiness. But as mentioned by Caballero (1999), the empirical corroboration of these simple adjustment rules is far from easy, as"...firms respond differently to similar imbalances over time and across firms". This leads Caballero and Engel (1999) to construct a stochastic version of the model with non-convex adjustment costs, where the regions of inaction and adjustment are not deterministically set, the basic idea being that large imbalances are more likely to induce investment. A simple way to randomize the latter model is to assume that the fixed cost variable is stochastic. Then, the analysis relies on the so-called hazard functions, *H(Z)*, which describe the probability to adjust when capital imbalance (or any other convenient function of it) is equal to *Z*.

2. In their celebrated 1999 paper, Caballero and Engel provide the necessary material to estimate these hazard functions and more importantly, to aggregate them. For a given imbalance *Z*, it is demonstrated that the expected investment by any firm can be written as basically the product of the adjustment to be done and the probability for the firm to undertake it (namely *H(Z)*). Then aggregation follows in two steps. Provided a large number of firms exist in the sample (which is the case in the empirical studies conducted on US micro data), so that the law of large numbers prevails, one can first take average investment over the establishments of the sample having approximately the same capital imbalance *Z*, as an estimate of expected investment (conditional to the level of imbalance). Then, using the above mentioned simple expression of expected investment in terms of the hazard function, one can precisely estimate the latter function. The second step simply requires averaging across all *Z*.

3. The results obtained by Caballero, Engel and Haltiwanger (1995) (corroborated by further empirical studies) seem to confirm the importance of non-convexities and, incidentally of irreversibility, both at the micro and aggregate levels. The main result is that the hazard functions are clearly increasing consistently with the «new» investment theories emphasizing the role of non-convexities and irreversibility. In particular, expected investment rises more that proportionally with capital imbalance. The linear specifications, consistent with the traditional formulations of the user cost and Tobin's q-theories, rather predict constant hazard functions, *ie.* the probability to adjust is the same whatever is the level of capital imbalance. The same conclusion is made at the aggregate level. Moreover, the estimated hazard functions are shown to be very low

for negative adjustment, suggesting irreversibility.

4. Despite this plausible evidences, more empirical work should be done, particularly in order to corroborate the irreversibility hypothesis. It is out of question that irreversibility matters in some circumstances. But it is also true that secondary markets exist for many capital goods, and this is likely to alleviate the effect of the irreversibility constraint. According to Chirinko (1996), 45% of nonresidential equipment purchases in 1993 were for information processing and related equipment, and secondary markets exist for such capital goods. Such markets plausibly exist for other capital goods like transportation and related equipment (20% of 1993 nonresidential equipment purchases) or tractors and agricultural and construction machinery (5%). Naturally, to quantify precisely the extent of irreversibility, it is necessary to go a step further and estimate the gap between the acquisition and resale prices. This is still not systematically done. Undoubtedly, Caballero's work with Engel, Bertola and Haltiwanger is fundamental in that it shows theoretically and empirically how accounting for non-convexities and irreversibility can be crucial in understanding investment behavior at the firm level. However, an accurate quantification of the real effects of both is not easy to produce, and Chirinko's objection is a good illustration of the reasonable doubts one can have about the recent investment theories.

5. Another questionable aspect of most of the models belonging to this literature stream is its treatment of technological progress. Technological choices affect capital accumulation exactly as in the early neoclassical theories, exclusively through the optimal stock of capital. However, it is now widely admitted that investing is also a technology choice because most innovations are embodied in capital goods. New capital goods are therefore likely to be more productive than old capital goods, and the age (or vintage) composition of the capital stock at all levels is potentially an important variable driving investment. This was recently pointed out in a seminal paper by Cooper, Haltiwanger and Power (1999). In contrast to Caballero and Engel, a new machine is more productive because of embodied technical change. Therefore, the age distribution of the capital stock does matter. Indeed, the hazard functions do no longer depend on the imbalance variable Z as in Caballero and Engel, but on the age of the capital stock and aggregate productivity. Cooper and his co-authors clearly show that the hazard functions are increasing with the age of the capital stock, which could be interpreted as a strong evidence in support of the role of embodiment in the investment decision. Moreover, ignoring the cross-sectional age distribution of capital is shown to yield predictable and non-negligible

errors in forecasting changes in aggregate investment after large swings in aggregate investment. In the next section, we provide a further empirical evidence in favor of the embodiment hypothesis. We shall review afterwards the new (rather) literature satisfactorily placing embodiment and vintage effects at the heart of investment and growth theory, specially after the rise of information and communication technologies in the 90s.

3. Vintage capital, embodied technical change and the 90's burst in ICT investment

As we have repeatedly mentioned before, technological progress is traditionally treated as part of the environment surrounding the firms just like government or weather. In such a context, a capital subsidy produces the same investment stimulus as an innovation boosting the marginal profitability of capital. The nonconvexities and irreversibility theories seen just above enrich considerably the analysis by showing that such fiscal and technical positive shocks are not necessarily followed by a rise in investment, as the simple (quasi-linear) traditional theories predict. But these new theories do not treat technological innovations in a very innovative way indeed, with the exception of Cooper, Haltiwanger and Power (1999).

The recent burst in ICT investment and its tremendous impact on the aggregate economy makes it necessary to think differently about how new technologies are brought into the market. In this specific case, it is clear that investment is the unique way to take advantage of the new technologies. It turns out that this is also the case for many other capital goods. When a firm acquires a machine, it also typically acquires a technology. Is it relevant to make the difference between embodied and disembodied technological progress? Is the embodiment characteristic so important to account for? The answer is nowadays clear: yes. It has been shown that around two thirds of the economic growth of the US economy over the period 1950-1990 is due to embodied technological progress (Greenwood, Hercowitz and Krusell, 1997). Since embodied technical progress has some specific implications at both the micro and macro level, it appears worthwhile to develop new approaches to investment, technological progress and growth. We summarize the main ideas of this recent research line in the following points. More details, including implications outside investment theory, can be found in Boucekkine *et al.* (2011).

3.1. The basic framework

There are basically two alternative strategies to model embodiment. The first one is extremely simple. It is mainly based on the concept of the relative price of capital, but it does not seem to be sufficiently comprehensive to capture all the implications of embodiment at the micro level. The second one exploits explicitly a vintage structure and as such, it is more suitable to deal with investment behavior at the plant level.

1. The main idea underlying the first strategy is the following: Embodied technical progress shows up specifically in the declining pattern of the relative price of capital, the price of capital goods in terms of consumption goods. This trend is impressive in the case of computers (an average decline rate of about 20% per year from 1990 to 1996 in the USA) but it is also observable in the aggregate, when one computes the evolution of a price index of capital in terms of a price index of consumption goods. And it traces back probably to the mid-seventies after the first oil shock.

Recall that the optimal capital accumulation rule in the basic Jorgenson model is

$$pMPK=s(\delta+r-\frac{s'}{s})$$

with p the output price, s the price of capital, δ the capital depreciation rate and r the interest rate. Assume for sake of simplicity that $p=1$, so that s actually measures the relative price of capital. An improvement in the disembodied component of technological progress propagates directly via MPK. An acceleration in the rate of embodied technical change is basically measured by a drop in s, namely by $\frac{s'}{s}$ Note that such a drop implies that the resale price is lower than the acquisition price of the capital goods, which tends to increase the user cost of capital. This features the famous obsolescence mechanism at work when technological progress is embodied, which was studied in details by Solow in 1960, and more recently in an optimal control set-up by Boucekkine, del Rio and Licandro (2003).

Will a drop in the relative price of capital stimulate equipment purchases, and through which channels if so? A priori, investment reaction is ambiguous since the user cost of capital, $c=s(\delta+r-\frac{s'}{s})$ is affected by two opposite effects: a negative level effect (via the first term s) and the positive effect arising from the obsolescence costs (the term $\frac{s'}{s}<0$). However, a truly rapid acceleration of the rate of decline of the relative price of capital should lower the user cost capital in the short run, inducing a massive accumulation of capital, as experienced by the US economy during the ICT boom episode. This is precisely the famous capital deepening engine of investment and growth, to which many analysts (notably, Gordon, 1999) attribute the impressive performances of the US economy during this episode. There is another and much more powerful reason to believe that an acceleration in the rate of embodied technical change can boost equipment purchases: One may think that the acquisition of more efficient and reliable machines will end up shifting upward the MPK curve[1]. This

1. Recall that an acceleration in disembodied technical progress yields directly this shift.

modernization channel is at the heart of the current debate on the viability of the New Economy (see Gordon, 1999, again, and Boucekkine, del Rio and Licandro, 2003 and 2005).

To conclude, one should keep the idea that the (very) rapid decline in the relative price of capital should undeniably matter significantly in shaping the investment decision, as the recent ICT boom in the US indicates. Hence, in contrast to the recurrent finding in the empirical investment literature according to which prices do not matter, one should expect to identify a much tighter relationship between the cost of capital and equipment purchases from the last decade as the relative price of computers sharply decreases, and ICT equipment purchases as a fraction of total capital expenditures markedly go up.

2. In the previous set-up, obsolescence operates through the loss in value of a fraction of the installed capital stock as the new capital goods embody the latest technological advances and are likely to be much more productive. One may legitimately think that a natural outcome of obsolescence is the scrappage of the oldest and least efficient machines. Curiously this does not happen in the previous set-up. All the capital goods are held for ever though the amount of labor assigned to a given vintage of capital tends to zero as times passes[1].Overall in such models, the vintage structure is not very active. Since the early 90's, many models have been proposed to get rid of this defect. Naturally the vintage approach is analytically much more demanding since capital is no longer homogenous in such an approach. A very simple description of a typical economic vintage model can be given to present the ideas. The technical details can be found in Malcomson (1975), Van Hilten (1991), Boucekkine, Germain and Licandro (1997), and Boucekkine, del Rio and Licandro (1999).

The vintage capital structure is introduced as follows. At any date, different vintages of capital coexist. Call v the vintage index: At t, typically the vintage index goes from $t-T(t)$ to t, where $T(t)$ is age of the oldest equipment still in use at t. Assume that a unit of capital of vintage increases output at t by $y(v,t)$ with the corresponding operation cost $c(v,t)$ at t. If $J(t)$ is the expected lifetime of the new capital goods at t, then the expected discounted profits from purchasing a unit of new equipment at t is:

$$\int_t^{t+J(t)} (y(t,\tau)-c(t,\tau))e^{-r(\tau-t)}\, d\tau$$

where r is the interest rate (assumed constant for sake of simplicity). Under perfect foresight, namely in the absence of any uncertainty, we have additionally the identity $J(t)=T(t+J(t))$. Embodied technical progress can be modelled by

1. This is essentially what happens in the Solow vintage capital model (1960), underlying the model seen just above.

assuming that new vintages either are less costly to operate, that is $c(v,t)>c(vv,t)$ if and only if , or more productive, if and only if $v<vv$, or both. The optimality condition for a strictly positive and finite investment in new equipment to occur equalizes the expected discounted profit given just above and the acquisition price of this new equipment. Assume that $s=1$ at t, then the optimality condition is simply:

$$\int_t^{t+J(t)}(y(t,\tau)-c(t,\tau))e^{-r(\tau-t)}\,d\tau = 1$$

A typical case studied in the economic literature is the case of operating cost saving technical progress. Whatever is the vintage index, the increment in output is the same but operating a new vintage costs less either in terms of labor or energy for example. In such a case and under further mathematical conditions on the cost function, one can prove that the optimal lifetime of machines is constant over time: $T(t)=J(t)=T, \forall t$, where t is a well specified constant[1].That is, the optimal scrapping time is constant over time, a result well known in the management literature as the Terborgh-Smith property (see Malcomson, 1975). The capital goods produced and acquired at t get obsolete at $t+T^*$, and are scrapped and replaced (ideally) by the vintages produced at $t+T^*$. In such a case, replacement investment (to be differentiated from the investment behavior consisting in augmenting the capacity of a firm, studied in the previous sections) is likely to be periodic, reproducing the infrequency and lumpiness characteristics of investment at the plant level.

Therefore, two main implications can be drawn from the canonical vintage model described above. First of all, it is possible to build a vintage theory comprehensive enough to understand how and when a firm decides to throw out a machine and to replace it by a more recent one. In particular, it is possible to identify the main determinants of the lifetime of capital goods and the corresponding average age of capital in the aggregate. A simple illustration helps understanding why the theory is so comfortable in this respect. Consider an increase in the interest rate. Such a shock decreases the left hand side of the optimality condition written above while the right hand side is constant. The optimal lifetime $J(t)$ should rise to re-establish equality. So an increase in the interest rate delays the scrapping of old machines, which is by no way surprising since a rise in r augments the opportunity cost of investing and requires a longer utilization of the machines to compensate this extra cost. Using simple analytical tools, one could indeed derive an accurate characterization of the optimal age distribution of machines mainly in terms of the parameters of the cost and production functions, which

1. The reader interested in the way the constant is computed can find the needed mathematics in Van Hilten (1991), and Boucekkine, Germain and Licandro (1997).

may be empirically tested[1].

Second, we have also mentioned that the same set-up allows for a deep theoretical inspection into how replacement investment is performed by the firms. It turns out that since in many simple but reasonable cases, the optimal scrapping time is constant, this theory produces the stylized facts of investment at the plant level, as documented by Doms and Dunne, infrequency and lumpiness[2].

3.2. Macroeconomic implications: Embodied technological change and the growth process

The macroeconomic implications can be summarized in three points.

1. Can we talk about a macroeconomic vintage effect? It is not a simple question. The results stated just above are valid at a firm level. Each firm decides about its optimal replacement policy given the technological trends. To rigorously assess the relevance of this theory at the macro level, one should resort to aggregation. There is a much more direct way to detect a vintage effect. According to vintage models, the new generations of capital are more efficient and more productive. Hence, it is in principle worthwhile to shorten the lifetime of machines so as to take advantage of the most recent technological advances. If this is true, one may detect a very significant negative correlation between the average age of capital in the considered sample of firms (or even at the macro-economy) and the growth rate of aggregate output. This is referred to as the vintage effect in the macroeconomic literature. A theoretical foundation for this effect in an optimal control set-up can be found in Boucekkine *et al.* (1998). An early empirical assessment of it has been provided by Wolff (1996) on the US economy. According to Wolff, the vintage effect is strongly effective in the US economy. A more recent assessment on the vintage effect on TFP growth, again on US data, has been provided by Gittleman *et al.* (2006). The authors show that the rigorous accounting of the vintage effect does prompt an upward correction of measured productivity growth in times of an aging stock of capital. This ultimately points at an important point: Treating the capital stock as an homogenous block without accounting rigorously for its age distribution may be highly misleading in interpreting and quantitatively characterizing GDP and TFP growth experience of a country.

2. Concerning the aggregation of

1. Another determinant of capital lifetime, not directly related to embodiment, but empirically relevant is capital maintenance, which has broad micro and macroeconomic implications on investment, see Albonico et al. (2014). It's not problematic to introduce such an important ingredient in vintage capital settings as demonstrated by Saglam and Veliov (2008) and Boucekkine et al. (2010).

2. Another determinant of capital lifetime, not directly related to embodiment, but empirically relevant is capital maintenance, which has broad micro and macroeconomic implications on investment, see Albonico et al. (2014). It's not problematic to introduce such an important ingredient in vintage capital settings as demonstrated by Saglam and Veliov (2008) and Boucekkine *et al.* (2010).

the replacement decisions and its impact on the patterns of aggregate investment, some very nice contributions have been done in the past few years. The most representative are certainly Adda and Cooper (2000), and Cooper, Haltiwanger and Power (1999). The main result brought out by these contributions is that aggregation does not eliminate the lumpiness and infrequency characteristics of investment patterns observed at the micro level[1]. One may go a step further and ask why the aggregation of individual investment patterns with a priori distinct periodicity features (due to a priori different scrapping time decisions) does not result in smooth aggregate investment dynamics. The main reason put forward by some authors is a kind of induced synchronization of scrapping decisions under aggregate shocks. That is, heterogeneous firms may be induced to take more or less the same timing of scrapping when they are submitted to the same aggregate shock. In the Adda and Cooper contribution for example, the resulting non-monotonic aggregate investment paths come from the application of scrappage subsidies by two successive French governments in a limited interval of time. Broadly speaking, this argument ultimately means that the aggregate shocks are more important than the idiosyncratic shocks in the scrapping decisions, a claim that certainly requires further corroboration.

3. Another important line of research, which has applied the previous investment models with vintage capital and/or embodied technical change to investigate whether an economic growth regime based on ICT equipment is sustainable in the long run. It is quite easy to see why those models are suitable to deal with the latter question: The technological advances conveyed by ICT are embodied in nature, and the replacement decision of the obsolete ICT tools is a key issue when one has to conduct a cost (obsolescence costs)/benefit (modernization) analysis of an economic growth regime driven by ICT. The important theoretical contributions regarding this issue are Krusell (1998), and Greenwood and Yorokoglu (1997); a much more empirical assessment is given by Gordon (1999). One of the main contributions of this literature is the incorporation into the benchmark vintage model seen above of the so-called adoption costs. In the benchmark model, when a machine gets obsolete, it is replaced without cost (except the acquisition price to pay) by a machine of the most recent vintage. However, as it is stated in Greenwood and Yorokoglu (1997), efficiently operating the new machines cannot be instantaneous and requires time since these machines eventually embody some innovative tools that may not be so easy to fully exploit from the

1. The reader can notice that this outcome is highly consistent with the aggregation results depicted in Caballero, Engel and Haltiwanger (1995) for example.

acquisition date[1]. For example, it could be the case that specific skills are needed to run efficiently the new machines, which induce the firms to spend an extra money in facilitating the adoption of these new technologies. In such a context, innovations can yield a productivity slowdown at least in the short run. Labor productivity and even total factor productivity may go down just after the costly adoption of the new technologies, and they would only recover after a relatively long period of time (some decades in the case of a radical innovation), as studied in Greenwood and Yorokoglu. In such a case, innovations will not be immediately followed by productivity improvements, as it is the case in the standard optimal control investment models. The tremendous rise of ICT investment from the early 90's has other crucial empirical consequences as for the validation of these traditional models, as it is explained briefly in the next sub-section.

3.3. More on the empirical ground: How to handle the burst in ICT investment

This sub-section is entirely based on the work of Tevlin and Whelan (2003). The empirical investment papers seem to deny any significant role to price variables and Tobin's q in explaining investment, specially in the 80's (see Chirinko's survey in 1993). Is this diagnosis acceptable for the more recent period, the 90's, where the relative price of capital has sharply decreased, following the even sharper decrease in the price of ICT equipment and the resulting massive investment in this type of equipment? For Tevlin and Whelan, the answer should be no. In particular, the user cost model should work during this episode. In order to make this property apparent however, one should treat properly some specific issues precisely coming from the very specific ICT boom episode in the 90's. First of all, capital depreciation should be seriously estimated (recall that the rate of capital depreciation enters the expression of the user cost of capital). Most empirical studies have tended to ignore the effects of capital depreciation, by assuming for example a constant pattern over time. This is definitely not true in the recent boom as the rise of ICT has been accompanied by a rise in the depreciation rate[2]. This increasing depreciation rate is shown by Tevlin and Whelan to have a first-order explanatory power of the recent trends in equipment investment.

However, to study this aspect properly, one has to take into account that the depreciation rates vary widely across different types of equipment. **Aggregation crucially matters.** In particular, the

1. The reader can notice the parallelism between the adjustment costs in the investment theories with disembodied technical progress and the adoption costs considered in the vintage approach.

2. Tevlin and Whelan report an acceleration of the (aggregate) depreciation rate from 0.13 in 1989 to 0.16 in 1997.

depreciation rate of ICT equipment is much higher than the depreciation rate of non-ICT equipment. The main contribution of Tevlin and Whelan is precisely to show"... that a two equation system for net and gross investment in computing and non-computing equipment, estimated through 1989, is capable of explaining the magnitude and pattern of the US equipment investment boom of the 1990's, **while aggregate models completely fail**".

4. Concluding remarks

In this survey, we have tried to pick up the main ideas and concepts which have prevailed in the recent theoretical and empirical investment literature. We have drawn several lessons along the way. First of all, it is fair to acknowledge that some dramatic advances have been made in the 1990s thanks to the efforts of some research teams. In particular, the implications of non-convex capital adjustment schemes are now much better understood. Nonetheless, this new literature has not satisfactorily accounted for the investment-specific nature of technical progress, with some very few exceptions. We do believe that the recent technological trends, notably the rise of ICT, have a heavy impact on the way the investment decision is taken and is to be taken. This is turn should imply the reconsideration of many empirical results, and a more careful modelling strategy taking into account the price variables and scrupulously choosing the most appropriate level of (dis)aggregation.

References

Abel, A. (1983). Optimal Investment under Uncertainty. *American Economic Review*, 73: 228-33.

Abel, A. (1985). A Stochastic Model of Investment Marginal q and the Market Value of the Firm. *International Economic Review*, 26: 305-22.

Abel, A. and Erberly, J. (1994). A Unified Model of Investment under Uncertainty, *American Economic Review* 84: 1369-1384.

Adda, J. and Cooper, R (2000). Balladurette and Juppette: A Discrete Analysis of Scrapping Subsidies. *Journal of Political Economy* 108: 778-806.

Albonico, A., Kalyvitis, S., and Pappa, E. (2014) Capital Maintenance and Depreciation over the Business Cycle. *Journal of Economic Dynamics and Control* 39: 273-286.

Boucekkine, R., Germain, M. and Licandro, O. (1997). Replacement Echoes in the Vintage Capital Growth Model, *Journal of Economic Theory* 74: 333-348.

Boucekkine, R., Germain, M., Licandro, O. and Magnus, A. (1998). Creative Destruction, Investment Volatility and the Average Age of Capital. *Journal of Economic Growth* 3: 361-384.

Boucekkine, R., del Rio, F. and Licandro, O. (1999). Endogenous Vs Exogenously Driven Fluctuations in the Vintage Capital Growth

Model, *Journal of Economic Theory* 88: 161-187.
(2003). Technological Change, Learning-by-doing and the Productivity Slowdown. The Scandinavian Journal of Economics 105: 87-97.
(2005). Obsolescence and Modernization in the Growth Process. Journal of Development Economics 77: 153-171.
Boucekkine, R., Fabbri, G., and Gozzi, F. (2010) Maintenance and Investment: Complements or substitutes? A Reappraisal. *Journal of Economic Dynamics and Control* 34: 2420-2439.
Boucekkine, R., D. de la Croix and Licandro, O. (2011). Vintage Capital Growth Theory: Three Breakthroughs. *Economic Growth and Development* 11, 87-116.
Caballero, R. Engel, E. and Haltiwanger, J. (1995). Plant-Level Adjustment and Aggregate Investment Dynamics. *Brooking Papers on Economic Activity*, 2: 1-54.
Caballero, R. and Leahy, J (1996). Fixed Costs: The Demise of Marginal q, NBER WP
5508.
Caballero, R. (1999). Aggregate Investment. In: Woodford, M. *Handbook of Macroeconomics*, vol.3
Caballero, R. and Engle, E. (1999). Nonlinear Aggregate Investment Dynamics: Theory and Evidence. *Econometrica* 67: 783-826.
Caballero, R. (2000). Aggregate Investment: Lessons from the Previous Millennium. American Economic Association Session. In Memoriam: Robert Eisner.
Chirinko, R. (1993). Business Fixed Investment Spendings: A Critical Survey. *Journal of Economic Literature* 31: 1875-1911.
(1996). Investment under Uncertainty: A Review Essay. *Journal of Economic Dynamics and Control* 20: 1801-1808.
Cooley, T., J. Greenwood and M. Yorukoglu. (1997). The Replacement Problem. *Journal of Monetary Economics* 40: 457-499.
Cooper, R., Haltiwanger, J. and Power, L. (1999). Machine Replacement and the Business Cycle: Lumps and Bumps. *American Economic Review* 84: 921-946.
Cruz, B., and Pommeret, A. (2010). Embodied Technology Adoption Under uncertainty. In: R. Boucekkine, N. Hritonenko and Y. Yatsenko (Eds.), *Optimal Control of Age-structured Populations in Economy, Demography, and the Environment.* Taylor & Francis: London.
Dixit, A. and R. Pindyck (1994). *Investment under uncertainty.* Princeton University Press.
Doms, M. and Dunne, T. (1998). Capital Adjustment Patterns in Manufacturing Plants". *Review of Economic Dynamics* 1: 409-429.
Gittleman, M., ten Raa, T., and Wolff, E. (2006) The Vintage Effect in TFP-Growth: An Analysis of the Age Structure of Capital. *Structural Change and Economic Dynamics* 17: 306-328
Gordon, R. (1999). Has the \New Economy" Rendered the Productivity Slowdown Obsolete? *Manuscript*, Northwestern University.
Greenwood, J., Hercowitz, Z. and

Krusell, P. (1997). Long Run Implications of Investment -Specific Technological Change. *American Economic Review*, 87: 342-362.

Greenwood, J. and Jovanovic, B. (2001). Accounting for Growth. In: E. Dean, M. Harper and C. Hult (eds), *New Directions in Productivity Analysis*, NBER Studies in income and Wealth Volume 63. Chicago: Chicago University Press.

Greenwood, J. and Yorukoglu, M. (1997): "1974". *Carnegie-Rochester Conference Series on Public Policy* 46: 49-95.

Hartman, R. (1972). The effects of Price and Cost uncertainty on Investment. *Journal of Economic Theory* 5: 258-66.

Haavelmo, T. (1960). *A Study in Investment Theory.* Chicago University Press.

Jorgenson, D. (1963) Capital Theory and Investment Behavior. *American Economic Review* 53: 247-259.

Krusell, P. (1998) Investment-speci_c R&D and the Decline in the Relative Price of Capital. *Journal of Economic Growth*, 3:131-141.

Licandro, O., Maroto Illera, M. and Puch, L. (2005) Innovation, Machine Replacement and Productivity. CEPR Discussion Papers 5422, C.E.P.R. Discussion Papers.

Malcomoson, J. (1975) Replacement and the Rental Value of Capital Equipment subject to Obsolescence. *Journal of Economic Theory* 10: 24-41

Oliner, S., Rudenbusch, G. and Sichel, D. (1995) New and Old Models of Business Investment: A Comparison of Forecasting Performance. *Journal of Money Credit and Banking* 27: 806-826.

Pindyck, R. (1988) Irreversible Investment, Capacity Choice, and the Value of the Firm. *American Economic Review* 79: 969-985.

Saglam, C. and Veliov, V. (2008) Role of Endogenous Vintage Specific Depreciation in the Optimal Behavior of Firms. *International Journal of Economic Theory* 4: 381- 410.

Solow, R. (1960) Investment and Technological Progress. In: K. Arrow, S.Karlin and

P. Suppes (eds.), *Mathematical Methods in the Social Sciences* 1959, 89-104. Stanford University Press, Stanford.

Tobin, J. (1969), A General Equilibrium Approach to Monetary Theory. *Journal of Money, Credit and Banking* 1, 15-29

Tevlin, S., and Whelan, K. (2003), Explaining the Investment Boom in the 1990s. *Journal of Money, Credit and Banking* 35: 1-22.

Van Hilten, O. (1991). The Optimal Lifetime of Capital Equipment. *Journal of Economic Theory* 55: 449-454.

Whelan, K. (2002), Some New Economy Lessons for Macroeconomists. *Recherches Economiques de Louvain*:68, 21-36.

Wolf, E. (1996) The Productivity Slowdown: The Culprit at Last? *American Economic Review* 86: 1239-1252.

Technology adoption in South Kivu province subsistence farming of DRC

Célestin BUCEKUDERHWA Bashige*

RÉSUMÉ/ABSTRACT

Objectives: Technology adoption offers considerable promise for increasing food production in South-Kivu. However, the packages of technology that have been promoted since several years produced limited success. Using cross-sectional data, this paper examines the factors affecting fertilizer's adoption among small scale subsistence farming.

Methodology: Logistic and mulivariate probit models are applied to the modeling of adoption decisions by farm households using technology such as fertilizer, which can be adopted in various combinations.

Results: The results show that there exist significant correlations between different types of fertilizers, suggesting that the adoption of fertilizers is interrelated. The livestock value and the number of crops grown per household have significant positive associations with the probability of adopting fertilizer, while the level of consumption, land access and off-farm employment negatively affect it. The contacts with extension services, farmer field school, credit and training access and education level of household head have positive effects. Moreover, social networks also play a critical role in the adoption of fertilizer and become U-shaped when the network increases. On the other hand, being a member of a farmer organization does not show any effect.

Limitation: An important limitation of the analyses in this paper is that they reveal very little about the direction of causality. Are subsistence farmer adopt more innovative because they have access to more resources and more information or thereby become more productive because they have access to fertilizer? Providing answers to this type of question requires panel data, which are hard to come by in the research context and experiment. Finally, the results in this paper are based on a relatively small sample of subsistence farming. Larger samples might yield markedly diverse results, confirming some of those presented herein while possibly confounding others.

Keywords: South Kivu, subsistence farming, multivariate probit, Fertilizers technology adoption.

JEL classifications: Q01, Q12, Q16, Q18.

* The author acknowledge the financial support of CUD now ARESS-CCD.

1. Introduction

Subsistence agriculture still continues to represent the primary source of income for many of low income countries. It represents an important source of employment and contributes more than 50% to their GDP. Its importance is distinguished by its spillover effects not only on downstream but also on upstream vis-à-vis to non-agriculture sector. Moreover, subsistence agriculture will continue to be the key factor for economic growth of low income areas during the next dedicates as more than 80% of their population are drawing their livelihood from crops and livestock production (Cunguara, 2012). Subsistence agriculture is there an important engine of poverty reduction.

However, the economic history of developing areas shows that subsistence farming are experiencing a decline in their productivity due to the collapse of the production mode and the low level of using technical progress. Therefore, Sub-Saharan African region food production levels for the majority of the countries have either declined or remained stagnant, while population growth continues to soar (Muzari and al., 2012). The region is doubtless experiencing a deep-seated crisis of food production [Mkandawire and Matlosa (1993) as expressed by Muzari (2012)]. Self-sufficient in production at independence, Sub-Saharan Africa is now a net food importer [Mkandawire and Matlosa (1993) as expressed by Muzari and al. (2012)]. In DRC, agricultural export declined from 40% of all exports in 1960 to only 10% in 2000, and the food surplus declined by 30% between 1975 and 2000. Around two thirds of the country lives on less than $1 per day, 70% face food insecurity, yields are a miniscule fraction of their potential, and the country imports around one-quarters of its cereal consumption (Ulimwengu *et al.*, 2009). The South Kivu province is not spared from this situation of productivity decline (Cox, 2008), poverty and food insecurity (Bucekuderhwa and Mapatano, 2013) in this region, despite the various interventions of development agencies and research institutions since 1960, remains one the highest in the countries (DSCRP, 2010) . In this province, due to a high population density, (300-500 inhabitants per km2); pressure on the land associated with poor cultural practices causes a rapid degradation of soils. Tuber and root crops which were already very important in this area have become increasingly so owing to their ability to use the marginal soils. For example, in this province potatoes yield decreased by -13% between 1985 and 1995 (Phezo, 2002). Moreover, banana bunchy top virus recently has begun to cause more significant yield losses (? 2010). In such a context of productivity slowdown, technology adoption is a more relevant strategy which will allow subsistence farming in the area to return on the path of economic growth and development.

The question of technology adoption, and in particular its effect on agricultural productivity dynamics, is strongly discussed in the literature on the analysis of increasing agricultural productivity. Technology adoption is relevant because it determines how the increase in agricultural output impacts on poverty levels and environmental degradation (Muzari and al., 2012). According to Christiaensen and Demery (2007) modern input, including fertilizer, is an important determinant of productivity, and continuing low agricultural productivity is an important contributor to poverty persistence, especially in agriculture based countries. For example, increased technology development and adoption of fertilizer can raise agricultural output (Larson and Frisvold, 1996); hence improve household food security and nutrition. Overall, the experience and evidence from countries within and around the sub-Saharan African region indicates that returns to agricultural technology development could be very high and far reaching. Technology adoption would transform not only the smallholder sector, but also in the entire national economies of countries in the region (Mazonde, 1993).

A huge literature on the determinants of technology adoption under subsistence farming from low income countries exists. Among different factors, economic, social, physical and technical aspects of farming are mentioned to have a significant effect on agricultural technologies, such as fertilizer [Rauniyar and Goode (1992), Nkonya*et al.* (1997), Adesina *et al.* (2000), Kaliba *et al.* (2000), Doss and Morris (2001), Croppenstedt *et al.* (2003), Asfaw and Admassie (2004), Fufa and Hassan (2006), Merenya and Barett (2007),Pender and Gebremedhin (2007), Shiferaw *et al.* (2008), Saka andLawal (2009), Ajewole (2010), Dercon and Christiaensen (2011), Asfaw *et al.* (2011), Thapa and Rattanasuteerakul (2011) and Bucekuderhwa (2013)]. Mbaga-Semgalawe and Folmer (2000) argue that participation in promotional activities of soil and water conservation programs influences the adoption decision process in Tanzania. Pender and Gebremedhin (2007), Matthews-Njoku *et al.* (2009), Asfaw *et al.* (2012) and Noltze *et al.* (2012) show that participating in training programs and household labor availability increase the probability and intensity of adoption. Moreover, Croppenstedt *et al.* (2003), Asfaw and Admassie (2004) their studies on fertilizer adoption in Tanzania found that education effect was substantial and statistically significant. In this regard they argue that the expansion of education in traditional areas may be more attractive than in modern areas since education is usually the only means to enhance the ability of farmers to acquire, synthesize and respond to innovations such as chemical fertilizer. Furthermore, the social network makes also the adoption of new technologies positive or negative among rural households [Isham (2002), Romani (2003), Bandiera and Rasul (2006), Matuschke *et al.* (2007)]. According to Bandiera and Rasul (2006) sunflower seed adoption in Mozambique and numbers of adoption is shaped like an inverse U, suggesting that social effects are positive when there are few adopters in the network, and negative when there are many. Matuschke *et al.* (2007) findings support this hypothesis. In the line with social network, Isham (2002) findings support that ethnically based and participatory affiliations is as form of social capital in the adoption decision of fertilizer in Tanzania. In addition, the recent literatures on technology adoption focus on the consumption erosion to explain why subsistence farms in low-income communities do not benefit from technical progress. In some case, adoption decisions are constrained by low consumption outcomes [Fafchamps (1992), Dercon and Christiaensen, 2011), whereas others found that neither farm size nor subsistence level influences the adoption decision (Matuschke *et al.*, 2007). [Duflo *et al.* (2011), Marenya and Barrett (2007)] found that household wealth is determinants for adoption of improved technologies. Doss and Morris (2000) evidence from Ghana suggests that gender-linked differences in the adoption of modern maize varieties and fertilizer result from gender-linked differences in access to complementary inputs. Little research regarding technology adoption, including fertilizer, has been published from South Kivu in recent years. In all most of the few existing studies, technology adoption has not been thoroughly investigated under different socioeconomic conditions. This research fills this gap using a cross-sectional data set collected from various parts of South-Kivu province (Bunyakiri, Idjwi, Kabare, Walungu and Uvira).

The objective of this chapter is to explore the empirical importance of factors in fertilizer adoption in South Kivu province, using a cross-sectional data set of 585 subsistence farming households. The approach is largely based on Doss and Morris (2001), Asfaw and Admassie (2004), Marenya and Barret (2007), Matthews-Njoku *et al.* (2009), Dercon and Christiaensen (2011) and Teklewold *et al.* (2013) who studied technology adoption using a binary model and that recognize the interdependence between different fertilizer and jointly analyses the decision to adopt different types of technology of fertilizer including inorganic and organic fertilizer and mixture of inorganic and organic fertilizer. On this basis, and through quantitative analysis, we glean the different types of fertilizer technologies used by subsistence farmers in their activities and identify both the factors of adoption all these fertilizers and variations of the factors with different fertilizers types.

Besides the present introduction, this paper is divided into six sections. Section two is devoted to theoretical and empirical framework. Section 3 deals with data and research hypotheses. Section 4 presents the empirical findings and section 5 reports the conclusions and implications of the study.

2. Conceptual framework

The adoption of technology in low-income countries can be associated with a number of constraints that find their origins in the basic elementary arguments relating both on the physical and organizational characteristics of the subsistence agriculture generally considered poor, backward and with limited services. These constraints, farm size, risk and uncertainty, human capital, labor availability, credit constraints, social networks, access to commodity markets, self-sufficiency and tenure security, are common to subsistence farming in low-income countries. Many studies have shown that each of these indicators influence significantly the agricultural technology adoption process.

Feder *et al.* (1985) consider adoption as the degree to which a technology is used in long-run equilibrium when farmers have complete information about the technology and its potentials. Under subsistence farming conditions, the objective of adoption study is to describe how each variable affects adoption, thus allowing actors to refine their strategies based on a wide body of empirical and qualitative results. For example, [Feder *et al* (1985), Feder and Umali (1993), Besley and Case (1993),Foster and Rosenzweig (1995), AdaduHgadil and Pannell (1999), Marra *et al.* (2003), Munshi, Conley and Udry (2010), Parvan (2011)] state that the behavior of adoption agricultural technologies in developing countries is often affected by two factors: those relating to the characteristics of individual farmers (leeway, personal attitudes to change risk and social attributes, etc.) and those relating to the characteristics to the technologies (technical features and performance related). From this point on view Perret and Stevens (2003) building on the findings of Milleville (1991) and Bosc and Amin (1995) show that technology adoption does not only involve a given technology. It rather supposes turning it into a practice, which most of the time supposes adaptation rather than mere adoption. The technology adoption is not addressing the technology as such but rather the organizational and managerial changes that are required so that the technology slots into the farming system and becomes a practice among others. Such process may even involve stakeholders beyond the farm boundaries if some form of collective action is required to implement the technology (Rasmussen and Meinzen-Dick, 1995). This emphasizes the complexity of subsistence farmers' decision-making with regard to the adoption fertilizer and related technologies such improved seed, soil conservation, row planting, etc. The complexity may even increase when one considers certain specific traits of African smallholder farmers, and especially markets failures. The technology must not only fit into the existing farming system, but also fit into the whole livelihood systems, matching the strategy developed by the family. Failures and successes of the so-called Green Revolution give vivid examples of that reality (Perett and Stevens, 2003). A successful adoption of technology, include fertilizer, requires also a high level of learning and knowledge, as well as some financial expenses. These may include additional investments, information gathering, initial loss of income due to trial errors, perceived usefulness which depends on individual attitudes. From the point of view of perceived usefulness, Davis (1986) emphasis that individual attitudes is not alone the determinant of the use of technology but it can based also to the impact it will have on its performance.

Several models have been developed for assessing technology adoption, including fertilizer. In such models adoption measures is obtain through the use of times series, panel and cross-sectional data studies [Besley and Case (1993) and Doss (2006)]. In time series studies, one observes only an aggregate measure of adoption, such as the percentage of farmers employing the new technology at each date. The study of hybrid corn in the United Stated by Griliches (1957) is classic study following Besley and Case (1993).

In panel data studies is forced to understand the dynamics of adoption decisions, rather than just developing static descriptions of particular area because technology adoption decisions are inherently dynamic (Besley and Case (1993) and Doss (2006). Among others studies, Marenya and Barrett (2007) were interested on the household determinants of adoption of improved natural resources management practices among smallholder farmers in Kenya using panel data. They found that there exists reinforcing feedback between investments in soil fertility and household wealth, as measured by asset endowments. Similarly, credit constraints and the possible outcomes of low consumption when crops fail appear as factors that discourage the use of fertilizers by farmers in Ethiopia (Dercon and Christiaensen, 2011). (Isham, 2002) findings support that ethnically based and participatory social affiliation act as a form of social capital in adoption decision of fertilizer in Tanzania using also panel data.

In contrast, cross-sectional studies provide insight into farm and farmer characteristic associated with ultimately accepting the new technology. According to Doss (2006) cross-sectional analysis can also answer important question about technology use and tell us about far preferences and perceptions of the constraints that they face. However, cross-sectional data do not and cannot address many other important research and policy questions. According to Besley and Case (1993) these data are available only at the time when the survey was done and their uses bias the parameters of interest. It also seems unlikely that the dynamics of adoption can be well captured by allowing time-varying coefficients on variables whose values are assumed to be constant over time. Thus, while one might be able to do better by having information about the year in which the technology was adopted, there are still problems. Authors like Nolte *et al.* (2012), Beshir *et al.* (2012), Admasie Asfaw (2004) used cross-sectional data to study the adoption of fertilizer and found that physical, economics and institutional characteristics of the farmers played a critical role in the adoption of fertilizer. For example, Nolte *et al.* (2012) found that participation in training and household labor availability increased the probability and intensity of adoption of rice intensification. Their findings suggest also that plot level data and plots conditions were important to understand the adoption of system technologies.

3. Methodology

3.1. Data

The data used here are from a survey conducted by the team of "Laboratoire d'Economie Apppliquée au Développement (LEAD)" of the Catholic University of Bukavu. This survey ought to describe the level of use of technology and evaluate the factors of fertilizer adoption under subsistence farming households. Given the poverty of the soil and few alternatives on soil management, understanding subsistence farmers' behavior in the adoption of fertilizer is important as the future of the rural area livelihoods in South-Kivu depends on the dynamics of subsistence agriculture growth. The construction of the sample meets the objective to measure the adoption of fertilizers.

Therefore, the sample thus constructed is from one of the major crops growing areas of South Kivu that supply the Bukavu town in basic foodstuffs, in this Bunyakiri, Kabare, Idjwi, Uvira and Walungu, based on the intensity of cereal, legume, tuber and root crops production, agro-ecology and accessibility. Although the selection of the areas of study was determinate by the project, the selection of the villages followed a multistage stratified random sampling, in which 3 villages were selected from each *territoire*, for a total of 15 villages. About 35 to 40 farmers were randomly sampled from a list of all farming families in each village, resulting in a total sample size of 600 households. Nevertheless, data on some households were dropped during the analysis because of lack of information on some of the variables of interest, such as household endowment and technologies used during the last two cropping seasons. Consequently, the results presented in this article are based on data from 585 farm households in five territories. The household data were collected using a structured questionnaire that sought information on general household characteristics, education, assets and land use, housing and consumption, crop and livestock production, awareness and use of fertilizer, social networks, access and use of improved inputs as well as credit.

Fertilizer technology on which information was sought includes agricultural compost (both livestock manure with crops residues) and inorganic fertilizer. The household head was interviewed sometime in the presence of other household members if they are present; this information on adoption is public within the household. The objective was to maximize the information from others members about the knowledge and use of fertilizer technologies by household. These different members may have different status in the household but only the response on the household head where maintained. In order to draw conclusions for policy makers at the farm level, and to allow the opening of any comparative studies, we considered as household head one of the spouse who was available the day of our visit. When both spouses were present, we considered as household head the spouse who had more information on available fertilizers and gave more explanations on our issues.

3.2. Description of variables

3.2.1. Dependent Variables (Regression)

The dependent variables included in the model have been chosen from the literature on the agricultural technologies adoption and in line with the elements within the questionnaire. The survey questionnaire asked subsistence farmers directly whether they used fertilizer during last two season's crops of 2011. Fertilizer adoption is broadly defined, in the context of this study, to include changes in technical and organizational practices on soil improvements with organic and inorganic materials. The basic requirement for any of these changes to be regard as fertilizer adoption is that newness under subsistence farming. Successful fertilizer adoption received a score of two, ongoing adoption a score of 1 and no adoption a score of 0. The questionnaire items allow us to distinguish three different types' technologies of fertilizer used by farmers in the study: compost (organic fertilizer), inorganic fertilizer and compost and inorganic fertilizer combined. The variables were created as follows. The sum of the scores for all items under each fertilizer use was computed for each subsistence farmer. These scores were then recoded as 0 (for no use) and 1 (for use). A binary variable, which indicates whether or not the farmer used any innovation at wall, was obtained by summing and recoding the three combinations. These four variables together form the dependent variables in the regression to address the research question.

In this study, adopters are classified as household who used agricultural compost, inorganic fertilizer and mixture of compost and inorganic fertilizer and non-adopters are those who did not use any of these three technologies fertilizer varieties. Use of compost depends mainly on the availability of livestock manure on which is added, crop residue, ashes from kitchen, household refuse and leftover mash from brewing banana beer. Composting is an agronomic practice development trough research, to promote efficient and sustainable agriculture through agricultural promotion of locally available resources. Essentially, the process involves encouraging materials like food waste and cuttings of grasses and branches to rapidly decompose, returning the nutrients bound in these materials to the earth in the form of soil. Manure is regularly included in compost heaps, furthering rapid breakdown. When a compost heap is well maintained and well balanced, it produces surprisingly minimal odor, and it can take less than three months for materials to break down, making composting a very efficient method for handling organic material. The application compost allows oxygen to get to the bacteria and organisms which break down the manure into soil-like structure. Geber (2008) puts in evidence that the technique is very labor-intensive as the farmer must cover the plant and animal raw materials during the entire process and mix it between each phase. Although it is difficult for the subsistence farmer to see the immediate effect of this technique on the output of the crops, the objective pursued by the subsistence farmers is to maximize yields and maintain soil health of their fields (Vanlauwe, 2004). The capacity of agricultural compost (both animals and crops materials) to supply nutrients, especially nitrogen (N), phosphorus (P) and potassium (K) is reported in Wubeneh and Sanders (2006), Marenya and Barrett (2007). According to Giller *et al.* (1998) as expressed by Wubeneh and Sanders (2006) manure for example can increase yields by improving the soil matter content. It also improves the soil water holding capacity and thus increases efficiency in the use inorganic fertilizer. In this line Marenya and Barrett (2007) found that the stable soil organic matter from manure stimulates the activities of soil macro fauna and microorganisms in soil, which in turn contribute to nutrient, realize and overall soil health. Furthermore, Geber (2004) found that since the farms are small, they apply an intensive system of production, in which the manure from their animals plays an important role in terms of soil fertility.

Inorganic fertilizer application is often available under subsistence farming with the help of research, peasant and non-government institutions. Subsistence farmers in the study area apply inorganic combined with compost on their plots to increase yields. Wubeneh and Sanders (2006) find that in Ethiopia sorghum yields were substantially higher for farmers who used manure and inorganic fertilizer in combination. Moreover, the integration of manure and fertilizer on maize in Zimbabwe resulted in a return of labor of about 1.35$ per day, while the best fertilizer-only or manure-only treatment yield only $0.25 (Mekuria and Waddington, 2002). These findings are also confirmed by Bossissi *et al.* (2011) for the South Kivu province by showing that the mixture of NPK and manure increased the yield of both beans and maize.

The use of fertilizer, especially compost, has been employed by subsistence farmers in South Kivu since several decades. This practice has been introduced by research institutions and development agencies to help farmers who are often confronted to problems of soil erosion and fertility. Kingombe wa Kingombe (2003) using the terms of Hendrickx and Colleaux found that because soil infertility, the "Institut d'Etudes Agronomiques du Congo (INEAC)" began around 1947 the initiatives to establish alley cropping, crops stabilize and soil enrichment. Moreover, Cox (2011) and Maas *et al.* (2012) put also in evidence that in traditional mixed farming in the region manure facilitates greatly reduced dependence on fallowing. Thus, every time when subsistence farmers go to the fields they usually carry in their basket ashes mixed with manure and plant residues from their compost. Taking into account the element mentioned above, we assume that fertilizer is mature technologies and so we can explore the question of its adoption to establish whether household endowments affect both uptake and continuation.

3.2.2. Independent variables

Several characteristics of the farmers are included as covariates. The farmer's gender is represented by a dummy variable. Instead of using the gender of the household head (the conventional practice in most adoption studies), we use the gender of the farmer. This allows us to examine the behavior of female farmers in both female- and male-headed households. According to Doss (2006) the literature on gender and farming in Africa suggests that men's labor and women's labor are not interchangeable. Generally, it is hypothesized that male-headed households are more likely to get information about new technologies and take risky businesses than female-headed households. However, however recent research is contesting this belief. Although, males may not be considered more efficient workers than females, they do have better access to organizational goods and capital resources. These opportunities may help males to access and adopt than females (Adesina and Djato, 1997).

As suggested by the literature, the age of the subsistence farmer is also included following Asfaw and Admasie (2004). Age is measured as a logarithm of the household subsistence farmer. As we are in rural area and considering that agricultural remain the main activity of farmer, age is usually taken as a proxy of experience and is expected to have a positive impact on adoption (Asfaw and Admassie, 2004). However, it is argued that there is a certain threshold of age beyond which the ability of farmers to take risk and adopt innovations decreases. This means that young farmers are more likely to face the risks associated with innovations (uncertainty in yield and unfamiliarity in technology) and to adopt them than their old counterparts [Matuschke *et al.* (2007) and Asfaw and Admassie (2004).

Included also are several other explanatory variables thought to affect technology adoption decisions most of these variables are extensively discussed in the adoption literature [Feder *et al.* (1985) and Feder and Umali (1993), Doss (2006)]. In their seminal review paper, Feder, Just, and Zilberman (1985) pointed out that individual variables like farm size and education are significant determinants of technology adoption in developing countries. Farm size, in terms of quantity and access, is measured as the total area of land (owned and rented) under cultivation. In the line with farm size, the number of field owned by the farmer is also included as explanatory variable because even though agricultural technologies are both expected to be scale-neutral, wealthier farmers (i.e. those with many lands) are more likely to be able to afford technologies as fertilizer. Number of fields may be an implication of land fragmentation. Moreover, if the major part of the field is rented, deciding to farm organically may raise objections from the landlord. This conflict may also have an impact on the decision process. Thus, land tenure is introduced to capture under which property mode the farmer manages the land. This is assumed to be a proxy to security of tenure which gives farmers ability and incentive to invest in productivity enhancing fertilizer. Its argue that periodic reallocation of rural land produces tenure insecurity, which in turn weakens farmers' incentives in the contracted plots (Prosterman, Hanstad, and Li (1996) and Wen (1995) reported in Kung and Cai (2000). Building on Asfaw and Admassie (2004) findings, education is measured in terms of the highest grade completed by any adult member of the household. It is hypothesized that education enhances the ability of farmers to acquire, synthesize, and quickly respond to disequilibria, thereby increasing the probability of adoption of innovation (Asfaw and Admasie, 2004). However, Basu *et al.* (2000) contend that literacy can spread in the household by virtue of certain kinds of decision-making on behalf on the household shifting toward literate. I hypothesize that decision whether to adopt a technology depends on the level of education attained by primary decision maker. Then Feder and O'Mara (1981), in their study on the adoption of high yielding varieties during the Green Revolution, emphasized also on the importance of proper access to credit as facilitating elements in the adoption process. The credit constraint variable is based on the farmers' self-reported access to a loan from the microfinance institutions or credit from the input dealer. Credit is assumed to be a proxy of financial access which assists farmers to purchase input to adopt fertilizer.

In addition, the number of crops grown by farmer, access to extension services and involvement in peasant institution are also integrated as factors influencing the adoption of fertilizer in order to light on the organization of the production and social structures. These two variables represent the formal source to access to information by farmers. Consistent with subsistence agriculture, farmers grow more than one crop, so production is not specialized. I hypothesize that the variety among crops may help to diversify away risk but it may result in misallocation of time and labor effort. To measure farmer access to extension services (public service and NGOs), I asked whether farmers had participated in training seminar on fertilizer use in the past years. Extension is assumed to be a proxy to access to technologies and is expected to increase the farmer's probability of adopting fertilizer. In addition, I hypothesis that by being involved in organizations (e.g., cooperatives and peasant organization), producers are introduced to advancements in technology and agricultural methods as well as provide access to new technology. Therefore, producer's involvement in organization is believed to enhance a producer's adoption. One question asked subsistence farmer whether or not they are engaged in peasant institution. The variable peasant institution is binary variable indicating whether or not a subsistence farmer is involved in peasant association during the reference period, which is? The binary variable value both for extension service and peasant institution were obtained from recoding sum scores reported on the whole observation. In the line with the institutional variable, the presence in the village of farmer field schools is also a channel that allows farmers to learn about fertilizer technology. Farmer field schools developed in Asia (Kenmore, 1996) are based on a learner-centered approach in which farmer's learn about new technology management options under realistic conditions, thereby improving their crop management decision-making skills (2005). Since this methodology promotes technology replicability in farmer's fields. Dummy variable representing availability of farmer field school to household, where availability of farmer field school =1, and lack of farmer field school=0. A positive relationship is expected.

In another question, several possible external sources of information where listed in the survey instrument among others farmers networks (family, neighborhood, religions, radio and phones calls). Each subsistence farmer was asked to list their main source of formations. Following previous work, such as Besley and Case (1997), Foster and Rosenzweig (1995), Conley and Udry, (2003), Munshi (2004), Bandiera and Rasul (2006) and Matuschke *et al.* (2007), I hypothesized that external formal source of information can be also completed by the family networks an informal information under which subsistence farming as learning from others. As a measure of the size of the individual network, following the approach of Bandiera and Rasul (2006) and Matusche *et al* (2007), I asked individual farmer in the village survey how many farmers who are using fertilizer they know. Social network include family members who are involved in farmer activity and who are using fertilizer in the one hand and friends and neighbors on the other. The sum of responses available to these questions measures the information on fertilizer technology available to each farmer from his social network following Bandiera and Rasul (2006).

In a context of extreme poverty, household consumption average, as a proxy for permanent income is included, in the model. Rich farmers are more likely to know about fertilizer than theirs poor counterparts. Moreover, since manure serves as an important source of organic fertilizer, the value of livestock hold by farmer is expected to be positively correlated with the probability of adoption. Livestock is measured by the value of all species of livestock (if sold at the market price during the survey time) owned by the household. This variable increases the credit worthiness of households and their ability to undertake risky businesses. For Dercon and Christiaensen (2011) livestock may be included separately in the regression to control for time-varying changes in wealth. Household consumption and livestock values reflect the relative poverty in the area. Since adopting a new technology often implies a need for additional labor, labor availability is frequently associated with successful adoption. In our study, the family size is used as a simple measure of labor availability. In addition, off-farm employment is hypothesized to be a source of cash to purchase; produce and transport input to adopt fertilizer for enhance crops yields. It is assumed to positively influence adoption of fertilizer. Off-farm employment which is an alternative job allowing farm to generate an alternative income also serves as a means of surviving of life when the income from the on farm activities couldn't be as expected. It is also believed that off-farm income can have a positive impact on resilience of rural households. When income opportunities increase, their risk taking behavior also increase; this may lead to a higher probability of modern agricultural inputs use. However, if the household generates more income on the off-farm activities than do the farm activities, they may not spend more time on the farm so that the probability of new technology adoption on the farm sector may be reduced.

Finally, the distance between homesteads and field is for importance in fertilizer adoption. The effect of distance to fertilizer use is hypothesized to be negative because fertilizer application implies to transport cost and subsistence farmers may be not able to afford it. The closer are the plots to the farmer's residence, the more likely is the farmer to use fertilizer. In other words, more intensive methods may be used on more accessible plots. Distance is estimated in minutes rather than kilometers (km). Indeed, in the study area subsistence farmers were not able to estimate the distance in km between their house and field in the one hand.

3.2.3. Econometrics models

The questions that this paper raises relate to search the fertilizer technologies and its probability adoption. This is explored first for the subsistence farming probability adoption of fertilizer at all, and the probability that the subsistence farming will adopt any compost fertilizer (organic fertilizer), inorganic fertilizer or mixture compost and inorganic fertilizer. For each farmer, fertilizer adoption is modeled within the framework of theories of discrete individual choice. The environment of the decision-maker determines the size of the non-empty universal set of available alternatives, among which any single decision-maker considers a subset, which constitutes his or her choice set (Ben-Akiva and Lerman, 1985). The feasibility and attractiveness of any alternative within the choice set depends on a variety of constraints, such as physical accessibility and the availability of financial resources or information, as well as on the technical and financial performance of each alternative (Marenya and Barret, 2007).

The underlying assumption is that farmers base decisions on utility rather than profit maximization. Thus each farmer makes different adoption decision based on their personal preferences and circumstances which depend on their friends and neighbor interactions as well as farm and household characteristics. This assumption is reasonable because farmers are producing for home consumption and contemplates the adoption of a new technology to improve the family's living standards. In addition, farmers are assumed to be risk averse, as the majorities of them are smallholders who operate in a poverty-stricken environment. As explained by Greene (2003), one can estimate a discrete choice process using latent regression modeling techniques. The problem analyzed, in this case, is the household *i*, who is involved in subsistence agriculture for at least one year. The last one is the confronted with following alternative: apply fertilizer or not. The adoption decision is then associated with a Bernoulli variable Y_i that can take two values: 1 if the household farmer applies fertilizer, 0 otherwise.

The decision to withdraw is then associated with a Bernoulli variable y which can take two variables: 1 if the household applies fertilizer, 0 otherwise, with:

$$Y_i^* = \beta'_i X_i + \varepsilon_i$$

Where y_n^* is the dependent variable, X_i is a matrix of independent variables containing household-specific characteristics that reflect constraints and preferences, β_i is a vector of parameter estimated, and ε_i is error term. However, we do not observe the net benefit of adoption, only the choice of whether or not the farmer chose the practice. Future profit flows after adopting the new milking technology are not known with certainty due either to ignorance of the exact technology performance or to the higher probability of technology failure as a consequence of errors in the use and maintenance of this technology. It is reasonable to assume that all farmers are seeking how they can improve their utility and production processes, even marginally. Under the revealed preferences assumption that the farmer use fertilizer technology that generates net benefits and does not use technology otherwise, I can relate the observable discrete choice of technology to the unobservable continuous net benefit variable as:

$$Y_i^* = \begin{cases} 1 \text{ si } y_i^* > y_0 & \textit{(household i used fertilizer), and} \\ 0 \text{ si } y_i^* \leq y_0 & \textit{otherwise} \end{cases}$$

In this formulation

$Prob\ (Y_0^* > 0) = Prob\ (\varepsilon_i > -\beta' X_i) = 1 - F\ (\beta' X_i)$

Where F is the cumulative distribution function of the error term μ_i. Various cumulative functions can be assumed for $F(\cdot)$. If we assume $F(\cdot)$ has a logistic distribution,

$$Prob(Y_i = 1/X_i) = \frac{1}{1 + e^{-\beta' X_i}} = \frac{e^{\beta' X_i}}{1 + e^{\beta' X_i}}$$

in the case of random sampling where all observations are sampled independently, the contribution of the th observations is written as $P_i^{Y_i}(1 - P_i)^{1-Y_i}$ and the likelihood function is simply the product of individual contributions. Thus, the likelihood function will be:

$$L = \prod_{i=1}^{n} P_i^{Y_i} (1 - P_i)^{1-Y_i}$$

Taking logarithms and replacing P_i by $e^{\beta' X_i}/1 + e^{\beta' X_i}$, the log-likelihood is

$$logL = \sum_{i=1}^{n} Y_i \beta' X_i - \sum_{i=1}^{n} log\left(1 + e^{\beta' X_i}\right)$$

In binary dependent variable models, the β cannot be interpreted as the marginal effect on the dependent variable. For instance, in the logit model, the marginal effect on the conditional probability is given by the rate change in probability as a result of unit change in dependent variable, i.e., dP/dx is given by $(\beta_j P_j)/(1-P_j)$ (Gujarati, 2012). This ensures that the predicted probability remains between 0 and 1 and thus the coefficients can be interpreted as log odds ratios. To test the reliability of the model one needs to conduct some diagnosis test. Unlike the standards regression model, the F-test cannot be used to test the overall fitness in a discrete choice model. The most popular diagnostic test in such cases is the χ^2_n statistic defined as:

$$\chi^2_{(n)} = 2ln\frac{L_R}{L_U} = -\ lnL_R - lnL_U$$

Where L_R and L_U are restricted and the unrestricted likelihood results, respectively [Murkerjee *et al.* (1998) as expressed by Asfaw and Admassie (2004)].

Given also that we investigated several different fertilizer technologies, it is worth mentioning that the three different fertilizer technology types are potentially interdependent. Then, it should be expected that the implementation of one type of technology will influence the likelihood of the other types. Moreover, in the empirical set-up of this paper, the same factors are assumed to be associated with all different technologies types of fertilizer, a scenario that makes interdependence even more likely. To account for this interdependence, a multivariate probit is analyzed. In this alternative empirical set-up, a simultaneous system of three probit equations is estimated instead of three separate one (see Table 10 for details). The results are not qualitatively different from those reported in Table 8. Consequently, I have chosen on assessing the logistic results for the additional benefit that the odds ratios are easily obtained and interpreted.

4. Results and discussion

4.1. Descriptive results

Summary statistics for continuous variables and binary variables for the whole sample are presented (Table 2). Some of these characteristics are the explanatory variables of the estimated model. Data cleaning before analysis was done following Neuman (2011), Tabachnick and Fidell (2012). The trends in several household variables show that about 41, 20% of the sample households are headed by females. The human capital resources in the region are poor in quality with low level of education and learned skills that have implications on agricultural productivity, food security and resources management. The average level of education is about 5, 74 years. About 48, 55% of household heads respondents have not attended primary school, 26, 32 % household heads had primary level education, while 25, 13% of household heads had least attended secondary and high school only. The majority of those surveyed consider farming as their main livelihood, about 85, 81% household heads are involved in agriculture. Since agriculture is the main activity in the study areas, fertilizer adoption should allow these populations to increase their yields and well-being and mitigate poverty. The average size of land (including banana and small afforestation) controlled by each household of our sample is around 1.45ha. The results are similar to Mass *et al.* (2012) findings who show that in the study area land property is small with a mean size of 1.5 ha and with an extremely skewed distribution. The data on average number of plots per farm for the different zones indicate that the degree of land fragmentation is largest in the study area. The overall average number of plots per farm of is 2, 63 with a standard deviation of 1, 97. These plots are governed by different land contracts. About 47, 01% farmers cultivate land under a lease contract which is called in the study area Bwasa. The fields held under Bwasa contracts are seldom fertilizer. According to Cox (2012) this is not just a matter of low incentive, but of active disincentive. Indeed, Bwasa tenants have to walk a fine line with regard to their production to avoid drawing the attention of the landlord who might want to take the plot back [Muheme (1996), Mugangu (1997), Bucekuderhwa (2005) and Cox (2012). The strategy is just to plant a patch of crops and leave it be.

The average of monthly household consumption expenditures is US$ 134.72 while the average value of total livestock owned by the household is estimated to US$ 159.75. However, there is no correlation between household consumption and livestock value. This indicates that holding livestock does not lead to consumption considering that animals induce wealth in the region. Dividing the value of consumption expenditures by the average number of people who are living in the household, it should be noted that the per capita consumption expenditures is far below (15492, 89 DCF, about 16, 84$ per month) the average required for a standard life. These results are similar to the World Bank (2012) findings that estimated the per capita income of DRC to 190$ on average per year. To this end, Marenya and Barrett (2007) conclude that if the propensity to use technologies depends on these attributes, this would not seem to bode well for the future of spontaneous uptake of technology.

The mean family size is about 7,11individuals for the whole sample showing that human population is larger in the study area. This implies the availability of labor that can be used by the farming for fertilizer transportation. Indeed, use of fertilizer increase the seasonal demand for labor, so that adoption could be attractive in this way. It worth mentioning that households are involved in growing crops production since 20 years on

TABLE 2
Select characteristics of sample farmers (n=585)

Variable	Mean	Std. Dev.	Min	Max
Age of primary decision maker	40,06	14,37	16	81
Gender of primary decision maker	0,58	NA	0	1
Education level	5,74	3,03	0	18
Number of household member per household	7,11	3,88	1	25
Number of adults member per household	4,92	1,42	1	5
Farm size	1,45	1,28	0,06	12
Number of field cultivated by farmer	2,63	1,97	1	13
Land tenure	47,01	NA	0	1
Experience in growing crops	20,03	13,19	1	65
Household consumption expenditures	134,72	335.81	21.74	1689.67
Livestock value	159,75	1.967	1	4518
Off-farm employment	14,20	NA	0	1
Number of crops grown per household	6,34	3,09	1	14
Organizational involvement	0,44	NA	0	177
Use of extension service	0,41	NA	0	87
Famer field schools	0,25	NA	0	1
Distance from home to the field	88,79	21,54	10	120
Adopters among family and friends	48,45	40,2	2	90
Adopters among family	6,58	74,47	1	14
Adopters among friends et neighbor	41,8	38,76	1	90
Number of crops grown per household	6,34	3,09	1	14

Source: Author's calculation from sample data 2011.

average. This implies that farmers are aware of the constraints on farming system in their communities. In addition, agriculture in our study area is dominated by the intercropping system. Household are growing more than 6 crops in average (Appendix 1). Only 10% of respondents are specialized in the cassava cultivation and 21% of the surveyed households are not intercropping producers although they are involved in several crops such as rice, maize and vegetables compared to 69% who are involved in intercropping system. In such situation one can expect a very low use of technologies as the requirements nutrients of crop varieties are different and then difficult for subsistence farmers to implement. In addition, only 44% of the respondents are members of rural institutions and 41% reported having a contact with extension service. To reach their fields, subsistence farmers make about 85 minutes of walking in average. This implies that application of fertilizer can be low in such situation because of physical, time and efforts. However, subsistence farmer is more connected with his social networks translated partly by the family, friend and neighbors networks. Households farmers are in contact with more than 48, 45 persons who used fertilizer in average.

The knowledge about available fertilizer technology is not important in our study area. Fertilizers that have been introduced and which are well-known by the respondent's farmers are presented in Table 2 below. While more than 60, 51 % of the respondents are aware of agricultural compost, only 46, 84% of this technology. Moreover, while inorganic fertilizer is known by 6, 50% of the sample 4, 27% is inorganic fertilizer users. The data show also only the half of the respondents who are aware of the mixture of inorganic and compost are not adopters. The number of respondents with no knowledge of any technology is about 22, 05%. A comparison between cumulative knowledge between compost and inorganic fertilizer lead to the conclusions that inorganic fertilizer is not widely known under subsistence because of use and access cost.

Although subsistence farmers are more aware of compost, the amount of its use by each remains questionable. The data on the quantity of fertilizer application and output by crops and plot are not available because subsistence farmer in the study area do not make calculation of the inputs and yields. Farmer use more organic fertilizer than inorganic. This is well illustrated more by the percent of farmers who use inorganic in the table above. This implies that poor subsistence farmer cannot afford the cost inorganic fertilizer. Dercon and Christiaensen (2011) found that inorganic fertilizer were low in Ethiopia due to fixed costs and marketing setup. Similarly, Bossissi *et al.* (2011) put in evidence that farmers cannot afford the fertilizers' cost at the recommended rate in the study area. In addition, the low level of use of inorganic fertilizer is also due to lack of the organized production, marketing setup of fertilizer, political insecurity and poverty that characterize the study area and then can partly explain the decline in

TABLE 3

Knowledge and use about available fertilizer in the study area (n=585)

Types	Adopters	Adopters	All
Manure and compost	279	78	357
Inorganic fertilizer	25	13	38
Agricultural compost and fertilizer	33	28	61
Do not know	0	129	129
All	325	260	585

Source: author's calculation from sample 2011

agricultural productivity and well-being that characterize the study area. While in principle farmers can buy fertilizer in the spot market, there are no enterprises which are involved in the production and marketing fertilizer. Supply of fertilizer is manly local belonging more from own production and their networks. These findings are in line with Shultz (1964) and Spio (1997) who find that small farmers in traditional agriculture remain poor mainly because of limited technical and economic opportunities. Moreover, Shively (2000) shows that payback periods for private investments in technology can be long, a feature that helps explain low adoption rates. This is confirmed by our survey data, showing that it is difficult to process for example on fertilizer adoption in the context of poverty. Therefore, the amount of technologies used by each farmer is insufficient to allow production efficiency. This merits further study using more appropriate data.

In addition to problems related to market and poverty, subsistence farmers are facing various difficulties which are mostly related to the lack of information, fertilizers, banana wilt, cassava mosaic, etc. (table 3). More than 98% reported facing the problems of technology in their village and surrounding areas although these problems do not have the same level of intensity. Subsistence farming is also experiencing lack of providers' services for both extension and training. Those who are confronted on the lack of access to credit, transport and bad quality of products are estimated to 23, 76% of the whole sample (Table 4).

Lack of information, production cost perception, etc. are key factor

TABLE 4

Main three reasons for not using fertilizer

Constraints	Percent
Lack of access to credit/Bad quality of products/ Lack of transport/Too expensive	23,76
Lack of information on technology and price/Lack of storage facility/ Fertilizers no available in the area and production cost	51,45
Plants disease/Soil erosion/Climate no suitable	23,59
Other	1,20

Source: Author's calculation from sample data 2011.

in the adoption process of fertilizer and their importance is raised by the surveyed households heads. The adoption or the implementation of fertilizer is not an easy task because they require enormous physical and economic efforts. More than 51, 45% declared to be confronted to the lack of information on price of inputs and commodities, storage facilities, fertilizers and others technologies. The percentage of farmers indicating plants disease, soil erosion and non-suitability of the agro-climatic conditions as reasons of non-adoption of fertilizer is about 23, 51%. Thus, daily use of technologies in this context turns out to be difficult or impossible given the almost nonexistence and poor coordination of technical, organizational and institutional supports to agricultural development, forcing farmers to work in the routine and context that do not allow them to capture the gain from technical progress. The costs of credit combine with the lack of information add the cost of fertilizer. Most of respondents who are using fertilizer mention the lack of access to credit, lack information on technology and production cost as the main reasons for not using fertilizer in the area.

Fertilizer use in the region is not only the prerogative of a single class of people, as is often the case in some rural areas for certain investment decisions. For example, focusing on the peasant institutions, more than 49, 24% of fertilizer adopters are involved in peasant institutions. This demonstrates the importance for farmer participation in social organization as a source of learning about techniques. Similarly, the owners of a village experimental field who have adopted technology are estimated to 25, 30% of the sample (table 1). With these results it seems necessary to document the source of information used by each farmer as the majority of fertilizer adopter does not have access to extension activity does not belong from institutions facilities. Thus, as noticed before the low level of institutions facilities leads also partly to the low level use of fertilizer in the study area.

On average, more than 45, 67% of adopters belong to peasant institutions indicated that agents from NGO were a source of information used to learn about new methods and practices relating to the fertilize use. From them, only 0, 89% of the adopters use extension services from the state agent. Socials networks with neighbors, family and religions are more used channel of communication (Table 6). Famers enhance their knowledge learning and observing others. The farmers use more than one source information to learn about the fertilizer technology. About 78, 87% of the whole sample used at least two sources, whereby there is great difference between adopters and non-adopters. However, religions are more used channel of communication by non-adopters than adopters' farmers. Indeed, 12, 34% of the adopters (24, 9%) of no-adopters)

TABLE 5

Sources of information used by adopters and non-adopters

Source	Adopters (N=336)	Non-adopters (N=249)
Don't now	3.27	43,78
Friends network	8.63	3,61
Family network	5.36	3,61
NGO	0.60	0,40
Peasant association	0.30	0,40
Religions	0.30	7,23
Traders supply	2.68	12,85
radio and phone calls	0.60	2,41
Friends and family networks	21.13	1,20
Friends and family networks, NGO and peasant institutions	23.51	2,41
Friends, NGO and peasant institutions	2.38	0,40
Friends and family networks, peasant institutions and religions	1.79	8,43
Friends and family networks and markets	7,9	1,61
Friends network, NGO, peasant institutions and religions	0.30	9,24
Friends and family networks, NGO, peasant institutions and Markets supply	11.31	0,40
Friends and family networks, peasant institutions, religions, radio and phone calls	2.38	0,00
Family, NGO, peasant institutions, religions and Markets supply	6,68	0,00
Family network, NGO, peasant institutions and state	0.89	0,00
Total	**100**	**100**

Source: author's calculation from sample data 2011.

said that religions were an important source of information. On the other hand, radio and phone calls do not represent an important role in diffusing basic information. Although 58, 23% of the respondents declared being in possession of a radio only 2, 98% of the sample cited it as a source of information. Moreover, their use by non-adopters is also very low (2, 41%). This show that listening to the radio is not necessary the way of getting basic on new techniques, but there are to question the broadcast programs in the study area who most of the time focus on the politics, security issues and music. Finally, the remaining source of information and which not less important in encouraging farmers to adopt are market supply on inputs. More than 25, 85% combine this kind of source of information with others channels. Only 2, 68% use it as a unique channel to access to information on fertilizer technology.

Regarding the adoption of fertilizer in each survey areas, location seems to be determinant factor of fertilizer adoption and its importance is revealed in the table below. Fertilizer is more important in Kabare, Walungu and Idjwi area than in Bunyakiri and Uvira. For example, the number of adopters of agricultural compost of the first three zones is for times the numbers adopters of Bunyakri and about the double of Uvira. The reason is that compost adoption is not an easy task because it requires enormous physical efforts for production and transportation.

Indeed, in these two areas (Bunyakiri and Uvira) were compost adoption is very low, the fields are more far from habitation and to reach them subsistence farmers have to walking more than an hour. Using compost become in this context leads to more investment both in production and transportation. Another way to explain this low usersn is that subsistence farmer from theses area still continues depending on fallow practice, then using fertilizer turns out to be lesser important. The percentage of adopter of compost is also higher in the first three areas because of soil erosion, land scarcity, soil infertility and demographic pressure. According to Wubeneh and Sanders (2006) in the area where land is scarce, small farmers are more likely to intensify production with fertilizer to compensate for their small land size. Households with larger farms may prefer extensive production methods because the fallow portions of their land use crop rotation to replenish the fertility of the soil.

The use of inorganic fertilizer alone or combined with compost in very low in the whole study area. Thus, on the 25 household farmers who adopted inorganic fertilizer, 7 are from Uvira, 6 from Bunyakiri, 5 from Walungu and 4 from Idjwi. Only three household farmers adopted this technology in Kabare. The adoption of inorganic fertilizer combined with compost seems to be the same in all surveyed area except

TABLE 6

Fertilizer technologies types by location

	Bunyakiri	Walungu	Idjwi	Kabare	Uvira	All	%
Manure and Compost	21	80	67	72	39	279	47,69
Inorganic fertilizer	6	5	4	3	7	25	4,27
Compost and inorganic fertilizer	2	8	9	8	6	33	5,64
Non-adopters	85	34	43	36	62	248	42,39
Total	**114**	**123**	**116**	**118**	**114**	**585**	**100**

Source: author's calculation from sample 2011

Bunyakiri where only 2 persons declared using mixture of inorganic fertilizer and compost technology. However, the quantity applied of both inorganic fertilizer and compost need to be documented. Overall, 44, 44% surveyed farmers are neither users of compost nor organic fertilizer suggesting that fertilizer technology adoption still continues to be low although farmers is study are experiencing soil degradation and productivity slowdown. This observation leads to analyze the next section, the factors that determine the adoption of fertilizer in the study area. The observation of the table 2 and 5 allow understanding the number of technologies adopted by household farmers, to maintain the quality of their land, which will be discussed in the econometrics estimates.

4.2. *Logistic regression for fertilizer adoption*

The result of estimation to assess the fertilizer technology adoption is reported in table 7 below. The logit estimates show that several variables are statistically significant associated with fertilizer technology adoption. Thus, the null-hypothesis that all variables can be dropped is rejected at less than the 1% level of significance. The results are represented in odds ratio, rather those coefficients. The odds ratio is the chance of the dependent variable – fertilizer adoption by subsistence farming household – changing in the independent variable. In contrast to regression based models where a statistically insignificant coefficient is zero, the statistically insignificant odds ratio is one – that is, a 1 – to – or even chance. Odds ratios that are less than one represent an inverse relationship between the independent and dependent variable, while odds ratios greater than one represent a direct relationship. The marginal effects simply capture the increase in the probability of adoption as the independent variables increase in value.

Seven variables of the seventeen variables influence the adoption of fertilizer at different levels of significance. Livestock value, land tenure and, access to extension activity, and the social networks variables are significant at 1% level, while the off-farm employment, consumption expenditure and number of field are significant at 5% level. However, the gender and age of the primary decision maker, his education level, total family size, farm size, number of crops grown, peasant institution, microcredit access, the existence of a farmer field schools square of social networks although it presents the hypothesized sign, and distance from the field are not significant.

Farmers who are involved in off-farm activity are less likely to adopt fertilizer. This result implies that the higher the capacity of households to develop alternative activity than agriculture the greater the likelihood for no adopting fertilizer. The odds in favor of fertilizer adoption, decreased by 0.56 ($p<0.05$) for farmers who had off-farm work.

The justification of this is that farmer behavior in the context of political instability may not be incited to invest as fertilizer adoption leads to more physical and financial efforts, and thus investing more in a business while the future is unknown and uncertain proves to be precarious. The result is consistent with the findings of Teklewod *et al.* (2006) and Daramola and Aturamu (2000), Abdulai and Fuffman (2005). High proportion of off-farm income suggests that incomes from farm investments are not enough to encourage farmers to take on some risks and adopt. However, Merenya and Barett (2007) and Beshir (2012) reported opposite effects and pointed that cash is essential in the hiring of labor for purchase of chemical fertilizer and related inputs. Moreover, increasing participation in off-farm employment (including self-employment) leads to rising costs of labor time and influences fertilizing practices (Kung and Cai, 2000).

In this study, in conformity with the hypothesis, the numbers of fields influences the use of fertilizer positively at less than 1% level significance. This may be due to the fact that fragmented land holdings allow producers to be more adaptive to certain circumstances such as adoption of new technology. The result goes in line with the findings of Kung and Cai (2000), Telda (2011) and Asfaw *et al.* (2012). However, Beshir (2012) find contradicts results. According to him the poor transportation access and the land fragmentation problems may increases the time required to reach the plots and then labor required increases.

Rented hectares have significant coefficients. Land rental imposes an additional payment burden in cash and crop-share, which may reduce the incentives for the adoption of fertilizer. Indeed, fertilizer adoption as a form of investment is expensive for poor subsistence farmers, and its application and transport are complex. Land rental puts subsistence farmer in a situation of high insecurity tenure because it gives no guarantee to farmer recover the invested the money in soil management. Land rental seems to be a hindrance agricultural intensification and the development urban-rural trade (Bucekuderhwa, 2005). Tenure insecurity appears here as element – among others – that blocks the process of agriculture intensification, renewal and management of natural resources. Without any real assurance to keep his land, every peasant will be reluctant to invest labor and capital for the improvement and sustainability of agricultural land [Teyssier (2000) and Goldstein and Udry (2008). For instance, compost acts slowly and helps to benefit from improving soil quality than directly feeding the plant. This amending power of the compost is much more over time. Only then the owners of the plots can easily take the initiative to use it since they are not bounded by the constraints associated with the rental of the plots. It is therefore the State to alleviate the conditions to access to land that most often do not motivate poor farmers. Howe-ver, Kung and Cai (2000) found in China that fertilizer application were explained by location of the field rather than property rights. Buliding on Kung's (1999) explanation Kung and Cai (2000) support that instead of applying an equal amount of organic fertilizer among the rice paddies, located near farmers' residence, and the dry hilly slopes, usually farther away, farmers apply a disproportionately larger amount of organic fertilizer to the paddies, with location being the main determining.

As hypothesized the consumption expenditures is negative and statistically significant for adoption of fertilizer. The negative coefficient indicates that poor farmer are less likely to adopt the fertilizer technology as the spend all of their income on consumption. As decision maker, subsistence farmers may maximize utility rather than profit and thus their planning horizon shrink and so the incentives for them to invest in future productivity of their farm diminish. Moreover, poor farmers may incur lower switching costs in implementing new practices since they only have limited assets and learning adjustment cost involved in adopting fertilizer may be lower for them. Finally, since fertilizer practices generally require more financial effort, the relatively wealthier subsistence farmers are more likely to implement than their poor counterparts. This raises an important extension policy. Extension systems must differentiate their clientele based on the critical economics and socials issues. If the objective of policy maker is to enhance the income of the poorest of the poor, perhaps extension messages can be accompanied by food distribution on certain income groups, especially in the early stages of technology development and dissemination. The result is consistent with the findings of Shively (2000), Lee (2005), Bucekuderhwa and Ngendakuriyo (2011) who found that consumption risk may limit adoption particularly among subsistence farmers due to their disproportionate sensitivity to short-term own-production losses.

The value of livestock is positively and significant ($p<01$) associated with adoption of fertilizer. Indeed, manure availability obviously depends in large measure on the size of the herd a household owns. Thus the size of the coefficient estimate for livestock is greatest in fertilizer regression because manure is the most important source of fertilizer for subsistence farms in this area. Moreover, livestock ownership is considered as an asset that could be exchanged for cash for the purchase of inputs whenever the need arose. The results are consistent with the findings of Marenya and Barett (2007), Dercon and Christiaensen (2011) and Beshir *et al.* (2012). The positive complementarily between livestock and crop enterprises as means for generating synergistic production relationships has been documented frequently (Kistjannson *et al.*, 2005).

According to Marenya and Barett (2007) crop enterprises generate both food and feed, while livestock enterprises yield both manure for replenishing soil fertility and cash for purchase of others inputs such as chemical fertilizer. This evidence is also found by Abaya and Assefa (2004) as reported by Beshir (2012). Similarly, Wubeneh and Sanders (2006) hypothesized that manure is positively related to the adoption of both the new cultivars and fertilizer because of the complementary effects. This has an important implication for the way crop and

TABLE 7

Logistic model estimates of adoption of fertilizer

Variables	Odds Ratio	Robust Std. Err.	Marginal effects	Robust Std. Err.
Gender of the household member	1,069798	0,219881	0,01625	0,04953
Log(age of the household member)	0,948623	0,268581	-0,01269	0,06810
Total family size	1,018241	0,022969	0,00435	0,00543
Education level	1,010338	0,034906	0,00247	0,00831
Off-farm employment	0,5772773**	0,159333	-0,13520**	0,06835
Farm size	0,930755	0,073829	-0,01726	0,01908
Log (Livestock value)	1,44825***	0,094870	0,08908***	0,01575
Number of field per household	1,142392**	0,066147	0,03202**	0,0139
Land tenure	0,5526011***	0,112648	-0,14126***	0,04767
consumption expenditures	0,9978142**	0,000941	-0,00053**	0,00023
Number of crops	1,018988	0,033209	0,00452	0,00784
Organizational involvement	1,303192	0,313507	0,06342	0,05722
Extension activity	1,928573***	0,375031	0,02228***	0,04449
Presence of a farmer field school	1,097543	0,307352	0,15486	0,06671
Social Networks	1,024617***	0,008955	0,00585***	0,0021
Square of social Networks	0,999921	0,000070	-0,00002	0,00002
Microcredit access	1,231411	0,245861	0,04984	0,04754
Log (Distance from home to field)	0,997264	0,003140	-0,00066	0,00076
Observations	585			
Pseudo R-squared	0,1662			
Model chi-square	106,39			
Log likelihood	-331,91			

Note: Statistical significance at 99 per cent (***), 95 per cent (**) and 90 per cent confidence levels.

livestock research is organized in low-income tropics. Cox (2011) found that given the poverty of the soil and few alternatives, bovine manure is becoming one of the most valuable resources in rural Kivu short of coltan and gold. The integration of natural resources management, crop and livestock research units at all stages of research and agricultural development continuum may yield important synergies.

Education, organizational involvement, contact with extension agents and social networks of the farmer were considered as proxies for access to information in formal and informal way. Two of these variables are significant in explaining the variation in the fertilizer adoption. Extension activity which is used as a proxy of access to formal information in the fertilizer adoption model is significant variable. The marginal values indicate that a 10% increase in the number of extension activity is expected to increase the probability of adoption by 19, 30%. Although the collapse of the government offices, agricultural extension services still remain a formal channel to access to information for improved agricultural technologies in the area study. Perhaps this can be explained by the fact that NGO allows farmers access to training activities. Building on Asfaw and al. (2012) findings, agricultural extension is the system of formal learning and building the human capital of farmers through the provision of information and demonstration, exposing farmers to technologies which can increase agricultural productivity and, in turn income and welfare. Farmers who are frequently visited by extension agents tend to be more progressive and more likely to experiment with fertilizer. This result is also consistent with the findings of Kaliba *et al.* (2000), Isham (2002), Abdulai and Huffman (2005), Tekelwold *et al.* (2006), Shiferaw *et al.* (2008), Thapa and Rattanasuteerakul (2011) and Beshir *et al.* (2012).

One of the most findings of this section is the positive and significant effect of social networks. A social network is an informal channels that farmer use to learn and build about fertilizer. The result implies that having one more adopter among family and friends, evaluated at the network mean, increases the propensity to adopt fertilizer by 10, 25% with social network. These are the initial effects, and there will also be multiplier effects as information spreads through the social network. Patterns of initial adoption decisions within and across social network may occur in other economic environments in which a new technology is introduced, information is a key barrier to adoption, and individuals can be expected to learn about the new technology from others. In particular, the possibility of nonlinearity in the relationship between the adoption decision and the number of adopters in the network should always be taken into account in contexts where social learning plays a key role. This result is consistent with Foster and Rosenzweig (1995), Lee (2005), Bandiera and Rasul (2006), Matuschke *et al.* (2007), Conley and Udry (2010), Thapa and Rattanasuteerakul (2011) findings. According to Thapa and Rattanasuteerakul (2011) farmers can also by themselves be the source of inspiration and serve as very influential agents for the promotion of any agricultural innovations. As a natural human behavior, farmers who have not yet adopted such innovation tend to seek the advice and recommendations of their fellow farmers, which are usually considered more convincing and reliable than the advice given by outsiders including GO and NGO officials (Jintrawet, 1995). More particularly in the developing countries where extension services have not been very effective due to resource and other constraints, farmers can play very effective role in the promotion of agricultural innovations as Adesina and Baidu-Forson (1995), Bewket (2007), Thapa and Rattanasuteerakul (2011) reported. For instance, Foster and Rosenzweig (1995) emphasized that neighbors, as part of social network, appear to be important sources of information about input use, as important as formal public information dissemination sources.

4.3. Multivariate probit of adoption of fertilizer technologies types

The act of adoption, observed variable by the direct response to the question "did you use at least compost (organic fertilizer)/inorganic fertilizer/ or both in the past two growing season?" is estimated by a multivariate probit regression (mvprobit). The estimates results are presented in table 9. The likelihood ratio test allows us to reject the hypothesis that the free equations are independent, at 1% level (see robustness checks). Note, however, that the discussion of the results is done by focusing on a logistic for obvious reasons that the odds ratio and the marginal effects are easily obtained and interpreted. Interestingly, the estimation of logistic model generated satisfactory and close results to those of multivariate probit regression. Indeed, the model is generally specified as the value of the statistic (df =51) was used to test the null hypothesis that all the coefficients of the explanatory variables are zero is significant at 1% and is equal to 182.58. We can therefore conclude that, statistically, all the coefficients of the explanatory variables are not zero simultaneously. The meaning of coefficients of the explanatory variables that determine the adoption of each type technology of fertilizer varies from one type of technology to another.

The first point that is in worth mentioning of the estimates from table 8 is the significant level education variable using the multivariate porbit regression. However, this relationship is negative for the use of compost while it is positive of inorganic fertilizer and mixture of compost and inorganic fertilizer. This implies that premium education induces subsistence farmer to adopt technology which requires more learning and building as is the case of inorganic and mixture fertilizer. The result is consistent with the findings of Doss and Morris (2001), Chianu and Tsujii (2004), Lee (2005), Marenya and Barret (2007) and Beshir *et al.* (2012) who found that system which are knowledge intensive and in which management ability may provide the key successful adaptation and adoption. Lee (2005) building on Van de Fliert (2003) and Barrett *et al* (2002) findings support that improved management begins with achieving simple literacy and numeracy, and can include observational, analytical, experimental, and communications skills. Policy marker may integrate farmer education in their agricultural development policy as education has important implications on technologies adoption.

Besides, in conformity with the hypothesis, livestock value positively and significantly affect the adoption of use of the three types of fertilizer. All things being otherwise, livestock ownership increases the probability of fertilizer adoption and then confirming in this way its importance at subsistence level. This is in line with previous work on the adoption of fertilizer [Marenya and Barret (2007), Wubeneh and Sanders (2006)]. Improving access to livestock is an alternative that may increase soil fertility for subsistence farming in rural South Kivu area.

As expected, the coefficient of access to extension is significant and positive in the sub-models of compost, mixture of compost and inorganic fertilizer (10%). As for the non-organic fertilizer, this coefficient is not significant, but keeps the positive expected sign. This result implies that the presence of extension services in a village influences the likelihood of adoption of fertilizer, and especially compost combined with inorganic fertilizer. Indeed, this variable promotes the exchange of information between farmers groups in different areas. In a word, it can convey information. The non-significant result in the sub-model of inorganic fertilizers has explanations. On the one hand, compost replaces organic fertilizer in areas where it does not exist. On the other hand, access to inorganic fertilizer is expensive under subsistence farmers and its application is unrelated to subsistence farms, which requires additional level of learning and financial expenses.

The multivariate estimates show that rented land and microcredit have significant effect for compost and the mixture of compost and inorganic fertilizer adoption, but no significant on inorganic fertilizer adoption. Although rented land remains with the expected negative and significant effect, microcredit access however presents an ambiguous effect with a positive sign for compost adoption and negative for mixture compost and inorganic fertilizer. In the absence of small ruminants that subsistence farmers sell to finance their activities, gets access to credit allow to cope with expenses related to the management of compost and purchase inorganic fertilizer. Credit availability to farmers is a measure of his financial worth and that most of them cannot adopt any innovations when their purchasing power is ineffective. This implies that policy interventions that make credit available to more subsistence farmers could facilitate adoption. This finding is consistent with the findings of Abay and Assfaw (2004), Teklewold *et al.* (2006) and Beshir *et al.* (2012). However, it should be noted that the variable access to credit is negative for mixture of compost and inorganic fertilizer. This can be partly explained by the fact that mixture of fertilizer requires an additional learning. Thus, farmers become skeptical to contact credit to finance technologies whose application leads to an increase of learning cost while they do not know well what will be their performances on crops yield. The finding appears to be consistent with the theoretical model of Feder following Abdulaiand Huffman (2005). According them where there is a binding credit constraint, farmers will devote proportionately less resources to the new technology, if the innovation is perceived to be sufficiently more risky than the traditional technology. Similarly, the facts that inorganic fertilizers are free distributed by non-government organization do not encourage famers to demand credit. These opposite signs in the use fertilizer technologies types therefore require special attention and need to be well documented in subsequent studies.

The results revealed also that the number of fields, off-farm employment, and consumption expenditures are only significant for compost, number of crops grown and the farm size for inorganic fertilizer, while social network is for mixture compost and inorganic fertilizer. While, there seems to be no significant difference between adopters of compost and inorganic fertilizer in terms of their social networks, this variable is significant for mixture manure and inorganic fertilizer. It actually seems obvious by merely looking at the estimates results that the square of social network reports now greater significance for adoption of fertilizer and mixture compost. Building on Matusche *et al* (2007) findings by using the square of social networks, I verified the Bandiera and Rasul (2006) hypothesis and I found that there exist an inverse-U shaped relationship between adoption and the numbers of adopt known.

In contrast with the simple model, the farmer field schools becomes significant for mixture of compost and inorganic fertilizer and while the numbers of crops grown by farmers is significant for inorganic fertilizer. The positive and significant effect of farmer field schools implies that farmers use more compost and inorganic fertilizer combined when there is in their

TABLE 8

Multinomial logistic regression, explaining fertilizer adoption by fertilizer type across South Kivu subsistence farming

Variables	Compost		Inorganic fertilizer		Mixture of compost and inorganic fertilizer	
		Robust SE	Odds ratio	Robust SE	Odds ratio	Robust SE
Gender of the household head	0,88391	0,17196	1,14449	0,46464	1,79232	0,69445
Log(age of the household head)	0,87852	0,24128	1,62133	1,06931	1,19115	0,60756
Total family size	1,01684	0,02358	0,96533	0,06752	1,00488	0,05795
Education level	0,94109*	0,03237	1,17758***	0,06904	1,14113***	0,05782
Off-farm employment	0,61522*	0,17016	0,42977	0,28884	1,56612	0,80759
Farm size	0,87103*	0,06766	1,23212*	0,13648	1,06869	0,17785
Log (Livestock value)	1,26974***	0,07992	1,41123***	0,18786	1,27015*	0,18553
Number of field per household	1,16616***	0,06082	0,93499	0,11129	0,92371	0,07067
Land tenure	0,68047**	0,13138	0,89397	0,39308	0,56124	0,2057
Consumption expenditures	0,99866	0,00087	0,99734*	0,0016	0,99855	0,0019
Number of crops	1,04804	0,03307	0,87452*	0,06452	0,97063	0,04782
Organizational involvement	1,36414	0,31791	1,20763	0,53841	0,71602	0,32184
Extension activity	1,36705*	0,25468	1,88458	0,83926	2,42924**	0,94146
Farm Field Schools	0,74183	0,19841	0,96215	0,54179	5,02099****	2,19097
Social Networks	1,00743	0,0119	1,01676	0,03817	1,11236****	0,03885
Square of social Networks	1,00007	0,0001	0,99981	0,00035	0,99901***	0,00031
Microcredit access	1,49311*	0,28801	1,08449	0,49196	0,29205***	0,14091
Distance from home to field	1,0003	0,00323	0,9966	0,00789	0,99199	0,00587

Note: Statistical significance at 99 per cent (***), 95 per cent (**) and 90 per cent (*) confidence levels.

village a community pilot field. The pilot field or farmer field school is site where of demonstration where farmers learn how they can simultaneously use compost and organic fertilizer. It is of paramount importance because it allows farmer to be aware of the potential benefits of each fertilizer technologies types. This finding is consistent with the finding of Nathaniels (2005). However, the farmer field school implies ownership by all stakeholders. This implies that collective action is possible in each village and leads to the problematic question of governing of the commons mentioned by Ostrom (1989). For instance, how to ensure that everyone is involved in the maintenance of the farmer field school and contribute to the different costs in order to make possible future tests? Research and extension services will need to compensate for this by making extra efforts to empower farmers, who are generally disadvantage in terms of social cohesion and coordination and skewed patterns of endowments of critical resources, need to make fertilizer adoption remunerative.

Interestingly, the coefficient on the number of crops grown by farmers confirms the hypothesis that the surveyed farmers emphasize ensuring basic subsistence. This implies that the greater the diversity of crops farm household grows, the low the probability of adoption of fertilizer by such household. As intercropping system is still dominated in study area and household pressure is very low, application of fertilizer may because of farmer vulnerability. However, this results contrast with others studies. Indeed, Chianu and Tsujii (2004) found that household may be usually open to new ideas and benefits derived from similar behavior in the past raise expectation form fertilizer. Besides, diversification into many crops implies diversification of income sources and income is needed to purchase fertilizer. Moreover, Marenya and Barret (2007) found that statistically significance of intercropping variable capture superior plot characteristics that influence farmer's choice of whether to invest integrated soil fertility management. According to him as farmers are more likely to invest in integrated soil fertility management on plots whose characteristics make them more productive, then the intercrop variable may merely proxy of unobserved plot characteristics. In the same line, Kung and Cai (2000) show that Chinese farmers applied disproportionate amount of their limited organic fertilizer to the plots that they believe will be most responsive to this soils nutrient. Because of ambiguous sign for the three different use of fertilizer, another thorough study with more data could help to confirm these results.

Consequently, in conformity with the hypothesis, farm size becomes significant for compost and inorganic fertilizer. From compost adoption there is a significantly negative response to farm size. The larger the farm the less inclined an operator is to adopt compost technology. But in inorganic adoption farm presents a positive sign for inorganic fertilizer. The possible justification is that the bigger the farm sizes, the more the flexibility for crop rotations and fallowing. The result is in the line with the findings Wanyama *et al.* (2010), Holloway *et al.* (2002) and Telda (2011). However, Asfaw *et al.* (2012), Beshir *et al.* (2012) found contrast results.

4.4. Robustness checks

A natural check for robustness of the conclusions above is required. I use two models to estimate the probability of adoption fertilizer by subsistence farmers. To capture the behavior on adoption I then first considered all fertilizer types as a unique technology. Therefore, adoption is estimated using logistic regression. However, subsistence farmers can use the technology in different level. To avoid this problem a multivariate probit is used to estimate the probability of adoption of fertilizer technologies types. Accordingly explanatory variables are checked for the problems of multicollinearity, endogeneity and heteroscedasticity. Following Gujarati (2012), I investigated the problem of multicollinearity for continuous explanatory variables using a technique of variance inflation factor (VIF) and tolerance level (TOL), where each continuous explanatory variable is regressed on all the other continuous explanatory variables. The larger is the value of VIF, the more worrying is the multicollinearity or collinear is the variable . As a rule of the thumb, if the VIF of a variable exceeds 10 and R^2 exceed 0.90 the variable is said to be highly collinear. The value of VIF were less than ten and hence no signals of multicollinearity problems (Appendix 3). To avoid the problems of heteroscedasticity, I calculated robust standards errors. The joint test of Wald that tests the global significance of the model on all zero alternative coefficients except the constant is significant to 1%. In addition the algorithm has converged after four iterations. The model is concave and the likelihood function reaches its maximum as showed by the negative value of the Log pseudo likelihood.

When farmer adopt fertilizer techniques, the resulting improvements in productivity affect household welfare through, for example, improved incomes, and increase ability to educate children, more health care access invest in livestock assets. It is therefore possible that some household variables such as livestock may be endogenous, a problem that remains unresolved in much adoption literature [Besley and Case (1993), Doss (2006) and Marenya and Barrett (2007). Due to the lack of panel data the problem of endogeneity an attempt was made to exclude dependent variable as explanatory variable. Similarly, as nothing allows concluding that available livestock under subsistence farming is the result of the increase in agriculture productivity due to the use of fertilizer, I maintained the variable. In addition, endogeneity due to positive, associative sorting along a characteristic correlated with fertilizer use (e.g., unobserved wealth) could produce a tendency for good news to be associated with either high or low fertilizer use, but we were unable to think of a scenario where it would induce both.

The discussion of results of the fertilizer technologies types focused on the logit models rather than the multivariate probit model. In Table 10, I present the same binary model as in table 8 but it is estimated using multivariate probit regression for checking robustness. As discussed before, multivariate probit model is desirable when the dependent variables in a set of otherwise independent equations are potentially interdependent. This is indeed the case in this paper since the three fertilizer technologies types being analyzed are not necessarily independent. In fact, to observe the degree of association between fertilizer technologies types of contingency coefficient are computed. Contingency coefficient is a chi-square based measure of association where a value 0.75 or above indicates a stronger relationship between explanatory variables (Healy, 1984). This is also checked and less than 0.7 (Table 9). Consequently, the multivariate specification that allows one to control for this interdependence takes the form

$$Y_n^* = \beta'_n X + \varepsilon_n$$

$$Y_n = \begin{cases} 1 \text{ si } y_n^* > y_0 \text{ (household i used fertilizer), and} \\ 0 \text{ si } y_n^* \leq y_0 \text{ otherwise} \end{cases}$$

Where y_n is the observed variable and is the unobserved latent variables. In this empirical set-up, n stands as n equation counter and range from 1 to 3 since there are three equations in total. Solving this system of equation requires the evaluation of multivariate normal distribution functions, a problem that is best solved by simulated maximum likelihood (SML).

The mvprobit routine in STATA performs this evaluation using the Geweke-Hajivassiliou-Keane (GHK) simulator (Cappellari and Jenkins, 2003). This method is known to be sensitive to the number of observations drawn in each step of the iteration procedure so the authors recommend using a draws at least as large as the square root of the total number of observations. For the analysis reported in Table 10, I have used 35 draws in the mvprobit routine instead of the default 5. It should be noted that probit models give estimates that are very similar to those of logit models (Cameron and Trivedi, 2005). Therefore, results from the mvprobit could be held up to those obtained from logit models in Table 8. The multivariate probit results (Table 10) suggest interdependence across the equations ($\rho > 0$, $p < 0.05$ for most of the equations).

Consequently, the apparent explanatory power of the separate equation models might be upward biased. To check this, I have obtained the normalized Aldrich-Nelson pseudo-R^2 (0,13) for the multivariate that I compared to separate models (Compost=0,13, Inorganic fertilizer=0,11, Mixture of compost and inorganic fertilizer=0,16; Average=13). This gives reliable approximations of the goodness of fit for models with discrete dependent variables [Veall and Zimmerman (1992), Hagle and Mitchell II (1992)]

TABLE 9

Contingency coefficients for different fertilizer technologies types

buVariables	Compost	Inorganic	Mixture compost and inorganic
Compost	1.0000		
Inorganic	23.8117***	1.0000	
Mixture compost and inorganic	33.9425***	1.6619	1.0000

Statistical significance at 99 percent (***)

TABLE 10
Multivariate probit of adoption technologies types of fertilizer

Variables	Compost		Inorganic fertilizer		Mixture compost and inorganic	
	Coeff.	Robust SE	Coeff.	Robust SE	Coeff.	Robust SE
Gender of the household head	-0,08331	0,11629	0,02242	0,17969	0,29947	0,18097
Log(age of the household head)	-0,07885	0,16216	0,10940	0,26551	0,11698	0,24922
Total family size	0,01296	0,01448	-0,01320	0,03049	0,00016	0,03764
Education level	-0,03409*	0,01937	0,07744***	0,02708	0,05714***	0,02332
Off-farm employment	-0,29821*	0,16303	-0,41242	0,29043	0,21230	0,26167
Farm size	-0,08174*	0,04287	0,11061**	0,04832	0,04036	0,05862
Log (Livestock value)	0,15472***	0,03720	0,15900***	0,06100	0,00033***	0,00014
Number of field per household	0,09039***	0,03049	-0,03065	0,04747	-0,04226	0,03447
Land tenure	-0,24140**	0,11532	-0,05963	0,19252	-0,30519	0,18248
Consumption expenditures	-0,00075	0,00048	-0,00092*	0,00062	-0,00018	0,00056
Number of crops	0,02714	0,01830	-0,04949*	0,03027	-0,00798	0,01986
Organizational involvement	0,16747	0,13599	0,06608	0,20648	-0,26828	0,19770
Extension activity	0,18953*	0,11153	0,20090	0,19896	0,33421**	0,16574
Farm Field Schools	-0,15320	0,15582	0,04708	0,24954	0,75576***	0,20230
Social Networks	0,00558	0,00638	0,00733	0,01661	0,04731***	0,01646
Square of social Networks	0,00003	0,00005	-0,00009	0,00015	-0,00044***	0,00015
Microcredit access	0,22217*	0,11592	0,08734	0,20204	-0,48819**	0,21553
Distance from home to field	0,00007	0,00190	-0,00056	0,00330	-0,00244	0,00274
Cons	-0,86524	0,68538	-2,94788	1,13330	-2,84931	0,98086

Note: Statistical significance at 99 per cent (***), 95 per cent (**) and 90 per cent (*) confidence levels.

and is very easy to calculate using the estimated log-likelihood for the null and alternative models. The results confirm the presence of upward bias in the separate equation models (Appendix Table 3). Notwithstanding, the results of the multivariate estimation differ from those obtained by estimating separate equations only in terms of the magnitude of the coefficients; the patterns and significance Levels remain the same. This suggests robustness of the results of the analyses. And for the added benefit that the can be easily obtained and interpreted (Cameron and Trivedi, 2005), I choose to discussed the logit models in the text.

5. Conclusion

This research aimed to explain the technology adoption in the context of subsistence agriculture in South Kivu province highlighting, from a cross-sectional data set, the different forms of fertilizer used by adopters' farmers and the variables that influence the adoption decision of fertilizer. The most important findings are that framers are subsistence oriented. They have small plots of lands which are disseminated within villages. The assets of these households are very limited and are largely dominated by livestock (large and small). Opportunities in terms of off-farm employment are limited and agricultural production remains the main source of livelihoods. The most important source of formal information for adoption technology of fertilizer is extension services and peasant institutions. Moreover, social networks as an informal source of knowledge represents important source information that subsistence farmer use to learn about fertilizer. Logistic and multivariate probit models were employed to study farmers' decision to adopt improved technologies. The logistic regression was employed to test a simple model of adoption of all different fertilizer technologies types, while the multivariate probit was used to assess adoption decision of each fertilizer technologies types.

The results of the logistic regression provided empirical evidence of the positive impact of livestock in enhancing the adoption fertilizer technologies to increase production. The study found availability of extension service and livestock value to be more powerful than other factors in explaining adoption fertilizer technology adoption. The results support the hypothesis of a positive relationship between the probability of a subsistence farmer adoption and his social network. The number of field was also powerful in explain the adoption fertilizer technologies suggesting that this input require additional plots for different crop operation. The consumption expenditures of the farmer significantly and negatively affected the use of fertilizer technologies. Poor farmers adopted less improved agricultural technologies than rich farmers suggesting that high level of consumption threshold delayed the adoption of improved agricultural technologies.

The results of the multivariate probit analysis show that the determinants and adoption rates of fertilizer technologies vary from one type of fertilizer to another. Thus, as in the unique model, the relationship between livestock value and adoption decision was also found to be positive for the three fertilizer technologies types considered in this paper. Explanations for this are found in the nature of the farming environment as well as the way in which farmers approach fertilizer technology. The results highlight the need for farmers to be more invested in livestock to access to more organic fertilizer. This has been the main conclusion from several previous studies but the present study confirms its relevance to South Kivu subsistence farming. The empirical results show that agricultural extension service significantly influenced agricultural technology adoption of compost, the mixture of compost with inorganic fertilizer. The development and dissemination of improved agricultural technologies should be given more emphasis to bring about a significant improvement in the productivity of smallholder mixed crop-livestock farming and eradicate the widespread poverty and food insecurity problem in the country in general and the study area in particular. The agricultural research and extension service should be given priority and emphasis ought to be placed upon fastening the production and dissemination of existing and newly developed improved technology. Focusing on market oriented interventions that motivate farmers to invest in improved agricultural technologies is a sensible policy option.

More importantly, the results of this multivariate analysis revealed also an important relationship education level and fertilizer technologies types. The positive significant of education is differentiated according to the fertilizer technologies types: education has positive effect on inorganic fertilizer and mixture compost and inorganic fertilizer, but the effect becomes negative for compost when used alone. Moreover, farm size revealed usefulness insights for compost and inorganic fertilizer. The negative significant sign for compost implies that compost management involves physical and financial efforts. Finally, the findings on mixture of compost with inorganic fertilizer point to the fact that social network is essentially for subsistence farmer adoption decision. Nevertheless, social network seems to be negative when technology users increase. This is could be probably due to the obsolescence of the technology. It is therefore necessary for the various stakeholders who are involved in agricultural research and development to make farmers aware about various new agricultural innovations to strength their network and stimulate their behavior in terms of adoption of technology.

An important limitation of the analyses in this paper is that they reveal very little about the direction of causality. Are subsistence farmer adopt more innovative because they have access to more resources and more information or thereby become more productive because they have access to fertilizer? Providing answers to this type of question requires panel data, which are hard to come by in the research context and experiment. Another shortcoming of the analyses is the usual problems of endogeneity and unobserved heterogeneity associated with the use of cross-sectional data. Quite regrettably, even if more waves of the fertilizer technology survey that has been used become available, they will most likely only provide repeated cross-sectional rather than true panel data. This creates the need for alternative data sources or a combination of complementary data sources. Finally, the results in this paper are based on a relatively small sample of subsistence farming. Larger samples might yield markedly diverse results, confirming some of those presented herein while possibly confounding others.

Bibliography

Abdulai, A. and W. E. Huffman (2005) The diffusion of new agricultural technologies: the case of crossbred-cow technology in Tanzania, *American Journal of Agricultural Economics*, Vol. 87, No. 3, 645-659

Adesina, A. A. and J. Baidu-Forson (1995) Farmers' perceptions and adoption of newagricultural technology: evidence from analysis in Burkina Faso and Guinea, *West Africa. Agricultural Economics,* 13, 1-9.

Abdoulaye, T. and J. H. Sanders (2005) Stages and determinants of fertilizer use in semiarid African agriculture: the Niger experience, *Agricultural Economics*, 32, 167-179.

Adesina, A. A., Mbila, D., G. BlaiseNkamleu, G. B. and D. Endamana (2000) Econometric analysis of the determinants of adoption of alley farming by farmers in the forest zone of southwest Cameroon, Agriculture, *Ecosystems and Environment*, 80, 255–265.

Ajewole, O.C. (2010) Farmer's response to adoption of commercially available organic fertilizers in Oyo state, Nigeria, *African Journal of Agricultural Research*, Vol. 5(18), 2497-2503.

Akpan S.B., Nkanta V.S. and U.A. Essien (2012) A Double-Hurdle Model of Fertilizer Adoption and Optimum Use among Farmers in Southern Nigeria, *Tropicultura,*30, 4, 249-253.

Alem, Y., Bezabih, M., Kassiea, M. and P. Zikhalic (2010) Does fertilizer use respond to rainfall variability? Panel data evidence from Ethiopia, *Agricultural Economics*, 41, 165-175.

Asfaw, S., M. Kassie, F. Simtowe and L. Lipper (2012) Poverty Reduction Effects of Agricultural Technology Adoption: A Micro-evidence from Rural Tanzania, *Journal of Development Studies*, Vol. 48, No. 9, 1288-1305.

Asfaw, A.and A. Admassie (2004) The role of education on the adoption of chemical fertilizer under different socioeconomic environments in Ethiopia, *Agricultural Economics,* 30, 215-228.

Asfaw, S., Shiferaw, B, Simtowe, F. and M. G. Haile (2011) Agricultural technology adoption, seed access constraints and commercialization in Ethiopia, *Journal of Development and Agricultural Economics*, Vol. 3(9), 436-447.

Bandiera, O. and I. Rasul (2006) Social Networks and Technology Adoption in Northern Mozambique, The *Economic Journal*, 116, 869–902.

Beshir, H., B. Emana, B. Kassa and J. Haji (2012) Determinants of chemical fertilizer technology adoption in North eastern highlands of Ethiopia; the double hurdle approach, *Journal of Research in*

Economics and International Finance (JREIF), Vol.1 (2), 39-49.

Besley, T. and A. Case (1993), "Modeling Technology Adoption in Developing Countries," *The American Economic Review*, Vol. 83, No. 2, 396-402.

Bewket, W. (2007) Soil and water conservation intervention with conventional echnologies in northwestern highlands of Ethiopia: acceptance and adoption by farmers, *Land Use Policy*, 24, 404-416.

Bossissi, K. Cidoro, V., Bashagaluke, J. Walangululu, J. and P. Pypers (2011) The best choice of fertilizer for maize (Zea mays) and climbing beans (Phaseolus vulgaris) rotation for rich, mean and poor farmers in South Kivu, D.R. Congo, *Increasing Agricultural Productivity and Enhancing Food Security in Africa: New Challenges and Opportunities.*

Bucekuderhwa, B.C. and Mapatano, S. (2013) Comprendre la dynamique de la vulnérabilité à l'insécurité alimentaire au Sud-Kivu, VertigO-la revue électronique en sciences de l'environnement, Hors-serie 17,

Bucekuderhwa, B.C. (2013) Is there a possiblity of technical progress for subsitence farming? Bukavu Journal of Economics and Social Sciences, n° 1, 148-180.

Bucekuderhwa, B.C. (2011) and Ngendakuriyo, F (2011) Technological change and subsistence farming: A two stage optimal control Approach.

Bucekuderhwa, B. C., (2005), La filière riz au Sud-Kivu : modes de production et localisation, LEAD, Projet PIC « Dynamique des filières productives et développement rural intégré », CUD, Document de travail, miméo, LEAD, UCB.

Byerlee, D., and E. Hesse de Polanco (1986) Farmers' Stepwise Adoption of Technological Packages: Evidence from the Mexican Atiplano. *American Journal of Agricultural Economics*, 68, 519–527.

Cameron, C. and P. K. Trivedi (2005) *Microeconometrics. Methods and Applications*, Cambridge University Press.

Conley, T. G. and Ch. R. Udry (2010) Learning about a New Technology: Pineapple in Ghana, *American Economic Review*, 100:1, 35-69.

Cappellari, L. and S. P. Jenkins (2003) Multivariate probit regression using simulated maximum likelihood, *The Stata Journal*, 3, Number 3, 278-294.

Cox, T.P. (2008) The land as casualty: Soil, cattle and the future in South Kivu, DRC. Unpublished MSc thesis, Department of Anthropology, University College London, UK. (cited 2013 February 23), available at:

http://www.cialca.org/files/files/Student%20Thesis/PaulCox-South-Kivu.pdf.

Cox, P. T. (2012) Farming the battlefield: the meanings of war, cattle and soil in South Kivu, Democratic Republic of the Congo, *Disasters*, 36, 2, 233-248.

Croppenstedt, A., Demeke, M. and M. M. Meschi (2003) Technology Adoption in the Presence of Constraints: the Case of Fertilizer

Demand in Ethiopia, *Review of Development Economics*, 7(1), 58-70.

Cunguara, B.(2012) An exposition of development failuresin Mozambique, Review of African Political Economy, Vol. 39, No. 131, 161–170.

Dercon,S. and L. Christiaensen (2011) Consumption risk, technology adoption and poverty traps: Evidence from Ethiopia, *Journal of Development Economics*, 96, 159–173.

Dorfman, J. H. (1996) Modeling Multiple Adoption Decision in Joint Framework, *American Journal of Agricultural economics*, Vol. 78,No. 3, 547-557.

Doss, C. R. and M. L. Morris (2001) How does gender affect the adoption of agricultural innovations? The case of improved maize technology in Ghana, Agricultural Economics, 25, 27–39.

Doss CR. (2006) Analyzing technology adoption using micro-studies: limitations, challenges, and opportunities for improvement, *Agricultural Economics*, 34:207-19.

Duflo, E., Kremer, M. & J Robinson (2011) Nudging Farmers to Use Fertilizer: Theory and Experimental Evidence from Kenya, *American Economic Review*, 10: 2350–2390.

Fafchamps, M. (1992). Cash crop production, food price volatility and rural market integration in the third world, *American journal of agricultural economics*, 74 (1): 90-99.

Feder, G. and D.L. Umali, (1993). The adoption of agricultural innovations: a review, *Technological Forecasting and Social Change*, 43, 215–219.

Feder, G., Just, R.E. and D. Zilberman (1985) Adoption of agricultural innovations in developing countries: a survey, *Economic Development and Cultural Change*, 33, 2, 255–298.

Foster, A. and M. Rosenzweig (1995) Learning by doing and learning from others: human capital and technical change in agriculture, *Journal of Political Economy*, 103,6, 1176-1209.

Fufa, B & R. M. Hassan (2006) Determinants of fertilizer use on maize in Eastern Ethiopia: weighted endogenous sampling analysis of the extent and intensity of adoption, *Agrekon*, Vol 45, No 1, 38-49.

Geber, J; (2008) *The role of information in the adoption of dairy related technology in Tanzania*, A dissertation thesis, Swiss federal institute of technology.

Goldstein, M. and Udry Ch. (2008) The profits of Power: Land Rights and Agricultural Investment in Ghana, *Journal of Political Economy*, Vol. 116, No. 6, 981-122.

Greene, W.H. (1994) *Ecometric Analysis*, second ed. Prentice-Hall, Englewood Cliffs.

Gujarati, D. (2012) *Econometrics by example*, Palgrave Macmillan, New York.

Hagle, T. M. and G. E. Mitchell II (1992) Goodness - of-Fit Measures for probit and Logit, *American Journal of political Science*, 36 (3), 762-784.

Holloway, G., Shankar, B. and S. Rahmanb (2002) Bayesian spatial probit estimation: a primer and an application to HYV rice adoption,

Agricultural Economics, Volume 27, Issue 3, 383–402.

Isham, J. (2002) The Effect of Social Capital on Fertilizer Adoption: Evidence from Rural Tanzania, *The Journal of African Economies*, Volume 11, Number. 1, 39-60.

Jintrawet, A. (1995). A decision support systems for rapid assessment of lowland rice based cropping alternative in Thailand, *Agriculture Systems*, 47, 245-258.

Kung, K-S. J. and Y. Cai (2000) Property Rights and Fertilizing Practices in Rural China: Evidence from Northern Jiangsu, *Modern China*, Vol. 26, No. 3, 276-308.

Kaliba, A. R. M., Verkuijl, H. & W. Mwangi (2000) Factors Affecting Adoption of Improved Maize Seeds and Use of Inorganic Fertilizer for Maize Production in the Intermediate and Lowland Zones of Tanzania, *Journal of Agricultural and Applied Economics*, 32,1, 35–47.

Kebede Y., Gunjal, K. and G. Coffin (1990) Adoption of New Technologies in Ethiopian Agriculture: The Case of Tegulet-Bulga District, Shoa Province, *Agricultural Economics*, 4, 27-43.

Kingombe-wa-Kigombe C.B. (2003) La réalité du génocide de la faim au Bushi (Sud-Kivu), Mouvement et enjeux sociaux, *Revue de la chaire dynamique sociale*, Numéro spécial, 1-18.

Kormawa, P., A. Munyemana and B. Soule (2003) Fertilizer market reforms and factors influencing fertilizer use by small-scale farmers in Bénin, *Agriculture, Ecosystems and Environment*, 100 129–136.

Larson, B.A. and G.B. Frisvold (1996) Fertilizer to support agricultural development in sub-Saharan Africa: what is needed and why, *Food Policy*, vol. 21, No. 6, 509-525.

Lee, D. R. (2005) Agricultural Sustainability and Technology Adoption: Issues and polices for developing countries, *American Journal of Agricultural Economics*, Vol. 87, No. 5, 1325-1334.

Maass B.L., D. M. Katunga, W. L. Chiuri, A. Gassner and M. Peters (2012) Challenges and opportunities for smallholder livestock production in post-conflict South Kivu, eastern DR Congo, *Trop Anim Health Prod*, 44, 1221–1232.

Matthews-Njoku, E. C., Adesope O. M. and C. Iruba (2009) Acceptability of improved crop production practices among rural women in Aguata agricultural zone of Anambra State, Nigeria, *African Journal of Biotechnology*, Vol. 8 (3), pp. 405-411.

Matuschke, I., Mishr R. R. & M. Qaim (2007) Adoption and Impact of Hybrid Wheat in India, *World Development*, Vol. 35, No. 8, pp. 1422–1435.

Mazonde, I. N. (1993) Food policy and agriculture in Botswana, Food policy and agriculture in Southern Africa, Harare: SAPES Books, ISBN 0797412255. - 1993, 5-108.

Mendola, M. (2008) Migration and technological change in rural households: Complements or substitutes? Journal of Development Economics, 85, 150–175.

Mbaga-Semgalawe, Z. and H. Folmer (2010) Household adoption

behavior of improved soil conservation: the case of the North Pare and West Usambara Mountains of Tanzania, *Land Use Policy*, 17, 321-336.

Mobambo, P., C. Staver, S. Hauser, B. Dheda and G. Vangu (2010) An Innovation Capacity Analysis to Identify Strategies for ImprovingPlantain and Banana (Musa spp.) Productivity and Value Addition inthe Democratic Republic of Congo, in T. Dubois, S. Hauser, C. Staver, D. Coyne (2010) 879International Conference on Banana and Plantain in Africa: Harnessing International Partnerships to Increase Research Impact, 821-828. (Cited 2013 February 24), available at:

http://www.actahort.org/members/buybook?booknr=879.

MUGANGU, M. S., (1997) *La gestion foncière rurale au Zaïre. Réforme juridique et pratiques foncières locales : Cas du Bushi*, Paris, L'Harmattan et Louvain-la-Neuve, Academia Bruylant.

MUHEME, B. G., (1996) *Comprendre l'économie informelle - Sociologie, économie et histoire de la filière Mboga*, Paris, L'Harmattan et Louvain-la-Neuve, Academia Bruylant.

Muzari, W., Gatsi,W. S. Muvhunzi (2012) The Impacts of Technology Adoption on Smallholder Agricultural Productivity in Sub-Saharan Africa: A Review, Journal *of Sustainable Development*, Vol. 5, No. 8, 69-77.

Nathaniels, N. Q. R. (2005) Cowpea, farmer filed schools and farmer-to-farmer extension: A Benin case study, Agricultural Research and Extension Network (AGRES), Network paper, No. 148.

Nkonya, E., Schroeder, T. andD. Norman (1997) Factors affecting adoption of improved maize seed and fertilizer in Northern Tanzania, *Journal of Agricultural Economics*, 48 (1), 1-12.

Noltze, M., Schwarze S. and M. Qaim (2012) Understanding the adoption of system technologies in smallholder agriculture: The system of rice intensification (SRI) in Timor Leste, *Agricultural Systems*, 108, 64–73.

Neuman, W. L. (2011) *Social research methods. Qualitative and quantitative approach,* Seventh Edition, Boston.

Oehmke, J. F.and E. W. Crawford (1996) The Impact of Agricultural Technology in Sub-Saharan Africa, *Journal of African Economies*, Volume 5, Number 2, 271-291.

Olagunju, F. I. and K. K. Salimonu (2010) Effect of Adoption Pattern of Fertilizer Technology on Small Scale Farmer's Productivity in BoluwaduroLocal Government, *World Rural Observations*, 2(3), 23-33.

Pender, J. and B. Gebremedhin (2007) Determinants of Agricultural and Land Management Practices and Impacts on Crop Production and Household Income in the Highlands of Tigray, Ethiopia, *Journal of African Economies*, Volume 17, Number 3, 395–450.

Perret, S.R. andJ. B. Stevens (2006) Socio-economic reasons for the low adoption of water conservation technologies by smallholder farmers in southern Africa: a review of the literature, *Development Southern Africa*, Volume 23, Issue 4, 461-476.

Rauniyar, G. P. and F. M. Goode (1992) Technology Adoption on Small Farms,*World Development*, Vol. 20, No. 2. pp. 275-282.

Romani, M. (2003) Love Thy Neighbor? Evidence from Ethnic information sharing within villages in Côte d'Ivoire, *Journal of African Economies*, Volume 12, Number 4, 533-563.

Saka J. O. and B. O. Lawal (2009) Determinants of adoption and productivity of improvedrice varieties in southwestern Nigeria, *African Journal of Biotechnology*, Vol. 8 (19), pp. 4923-4932.

Sakurai, T. (2006) Intensification of rainfed lowland rice production in West Africa: present status and potential green revolution , *The Developing Economies*, XLIV-2, 232–251

Sanni, S. A. and W. Doppler (2007) Socio-economic determinants of household fertilizer use intensity for maize-based production systems in the Northern Guinea Savannah of Nigeria, *Journal of Applied Sciences*, 7 (13), 1774-1779.

Shiferaw, B. A., Kebede T. A. and L. You (2008) Technology adoption under seed access constraints and the economic impacts of improved pigeonpea varieties in Tanzania, *Agricultural Economics*, 39, 309–323.

Shively, G. E. (2000) Soil conservation and consumption risk in a model of low income agriculture, *Environmental Monitoring and Assessment*, 62: 55–69.

Shively, G. E. (2001) Poverty, consumption risk, and soil conservation, *Journal of Development economics*, Vol. 65, 267-290.

Smale, M., Just R. E. and H. D. Leathers (1994) Land Allocation In HYV Adoption Models: An Investigation Of Alternative Explanation, *American Journal of Agricultural Economics*, 76, 535–547.

Spio, K. (1997) The low input farming sector in Sub-Saharan Africa: lessons and experiences, *Agrekon,* Vol 36, No 3, 231-251.

Tabachnick, B.G. and Fidell, L.S. (2012) *Using Multivariate Statistics*, 6thEdition, 2012.

Thapa, G. B. and K. Rattanasuteerakul (2011) Adoption and extent of organic vegetable farming in Mahasarakham province, Thailand, *Applied Geography*, 31, 201-209.

Teklewold, H., L. Dadi, A. Yami and N. Dana (2006) Determinants of adoption of poultry technology: a double-hurdle approach, *Livestock Research for Rural Development* 18, (3), http://www.lrrd.org/lrrd18/3/tekl18040.htm.

Teyssier, A.., (2000) Quelques éléments pour un programme de sécurisation foncière », Contribution à la mission de pré-évaluation du Projet Sectoriel de Développement Rural, mission Banque Mondiale/ Coopération Française, miméo.

Ulimwengu, J., Funes, J., Headey, D. and L. You (2009) Paving the Way for Development: The Impact of Road Infrastructure on

Agricultural Production and Household Wealth in the Democratic Republic of Congo, *IFPRI Discussion Paper 00944*. (Cited 2013 February 20), available at:

http://www.ifpri.org/sites/default/files/publications/ifpridp00944.pdf,

Veall, M. R. and K. F. Zimmerman (1994) Evaluating Pseudo-R2 for binary probit models, *Quality & quantity*, 28: 151-164.

Wanyama, J.M., L. O. Mose, S. C. Rono, A. A. O. Masinde and N. Kariuku (2010) Determinants of Fertilizer Use and Soil Erosion Measures in Maize Based Production System in Greater Tans Nzoia District, Kenya, *Middle-East Journal of Scientific Research*, 5 (5), 425-434.

White, S.D., Labarta, R. A. and E. J. Leguia (2005) Technology adoption by resource-poor farmers: considering the implications of peak-season labor costs, *Agricultural Systems*, 85, 183-201.

www.worldbank.org.

Wubeneh, G.N. and J.H. Sanders (2006) Farm-level adoption of sorghum technologies in Tigray, Ethiopia, *Agricultural Systems*, 91, 122-134.

Relation entre la satisfaction des employés et leur intention de départ des institutions de microfinance au Kivu en RDC

Effets modérateurs des variables sociodémographiques

Eddy BALEMBA Kanyurhi & Déogratias Bugandwa Munguakonkwa

RÉSUMÉ

Objectif : Cet article poursuit un triple objectifs : développer préalablement une échelle pour mesurer la satisfaction des employés en microfinance (a) ; tester la nature des relations existant entre la satisfaction des employés et leurs liens avec les intentions de départ (b) et tester si certaines variables sociodémographiques peuvent modérer cette relation (c).

Implémentation/Méthodologie/Approche : Les données ont été collectées auprès de 419 employés issus de 53 institutions de microfinance au Kivu en République Démocratique du Congo (RDC). Le traitement des données a été obtenu en recourant à la fois à une analyse par les équations structurelles et la régression hiérarchique.

Résultats : Les résultats montrent que la satisfaction des employés dans les IMFs est un construit multidimensionnel composé de 43 attributs subdivisés en dix dimensions. Les résultats révèlent que la circulation de l'information et la sécurité du travail constituent les deux premières dimensions de la satisfaction des employés dans les IMFs du Kivu. Les résultats montrent qu'il existe une relation négative significative entre la satisfaction des employés et leur intention de départ des IMFs. Les résultats indiquent que le niveau d'études des employés influence positivement leurs intentions de départ. Les résultats confirment que la satisfaction des employés a un impact d'autant plus important sur les intentions de départ que le niveau d'études des employés est élevé.

Limites/Implications : Cette étude ne teste que l'effet interactif des variables sociodémographiques sur la relation entre la satisfaction des employés et leur intention de départ. Cette étude n'analyse pas non plus l'influence directe du comportement des gérants des IMFs sur la satisfaction des employés.

Implications pratiques : Les dimensions de la satisfaction des employés qui ont été identifiées offrent aux gestionnaires des IMFs un outil managérial qui leur permet de répondre aux besoins et aux préférences des employés. Les gestionnaires devraient se focaliser principalement sur la circulation de l'information et de la sécurité de l'emploi pour satisfaire leurs employés. La capacité du niveau d'étudess à influencer négativement l'intention de départ et à tempérer la relation entre la satisfaction et l'intention de départ rappelle aux managers des IMF de recruter des personnes compétentes et bien formées et de les placer dans des postes qui sont compatibles avec leur niveau d'étudess. Cela pourrait se traduire par un attachement exclusif à leurs IMFs avec des répercussions positives sur la performance des IMFs.

Originalité/valeur : Cette étude est la première, à notre connaissance, qui tente d'identifier les dimensions de la satisfaction des employés et de lier ces dernières avec les intentions de départ dans le secteur de la microfinance. Les résultats confirment donc l'importance capitale des ressources humaines dans le secteur de la microfinance et invitent ainsi les IMFs à la valorisation de leur personnel.

Mots-clés : Satisfaction des employés, intentions de départ, Microfinance, Kivu, RDC.

1. Introduction

La relation entre la satisfaction des employés et leurs intentions de départ ou les départs effectifs a déjà fait l'objet de plusieurs études (Clark, 2001 ; Mohsina *et al*, 2013 ; Lambert *et al*, 2001 ; Jang et George, 2012 ; Yucel et Bektas, 2012 ; Muchinsky et Tuttle, 1979, notamment). Les résultats agrégés montrent que certaines dimensions de la satisfaction des employés seraient les principaux déterminants de la mobilité des employés (Alfonso Sousa-Poza, Andres A. Sousa-Poza, 2007). L'argument sous-jacent est lié au fait que des employés satisfaits sont enclins à s'attacher à leur entreprise et à réduire significativement leurs intentions de départ et inversement (Chan Yin-Fah *et al*, 2010 ; Adams, 1963 ; Withey et Cooper 1989 cités par Arndt *et al*, 2006).

La présente étude porte sur la satisfaction des employés « front line employees » (agents de crédit, caissiers, chargés de la clientèle) et autres employés et ses liens avec les intentions de quitter les institutions qui les emploient. Ce choix est dicté par l'importance que revêtent ces employés pour les IMFs (Heskett *et al*, 1994 ; Hoffman et Ingram, 1992 ; Schneider et Bowen, 1993 cités par Bettencourt et Brown, 1997 ; Burmann et Konig, 2011 ; Fang *et al*, 2011 cités par Malhotra *et al*, 2013). Ils sont « les premiers, si pas les seuls points de contact entre l'IMF et ses clients. Ils sont chargés à la fois de la promotion, de l'analyse, de l'acceptation, de la gestion et des activités de recouvrement du crédit » (Canales, 2010 ; Beck *et al*, 2011). Les employés constituent peut-être la ressource la plus importante dont disposent les IMFs. En effet, les IMFs doivent compter sur leurs employés pour offrir les produits et services financiers qui rencontrent les besoins des clients (Ross et Denzer, 2011).

Malgré l'importance manifeste des « front line employees » et autres employés au sein des IMFs, très peu d'études leur ont été consacrées (Canales, 2010 ; Dixon *et al*, 2007 ; Abbing, 2011 ; Uchida *et al*, 2012). Celles qui existent portent sur :

(a) les difficultés ou les problèmes que les agents de crédit éprouvent dans l'exercice de leur travail (Dixon *et al*, 2007 ; Abbing 2011) ;

(b) la possibilité de voir les agents de crédit discriminer certains emprunteurs potentiels en fonction de la position stratégique qu'ils occupent dans le processus de crédit (Labie *et al*, 2009 ; Beck *et al*, 2011) ;

(c) la problématique de la rémunération et des récompenses monétaires accordées aux agents de crédit (McKim et Hughart, 2005 ; Aubert *et al*, 2009 ; Armandariz et Morduch, 2005, entre autres). Les études qui analysent directement la satisfaction des employés au-delà des récompenses des agents et ses liens avec les intentions de départ sont, à notre connaissance, inexistantes en microfinance. Cette étude veut donc combler ce gap.

L'objectif de cette étude est double : (a) développer préalablement une échelle permettant de mesurer la satisfaction des employés des IMFs et tester la nature des liens existant entre la satisfaction des employés et leurs intentions de quitter les IMFs et (b) vérifier si les variables sociodémographiques (l'ancienneté, l'âge, le sexe, le niveau d'études, le degré de parenté avec les responsables) constituent des variables pouvant modérer ou amplifier cette relation (Mohsin Bashir *et al*, 2011 ; Yucel et Bektas, 2012). L'importance de cette étude est double. Premièrement, elle aborde un sujet qui a été très peu ou pas analysé dans la littérature de la microfinance (Mansor *et al*, 2012).

Cette étude a l'ambition d'identifier les dimensions de la satisfaction des employés que les IMFs peuvent utiliser pour retenir les meilleurs employés (Ross et Denzer, 2011). Deuxièmement, elle est conduite dans un contexte urbain du Kivu qui a peu ou pas été étudié. Ce contexte est caractérisé par un taux de chômage élevé (Makabu ma Nkenda, Mba et Torelli, 2005) à telle enseigne que des employés, même insatisfaits, auraient tendance à rester au sein de leur IMF. Pareil comportement justifie l'importance d'analyser la problématique des intentions de départ plutôt que celle des départs effectifs car les employés auraient de la peine à quitter réellement leurs IMFs par manque d'alternatives.

Les intentions de départ sont analysées selon qu'elles sont orientées vers d'autres IMFs qui offrent de meilleures perspectives d'emploi (mobilité intrasectorielle) ou vers les banques commerciales et d'autres secteurs dans lesquels les employés espèrent se réaliser pleinement. La population cible est composée des agents de crédit et des autres agents (caissiers, chargés de la clientèle, entre autres) permanents issus de 53 IMFs du Kivu. Les données ont été collectées auprès d'un échantillon de 419 « front line » et autres employés. Le traitement des données a été obtenu en recourant successivement aux équations structurelles et à la régression hiérarchique.

Outre la présente introduction, cette étude s'articule autour de quatre sections. La deuxième présente le modèle théorique ainsi que les différentes hypothèses testées dans ce chapitre. La troisième section présente la méthodologie. La quatrième section présente et discute les résultats alors que la cinquième section donne les principales conclusions, les limites ainsi que les pistes pour les études futures.

2. Modèle théorique et développement des hypothèses

La satisfaction des employés est l'un des concepts les plus étudiés en gestion des ressources humaines, en Psychologie du travail et en Marketing (Sepctor, 1997). Ce terme remonte aux travaux pionniers de Hoppock (1935) qui en offre aussi la première définition : « la satisfaction au travail est la combinaison des circonstances psychologiques, physiques et environnementales qui amènent une personne à dire : « je suis satisfait de mon travail ». Locke (1969) complète cette définition en mettant en exergue le processus d'évaluation qui caractérise la satisfaction des employés. Ainsi définit-il la satisfaction au travail comme « un sentiment émotionnel positif résultant de l'évaluation que l'individu fait de son travail en effectuant une comparaison entre les avantages qu'il espérait en retirer et ce qu'il en tire réellement ». Cette définition a été reprise plus tard par Igalens (l999) cité par Moutte (2010) quand il affirme que la satisfaction au travail est « une réponse émotionnelle positive résultant de l'évaluation du travail ou des expériences de travail ».

La satisfaction des employés est souvent mesurée à travers des échelles multidimensionnelles ou non visant à offrir une vue d'ensemble sur les variables qui satisfont les employés au travail. Les premières échelles ont été forgées dans les années 1960 (USA). Parmi les échelles les plus populaires, on cite généralement : Job Satisfaction Survey, Job Descriptive Index, Minnesota Satisfaction Questionnaire, Job Diagnostic Survey, Job in General Scale et le Michigan Organizational Assessment Questionnaire Subscale (Spector, 1997). Même si la plupart de ces échelles ont été élaborées il y a plusieurs années, elles servent encore de base pour des études destinées à évaluer la satisfaction des employés dans plusieurs pays et secteurs d'activités.

L'intention de quitter une entreprise est souvent définie comme une force individuelle interne qui pousse un employé à vouloir quitter son emploi actuel et à chercher activement d'autres opportunités d'emplois répondant à ses attentes.

Il s'agit donc d'une tendance continuelle des employés à se résigner à leur emploi actuel (Ching-Li Fan, 1978 ; Tzu-Chi Wang, 2000 ; Caplan et Jones, 1975). Mobley *et al* (1978) cités par Gao-Liang Wang *et al* (2012) définissent l'intention de quitter l'entreprise comme « l'agrégation de l'insatisfaction au travail, la tendance à chercher d'autres emplois et la possibilité de trouver un autre travail ». Williams et Hazer (1986) cités par Gao-Liang Wang *et al* (2012) corroborent cette définition en concluant que l'intention de départ est un plan que les employés se forgent au sujet de la volonté de quitter leurs emplois. Ahmad *et al* (2012) confirment ces faits quand ils affirment que « l'intention de quitter l'organisation se rapporte à la volonté de quitter l'organisation de manière permanente ».

Lambert *et al* (2001) soutiennent qu'il existe trois variables qui sont susceptibles d'expliquer l'intention de départ au sein d'une entreprise : les caractéristiques démographiques des employés, la satisfaction au travail et l'environnement du travail. Le schéma ci-après nous donne de plus amples informations sur les relations entre les variables ainsi que sur les hypothèses qui les sous-tendent.

SCHÉMA 1

Modèle théorique (Muchinsky et Tuttle, 1979 ; Spector, 1997 ; Karapate, 2011)

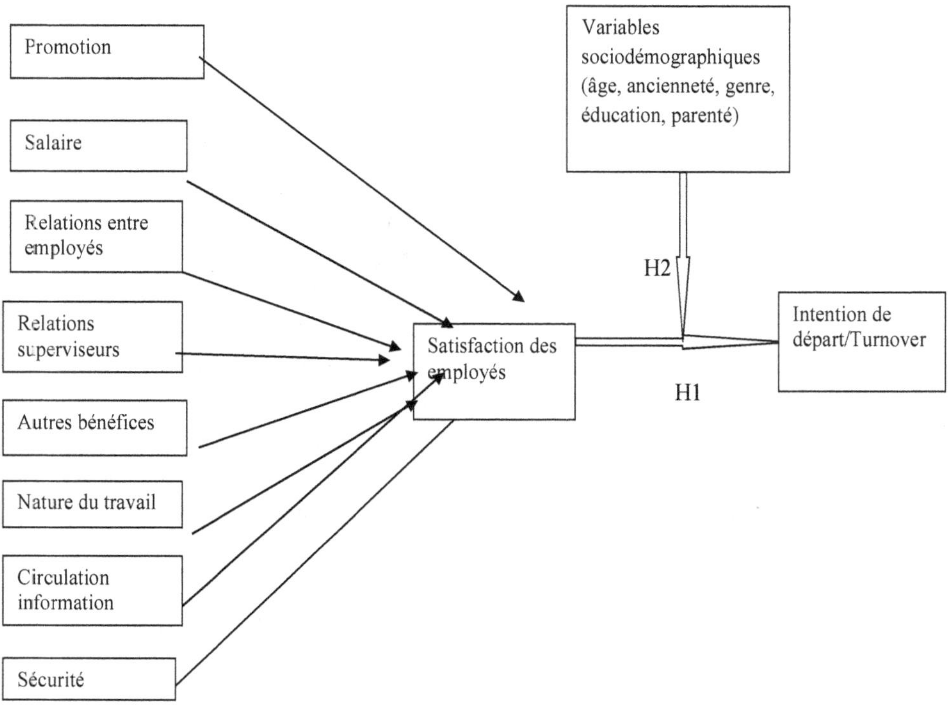

2.1. Relation entre l'intention de quitter l'entreprise et la satisfaction des employés

Très peu d'études ont été conduites sur la relation entre les intentions de quitter une entreprise et la satisfaction des employés dans le secteur de la microfinance. La seule étude qui existe, à notre connaissance, est celle de Heyns (1996) citée par Abbing (2011). Même si cette étude ne teste pas directement le lien entre l'intention de départ et la satisfaction des employés, elle offre une liste plus ou moins exhaustive des facteurs qui poussent les agents de crédit à quitter les IMFs au Bangladesh. Les résultats révèlent que les agents de crédit quittent les IMFs car ils sont mal payés, sous-évalués, moins appréciés, sur-utilisés et exploités. Les résultats de cette étude montrent indirectement qu'il existe une relation positive entre les mauvaises conditions de travail et l'intention de quitter les IMFs. Ainsi, « les employés qui sentent qu'ils sont sous-récompensés par leur travail devront tenter de restaurer l'équilibre en réduisant les efforts et en accroissant par exemple le taux d'absentéisme, en venant en retard au travail, en prenant de longues pauses et donc en réduisant la productivité… » (Greenberg, 1990 ; Lawler, 1990 ; Lum *et al*, 1998 cités par Singh et Loncar, 2010). Puis s'ensuivra le départ qui est la fin du processus d'incompatibilité entre les attentes des employés et les bénéfices qu'ils retirent du travail.

Les études qui testent le lien entre la satisfaction des employés et l'intention à quitter les organisations dans des secteurs autres que la microfinance sont nombreuses (Lambert *et al*, 2001). Muchinsky et Tuttle (1979) offrent la quintessence de la nature des relations entre ces deux construits dans une méta-analyse qu'ils ont conduite sur plus de 150 articles relatifs aux déterminants des intentions de turnover et du turnover lui-même. Les résultats agrégés révèlent qu'il existe une relation négative entre la satisfaction des employés et leurs intentions de turnover. Les auteurs montrent, sur base des résultats de l'étude de Hulin (1966) que le score moyen de satisfaction des employés qui ont quitté l'organisation est significativement plus faible que celui de ceux qui sont restés.

La primauté de la satisfaction des employés dans l'explication des intentions et du turnover est aussi mise en exergue par des études plus ou moins récentes. Lambert *et al* (2001) affirment que la satisfaction des employés est le meilleur déterminant de l'intention de turnover. Alfonso Sousa-Poza, Andres A. Sousa-Poza (2007) corroborent cet argument en démontrant que « … certaines dimensions de la satisfaction des employés sont peut-être les meilleurs déterminants de la mobilité au travail …. ». Des résultats similaires avaient déjà été trouvés par Rose et Hulin (1985) qui soutenaient que « la satisfaction globale des employés expliquait à elle seule 45 % de la variance des décisions de quitter l'organisation ». Griffeth *et al* (2000) corroborent l'argument ci-avant en démontrant que la satisfaction globale au travail était le principal déterminant de la volonté de quitter la firme comparativement aux autres attitudes au travail.

Les résultats ci-dessus confirment ceux trouvés par Shields et Ward (2001) qui ont montré que la satisfaction au travail était la variable la plus importante qui détermine l'intention de quitter le travail. En abondant presque dans le même sens, Yucel et Bektas (2012), sur base des résultats des études antérieures (Hellriegel et Slocum, 2004 ; Wagner et Hollenbeck, 2005 ; Smith *et al*, 1969) soutiennent que les employés insatisfaits ont des niveaux plus élevés de turnover et d'absence que ceux qui sont satisfaits. Karatepe et Uludag (2007) corroborent cet argument en affirmant que « les employés de contact qui exhibent de faibles niveaux de satisfaction et un faible niveau d'attachement affectif à leur organisation réfléchissent toujours sur la possibilité de quitter leur organisation ». Lam *et al* (2001) et Jang et George (2012) soutiennent qu'il existe une relation significative négative entre la satisfaction des employés et l'intention de quitter la firme.

Yang (2008) arrive presque au même résultat en démontrant que les employés qui ont un niveau élevé de satisfaction sont plus motivés à rester avec leur organisation. Ahmad *et al* (2012) soutiennent que "la satisfaction au travail et l'intention à quitter l'organisation présentent une corrélation innée, la satisfaction au travail influençant négativement la volonté des employés à quitter les organisations ». Hom *et al* (1992) cités par Khiljia, Xiaoyun Wang (2007) démontrent qu'il existe une relation positive linéaire entre la décision de turnover et l'insatisfaction des travailleurs. Wong (1989) cité par Ahmad *et al* (2012) corrobore cet argument en prouvant que plus les enseignants sont insatisfaits de leur travail, plus leur niveau d'attachement organisationnel diminue ; ce qui les contraint à chercher d'autres opportunités d'emplois ailleurs. Singh et Loncar (2010) abordent dans le même sens en concluant que les intentions de quitter une organisation décroissent avec l'augmentation des salaires et vice versa (Dailey et Kirk, 1992 ; Motowildo, 1983). Chan Yin-Fah *et al* (2010) arrivent presque aux mêmes conclusions en démontrant que plus les employés sont satisfaits, plus ils s'attacheront à leur organisation et penseront peu ou pas à quitter leurs emplois actuels. Prenant appui sur les résultats des études antérieures, nous formulons donc l'hypothèse suivante :

H1 : Il existerait une relation négative entre la satisfaction des employés et l'intention de quitter les IMFs.

2.2. Rôle modérateur des variables sociodémographiques

Les variables sociodémographiques qui sont susceptibles de modérer ou d'amplifier la relation entre la satisfaction et les intentions de départ des employés sont extraites à la fois des études de Muchinsky et Tuttle (1979) et de Jang et George[1] (2012). Les auteurs reconnaissent que l'âge, le genre, l'ancienneté, le niveau d'études, la taille du ménage et les responsabilités familiales sont des variables sociodémographiques susceptibles d'expliquer l'intention de turnover. En prenant appui sur ces résultats et en tenant compte du contexte de l'étude, nous avons décidé d'examiner l'effet modérateur des variables ci-après :

Le rôle interactif de l'ancienneté

Plusieurs auteurs soutiennent que les intentions de turnover varient significativement en fonction de l'ancienneté des employés (Chia-Shang Chen, 1985 ; Gao-Liang Wang *et al*, 2012). Ces résultats ont été confirmés par la méta-analyse réalisée par Muchinsky et Tuttle (1979). Les auteurs soutiennent que dans toutes les sept études portant sur la relation entre le turnover et l'ancienneté qu'ils ont analysées, l'ancienneté était négativement corrélée à l'intention de quitter une organisation. Les conclusions de l'étude de Mangione (1973) corroborent les résultats ci-dessus en affirmant que l'ancienneté des employés était le meilleur déterminant de leur turnover. L'explication probable est liée au fait que le nombre d'années passées au sein d'une organisation est interprété comme un investissement dans le chef des employés (Valle et Perrewe, 2000). La peur de découvrir de nouveaux horizons et de nouvelles expériences de travail peut les dissuader à ne pas quitter leur organisation actuelle.

L'étude conduite par Ahmad (2002 et 2003) sur les agents de crédit des IMFs au Bangladesh semble toutefois contredire les résultats des études antérieures. L'auteur trouve que les IMFs discriminent les anciens agents de crédit, ce qui pourrait les pousser à de plus fortes intentions de turnover. A la suite des arguments d'Ahmad, on peut conclure que les anciens employés exprimeraient plus d'intentions de turnover que les jeunes. En effet, comme les employés nouvellement engagés savent que la promotion est souvent fonction de l'ancienneté dans certaines IMFs, ils pourraient accepter de faire carrière dans les IMFs. Ils pourraient travailler dur, confirmer leur performance, mériter une augmentation de salaire et accéder même au poste de gérant de leur IMF. Cela étant, ils peuvent être plus satisfaits que les anciens pour lesquels les possibilités d'évoluer et de faire évoluer leurs salaires sont limitées.

Plusieurs études empiriques reconnaissent aussi l'importance de l'ancienneté comme facteur modérateur des relations entre la satisfaction des employés et les intentions de départ (Ferris *et al*, 1987 ; Hackett, 1990 ; Bender et Heywood, 2006 ; Cossette et Gosselin, 2012).

1. Jang et George (2012) s'inspirent fortement des études de Arnold et Feldman, 1982 ; Parasuraman et Futrell, 1983 ; Williams et Hazer, 1986).

Les résultats agrégés de ces études montrent que plus les employés sont satisfaits, moins ils ont tendance à quitter et plus ils jouissent d'une longue ancienneté au sein de leurs entreprises. L'argument ci-dessus est classique en microfinance. L'expérience montre que les promotions et les autres avantages sont accordés souvent en fonction de l'ancienneté des employés des IMFs. L'employé jouissant d'une longue ancienneté a eu la chance de gravir les échelons de la hiérarchie, il reçoit des avantages liés à son rang (en matière de formation, de rémunération, entre autres) et serait donc plus associé à la gestion de son IMF en ce sens qu'il en constitue la mémoire vivante.

Tous ces éléments accroissent son niveau de satisfaction et son attachement envers l'IMF de sorte qu'il lui soit difficile de quitter cette dernière à cause de nombreuses barrières à la sortie (perte de statut privilégié et autres avantages). En effet, les employés qui ont longtemps travaillé pour une organisation développent un attachement affectif à l'égard de cette dernière, et par conséquent, ils tendent à y être rattachés d'autant plus que leurs niveaux de satisfaction sont élevés (Yucel et Bektas, 2012). Sur base des arguments ci-avant, nous formulons donc l'hypothèse ci-après :

H2 (a) : Le lien entre la satisfaction des employés et leur intention de quitter l'IMF serait plus élevé pour les nouveaux que pour les anciens employés.

Le rôle interactif du niveau d'études

La théorie du capital humain soutient que plus les travailleurs sont qualifiés plus ils deviennent productifs (Becher, 1964). Par conséquent, les travailleurs très instruits et hautement qualifiés seront aussi naturellement plus exigeants que d'autres en termes de revendication salariale et de meilleures conditions de travail. L'incapacité des IMFs à répondre à leurs exigences peut créer des frustrations dans le chef de ces employés et les entraîner à quitter leur emploi actuel. Poussés par leurs qualifications, ces employés s'estiment capables de trouver d'autres opportunités d'emploi répondant à leur statut. Des études récentes relatives à la relation entre les intentions de turnover et le niveau d'études confirment ces faits. Ying-Cheng Chen (2001) cité par Liang Wang *et al* (2012) montre que les employés plus scolarisés[1] seraient plus stressés par les mauvaises conditions de travail et réagiraient directement à l'insatisfaction en exhibant des taux très élevés d'intentions de turnover.

Le niveau d'études peut aussi exercer un effet interactif sur la relation entre la satisfaction des

1. On peut classer les employés expérimentés mais qui n'ont pas nécessairement un niveau d'études élevé dans cette catégorie. En effet, en l'absence des universités et des instituts supérieurs qui formaient jadis en Microfinance, la formation sur le tas à travers des séminaires accroît le niveau des employés qu'ils peuvent brandir à l'égard de plusieurs institutions qui recrutent sur base d'expérience.

employés et leur intention de départ. Ainsi, plus les employés sont satisfaits moins ils sont prédisposés à quitter leurs IMFs bien qu'ils soient de niveaux d'étude élevés. En effet, les employés ayant des niveaux d'études élevés occupent quelquefois des postes hiérarchiques élevés (Hersh, 1991). Les avantages monétaires et non monétaires qu'ils retirent de ces postes sont élevés comparativement aux autres catégories d'employés. Par conséquent, ils présenteraient aussi des niveaux de satisfaction élevés, les persuadnt à rester au service de la même IMF et à continuer ainsi à jouir des mêmes avantages (Theodossiou et Vasileio, 2007). Les arguments ci-dessus nous permettent donc de définir l'hypothèse suivante :

H2 (b) : Le lien entre le degré de satisfaction des employés et leur intention de quitter l'IMF serait plus élevé pour les employés plus instruits que pour les moins instruits.

L'effet interactif du genre

Il existe très peu d'études qui testent le lien entre la satisfaction des employés et leur intention de turnover en utilisant la variable genre comme variable interactive de cette relation (Alfonso Sousa-Poza, Andres A. Sousa-Poza, 2007). Les quelques études qui existent aboutissent très souvent à des résultats mitigés, voire controversés (Khiljia et Wang, 2007). En effet, certaines études nient carrément l'existence d'une préalable relation entre le genre et les intentions de turnover alors que d'autres montrent que le genre est une variable importante dans l'explication du turnover. Campbell (2003) cité par Khiljia et Wang (2007) a trouvé que le genre n'exerçait aucun effet modérateur sur la relation entre la satisfaction des employés et l'intention de départ des employés. Booth et Francesconi (1999) cités par Alfonso Sousa-Poza, Andres A. Sousa-Poza (2007) révèlent que les taux de turnover sont similaires chez les hommes comme chez les femmes.

D'autres études, par contre, postulent l'existence d'une relation significative entre le turnover et le genre. Les résultats des études de Cotton et Tuttle (1986), Weisberg et Kirschenbaum (1993) repris récemment par Khiljia et Wang (2007) montrent que les femmes étaient plus motivées à quitter leurs emplois que les hommes en raison de faibles niveaux de satisfaction. Kuo-Yang Wang (2002) cité par Gao-Liang Wang *et al* (2012) corrobore ces résultats et soutient que les femmes exhibent des taux plus élevés d'intention de départ que les hommes. Les résultats des études d'Elaine (1997) et Khatri *et al* (2005) cités par Khiljia et Wang (2007) arrivent plutôt à des conclusions contraires en précisant que ce sont les hommes qui exhibent des taux significativement plus élevés de turnover lorsqu'ils ne sont pas satisfaits des conditions de travail.

Toutefois, ces résultats peuvent être relativisés par les arguments issus du contexte de cette étude. En effet, la RDC, comme la plupart des pays en développement, est caractérisée par de fortes inégalités de genre, les femmes n'accédant presque pas aux opportunités d'emplois comparativement aux hommes. Dès lors, elles s'attacheraient presque naturellement à des postes d'emplois actuels quel que soit leur niveau de satisfaction. Le sexe de l'employé peut aussi jouer un rôle interactif entre la satisfaction et l'intention de départ de l'employé. En fait, plus l'employé n'est pas satisfait de son travail, moins il a tendance à quitter son emploi s'il est de sexe féminin. Ce raisonnement n'a de sens que lorsqu'il s'applique à certaines fonctions au sein des IMFs (caissière, secrétaire de direction, entre autres), fonctions pour lesquelles les femmes détiennent un avantage comparatif par rapport aux hommes.

En effet, dans la majorité des IMFs, les caisses sont tenues par les femmes. Ces dernières brillent par leur honnêteté et par leur bravoure et finissent par s'imposer à travers un travail bien fait. C'est pourquoi reçoivent-elles des primes de caisse ainsi que des récompenses monétaires et non monétaires (meilleure caissière de l'année) diverses. Certaines d'entre elles arrivent à gravir les échelons de la hiérarchie jusqu'à devenir gérantes ou chefs d'agences, fonctions, jadis réservées aux seuls hommes. Les récompenses ainsi reçues valorisent les femmes, accroissent drastiquement leur niveau de satisfaction comparativement à leurs collègues hommes et les prédisposent à rester au sein de leurs IMFs. Cela nous permet donc de formuler l'hypothèse suivante quelque peu en marge de la théorie existante :

H2 (c) : Le lien entre le degré de satisfaction des employés et leur intention de quitter l'IMF serait plus élevé pour les hommes que pour les femmes.

Effet interactif de l'âge

L'âge est la variable qui a été la plus étudiée en lien soit avec la satisfaction des employés soit comme médiatrice de la relation entre la satisfaction des employés et leur intention de turnover. Muchinsky et Tuttle (1979) révèlent que neuf études sur les onze qu'ils ont passées en revue confirment qu'il existe une relation négative entre l'âge et les intentions de turnover. La revue des études antérieures effectuée par Yucel et Bektas (2012) montre qu'il existe « une relation linéaire positive entre l'âge et la satisfaction au travail...» (Herzberg, Mausner *et al*, 1987 ; Rhodes, 1983). Yucel et Bektas (2012) et Bedeian *et al* (1992) et Jang et George (2012) reprennent presque le même argument quand ils affirment que « les employés âgés considèrent les années passées au service d'une organisation comme un investissement rendant ainsi leur emploi actuel très attractif (Mathieu et Zajac, 1990 ; Lew Tek Yew, 2007). Par conséquent, ils seraient soumis à une barrière psychologique qui les empêcherait de quitter leur organisation actuelle et d'aller vers d'autres. Ce constat serait encore vrai dans le contexte socio-économique du Kivu où il n'existe pas d'indemnités de retraite et où l'Institut National de Sécurité Sociale (INSS) fonctionne au ralenti. Par conséquent, les employés âgés sont obligés de s'accrocher à leur emploi quand ils en ont encore la force.

Les jeunes, quant à eux, exprimeraient une forte mobilité au travail (intention de quitter) liée au fait qu'ils sont au début de leur carrière. Les jeunes sont donc dans un processus de recherche actif pour un emploi qui rencontre leurs attentes dans d'autres organisations (Theodossiou et Vasileio, 2007, Mohsina *et al*, 2013). L'âge peut aussi jouer un rôle interactif dans la relation entre la satisfaction des employés et leur intention de départ. En effet, plus l'employé est plus âgé, plus l'effet négatif de la satisfaction sur les intentions de départ sera grand. Les employés plus âgés attachent plus d'importance à la securité de leur carrière et tendent à avoir des niveaux de satisfaction plus élevés. Par conséquent, leurs intentions de départ seront plus négativement affectées par leur niveau de satisfaction comparativement aux jeunes (Martins, Eddleston et Veiga, 2002).

Le soubassement d'une telle relation en microfinance repose sur le fait que les IMFs récompensent leurs employés en fonction de l'expérience et donc de l'ancienneté (voir supra). Cela étant, les employés plus âgés[1] accèdent souvent aux postes hiérarchiques les plus élevés (gérant, président du conseil d'administration, entre autres), perçoivent des salaires élevés et sont dès lors plus préoccupés par des objectifs de stabilité de l'emploi. C'est pourquoi ces employés expriment moins de revendication salariale et présentent[2] souvent des niveaux de satisfaction élevés comparativement aux jeunes. Ces employés sont aussi peu ou pas sensibles aux mauvaises conditions de travail (ils s'y habituent) et s'accrochent à leur emploi actuel car ils savent que, compte tenu de leur âge, il leur sera très difficile de trouver un autre emploi dans une autre IMF (Ferlie et Rosenberg, 2008). Tous ces arguments confirment que la relation entre la satisfaction des employés et les intentions de départ sera plus négativement prononcée que les employés sont plus âgés.Les arguments ci-haut nous permettent donc de formuler l'hypothèse ci-après :

H2 (d) : Le lien entre le degré de satisfaction des employés et leur intention à quitter l'IMF serait plus élevé pour les jeunes employés que pour les employés plus âgés.

1. Une acception populaire estime que les employés les plus âgés seraient plus sages et seraient donc plus aptes à diriger une IMF.
2. D'autres études indiquent que cette relation prend parfois la forme de U. Ce qui pose la problématique de l'âge chronologique au travail.

L'effet interactif de la relation de parenté/amitié avec les responsables des IMFs

Les institutions de microfinance ont toujours commencé leurs activités par une taille réduite. Au stade de lancement, elles ne peuvent pas attirer des employés hautement qualifiés car leurs cash-flows ne sont pas en mesure de couvrir les hauts salaires et les autres dépenses relatives au bon fonctionnement de l'IMF. Les IMFs recourent souvent à des frères et amis qui acceptent de toucher de bas salaires. Lorsque les IMFs croissent et atteignent une taille critique, elles doivent soutenir la croissance et sont donc obligées de recourir à des personnes qualifiées qu'elles identifient souvent en dehors du cercle familial et amical. Comparativement aux autres employés, les nouveaux venus comptent sur leurs compétences pour s'imposer dans l'organisation et seraient prêts à quitter l'IMF si leurs attentes ne sont pas réalisées.

Les employés qui entretiennent des relations avec les gérants seraient tentés de rester au sein de leur IMF ne fût-ce que pour plaire à leur mentor. Le niveau de parenté avec les gérants des IMFs peut exercer aussi un rôle modérateur dans la relation entre la satisfaction des employés et leur intention de départ. En effet, la relation négative entre la satisfaction des employés et leur intention de départ serait plus forte pour les individus qui ont des relations de parenté et ou d'amitié avec les gestionnaires des IMFs (Martins, Eddleston et Veiga, 2002) que d'autres catégories d'employés. Ces types d'employés poursuivent deux objectifs complémentaires : premièrement, ils travaillent dur pour réaliser les objectifs organisationnels et participer ainsi à la performance de leur IMF ; deuxièmement, ils ont l'intention de pérenniser les liens sociaux et familiaux avec leurs "parrains". Pour ces employés, l'IMF est confondue avec la personnalité du mentor de sorte qu'ils s'engagent à rester à son service aussi longtemps qu'il le voudra.

Par conséquent, ces employés auraient une prédisposition positive envers leur travail et exprimeraient un attachement moral très fort envers l'IMF en qu'ils reconnaissent la personnalité de leur mentor. Ces employés auraient donc des niveaux de satisfaction plus élevés que les autres qui n'ont aucune relation sociale avec les autorités hiérarchiques. Ces employés voient en l'IMF une extension de leur famille et expriment peu ou pas d'intention à quitter actuellement leur IMF. La peur de ne pas trouver un autre emploi en dehors du cercle familial et amical pousse ces employés à exprimer plus de satisfaction envers leur IMF et s'y attachent presque naturellement. Les arguments ci-avant nous permettent donc de formuler l'hypothèse suivante :

H2 (e) : Le lien entre le degré de satisfaction des employés et leur intention à quitter l'IMF serait plus élevé pour les employés indépendants que pour ceux qui sont liés aux responsables des IMFs par un lien de parenté ou d'amitié.

3. Approche méthodologique

Nous présentons respectivement les techniques utilisées pour collecter et traiter les données ainsi que la mesure des variables mobilisées dans cette étude.

3.1. Echantillon et collecte des données

Les données ont été collectées en trois étapes : l'enquête qualitative, la pré-enquête et l'enquête proprement dite. L'enquête qualitative a été conduite auprès de 105 employés du Kivu. Cette enquête visait à identifier les attributs de la satisfaction tels que perçus par les employés. La pré-enquête[1] a été conduite auprès de 40 employés et ses résultats (*moyenne = 3.26 ; Ecart-type = .65*) nous ont permis de déterminer la taille de l'échantillon en utilisant la formule ci-contre (Vernette et Giannelloni, 2012) : $n = [z^2_{\alpha/2.}\ s^2_X]/e^2]$. En appliquant cette formule, nous avons trouvé un échantillon total de 650 employés.

L'enquête a été conduite dans 53[2] IMFs localisées dans cinq centres urbains du Kivu : Bukavu, Goma, Uvira, Beni et Butembo[3]. L'enquête s'est déroulée directement dans les IMFs durant les heures de travail. Nous avons contacté en avance les directeurs ou gérants de différentes IMFs pour obtenir la permission d'administrer le questionnaire à leurs employés. Pour certaines institutions, les questionnaires étaient déposés auprès du chargé de l'administration et des ressources humaines[4] qui en assurait ensuite la distribution auprès du personnel. Les enquêteurs s'évertuaient à expliquer à ces responsables les objectifs de l'étude et surtout les méthodes de son administration. Compte tenu de la charge de travail particulière des agents de crédit et caissiers, nous avons décidé de leur laisser un délai de trois semaines pour compléter et nous retourner le questionnaire. Un suivi régulier a été effectué en passant un coup de téléphone aux responsables et employés au bout de 15 jours[5].

1. La pré-enquête a été conduite dans six IMFs de Bukavu et d'Uvira. Deux objectifs étaient assignés à la pré-enquête : tester le questionnaire et déterminer la taille de l'échantillon. Les points de vue issus des employés nous ont permis de corriger et/ou de supprimer certains items ambigus.

2. Ces IMFs sont les mêmes que celles qui ont été mobilisées dans le chapitre 1 portant sur la satisfaction des clients.

3. Le choix de ces villes a été motivé par deux arguments : la concurrence entre IMFs et banques classiques s'installe peu à peu dans ces zones (a), elles sont facilement accessibles sur le plan sécuritaire (b).

4. Cette procédure n'a été utilisée que dans les cas extrêmes où les responsables étaient exigeants et ne pourrait donc pas biaiser les résultats.

5. L'objectif était de se rassurer que le questionnaire n'avait pas été égaré, ce qui pourrait accroître le taux de non réponses. Dans les autres IMFs, le personnel a été directement contacté après les heures de travail et a complété le questionnaire sur le champ. Cela permettait d'avoir une variété des points de vue en fonction de la fonction occupée par l'agent.

Le choix des employés a été effectué par un tirage stratifié proportionnel. Ainsi, les IMFs qui emploient plus d'employés ont été surreprésentées dans l'échantillon. Les employés ont été choisis sur base de leur ancienneté et de leur fonction. Seuls les employés ayant au moins une ancienneté minimum de trois mois ont été appelés à participer à l'enquête. Les agents de crédit, les caissiers et les chargés de clientèle ont été ciblés en majorité en fonction de leur interaction régulière avec les clients. D'autres catégories d'employés[1] ont aussi été interrogées (gérants, comptables, chargés d'administration et finance, notamment). L'enquête a été conduite par 38 étudiants en licence. Ces derniers ont reçu une formation sur le mode d'administration du questionnaire et surtout sur les erreurs à éviter à l'enquête. Un suivi et des appels réguliers ont permis de récupérer 450 questionnaires. Sur les 450, 31 étaient mal complétés ou certaines informations manquaient. Après avoir exclu ces questionnaires non exploitables, nous sommes resté avec 419, ce qui nous a donné un taux de réponse de 64 %.

Les résultats révèlent que 74 % des employés sont des hommes et 26 % seulement des femmes. La majorité des employés, soit 43 %, ont un âge compris entre 21 et 30 ans et 42 % ont un âge compris entre 31 et 40 ans. 85 % des employés ont un bon niveau de formation, soit 45 % des licenciés contre 40 % des gradués. La plupart des employés, soit 59 %, sont mariés contre 36 % de célibataires. 3 % des employés sont divorcés alors que 2 % sont séparés. Les « frontline » constituent la majorité des employés enquêtés, soit 62 % des cas (31 % d'agents de crédit, 19 % de caissiers, 12 % de chargés de clientèle). Les résultats révèlent que 45 % des employés travaillent dans leurs IMFs depuis une période comprise entre 1 et 3 ans. Les employés ayant une ancienneté de moins d'un an représentent 15 % de l'échantillon contre 5 % des employés ayant une ancienneté de 10 ans et plus. 86 % des employés disent n'entretenir aucune relation de parenté ou d'amitié avec les gérants/directeurs.

3.2. Mesures des variables

L'intention de départ des employés

Elle a été mesurée par trois items inspirés des études antérieures (Jaramillo *et al*, 2009 ; Mitchell, Brooks *et al*, 2001 ; Jang et George, 2012 ; Yin-Fah, Foon *et al*, 2010 ; Alniacik *et al*, 2011 ; Newazi et Akhter, 2007 ; Athanassopoulos *et al*, 2001 ; Vidal *et al*, 2007 ; Khiljia et Xiaoyun Wang, 2007). Ces items permettent d'identifier jusqu'à quel niveau les employés étaient sérieusement impliqués dans la recherche d'un autre emploi dans une autre institution dans un futur proche (Singh et Loncar, 2010). Les items utilisés sont : « *je ne pense pas que*

1. Cela permettait d'avoir une vue d'ensemble de la satisfaction des employés en récoltant les points de vue de toutes les catégories d'employés.

je pourrais passer l'entièreté de ma carrière dans cette IMF » ; « *si très prochainement je n'obtiens pas de promotion, je pourrais chercher un autre emploi ailleurs* » et « *je considère que je ne pourrais pas continuer à travailler avec mon IMF dans les cinq années à venir* ». Les employés devraient exprimer leur degré d'accord et désaccord sur une échelle de Likert à 7 points allant de « Pas du tout d'accord » (1) à « Tout à fait d'accord » (7). Les trois items retenus exhibent une bonne fiabilité, soit α = .80.

La satisfaction des employés

Elle est mesurée par une échelle développée grâce aux résultats des interviews conduites auprès de 103 employés issus de 26 IMFs du Kivu, de trois directeurs[1] de deux IMFs du Kivu et grâce aux items identifiés dans la littérature (Churchill, 1979). Les interviews[2] ont porté sur les aspects positifs, négatifs du travail ainsi que sur les modifications à porter au travail pour qu'il soit conforme aux attentes des employés (Sower *et al*, 2001 ; Mittal *et al* ,1998). La codification des données a été obtenue grâce à une analyse de contenu. L'unité d'agrégation était composée des phrases qui se rapportent, de près ou de loin, à un aspect de la satisfaction des employés. L'importance de chaque item était appréciée par sa fréquence d'apparition (Neuman, 2010 ; Evrard *et al*, 2009). Les résultats des interviews ont abouti à une échelle provisoire composée de 114 items subdivisés en neuf dimensions.

Les items issus de la littérature ont été empruntés principalement à trois principales échelles de mesure : Job Satisfaction Survey, Job Descriptive Index et Minnesota Job Satisfaction Questionnaire. Des items se rapportant à la circulation de l'information et au développement du personnel ont été extraits respectivement des études de Jaworski et Kohli (1993) et de Tsui *et al* (2001). En confrontant les résultats issus des interviews et ceux issus de la littérature, nous avons finalement abouti à une échelle composée de 172 items subdivisés en 11 dimensions (Black et Sherwood, 2010 ; Korda et Snoj, 2010 ; Verhoef, 2003). L'échelle ainsi constituée a été envoyée à deux professeurs d'Universités ainsi qu'à deux directeurs d'IMFs au Kivu en vue d'en assurer la validité faciale et de construit (Neuman, 2010 ; Devellis, 2011 ; Black et Sherwood, 2010 ; Korda et Snoj, 2010 ; Bahia et Nantel, 2000).

L'échelle a été ensuite soumise à quarante employés de Bukavu et d'Uvira afin d'identifier les items qui étaient mal formulés et donc incompréhensibles du point de

1. Nous avons discuté avec messieurs Remy Mpanano et Ramazani, directeurs du Pogramme d'Appui aux Initiatives de Développement au Kivu (PAIDEK), l'une des plus anciennes et la plus prospère des IMFs de Bukavu. Les entretiens ont eu lieu aussi avec monsieur Déogratias Katulanya, initiateur et directeur général actuel de la MECRECO, la plus grande coopérative d'épargne et de crédit au Congo.

2. Les entretiens ont eu lieu dans l'enceinte des IMFs et pendant les heures de service.

vue des employés (TOPCO, 2010 ; Rossister, 2002 ; Evrard *et al*, 2009). Au bout de ce processus, nous avons obtenu une échelle composée de 128 items[1] subdivisés en dix dimensions : rémunération (10), autres avantages monétaires et non monétaires (6), relations et respect envers les collègues de même niveau (13), possibilités de formation (4), conditions de travail (20), formation et développement du personnel (8), circulation et partage de l'information (19), relations et respect provenant des superviseurs (17), sécurité de travail et conformité à la loi (8) et nature du travail (22). L'échelle a enfin été soumise à 419 employés à travers une enquête quantitative. Pour chaque item, les employés devraient donner leur degré d'accord ou de désaccord sur une échelle de Likert à sept points allant de « Pas du tout d'accord » (1) à « Tout fait d'accord » (7).

L'échelle a été soumise à une analyse factorielle exploratoire en vue de réduire le nombre d'items et d'être purifiée (Lings et Greenly, 2005)[2]. Les résultats montrent que tous les items retenus ont des communalités supérieures à .5 prouvant que la part de variance que chaque item partage avec les autres est grande (Carricano et Poujol, 2008 ; Parasuraman *et al*, 1988). Les communalités vont de .52 pour l'item 8 à .76 pour l'item 123. Toutes les dimensions extraites ont des valeurs[3] propres supérieures à 1, indiquant qu'elles valent mieux qu'un seul item (Evrard *et al*, 2009). Les résultats révèlent aussi que tous les items retenus sont fortement corrélés à leurs dimensions avec des coefficients structurels supérieurs ou égaux à .5 (Matzler et Renzl, 2007 ; Evrard *et al*, 2009). Au bout de ce processus, nous avons obtenu une échelle composée de 43 items subdivisés en dix dimensions expliquant 65 % de la variance totale de la satisfaction des employés dans les IMFs. Les dimensions « rémunération » et « avantages monétaires et non monétaires » ne forment plus qu'une seule dimension « rémunération » alors que la dimension « conditions de travail » se mue en deux dimensions différentes. Les résultats issus de l'analyse de la fiabilité sont satisfaisants et aboutissent à un α =. *83*.

L'échelle ainsi purifiée a été soumise à une analyse factorielle confirmatoire. Tous les indices de la qualité d'ajustement sont bons (*CFI = .94 ; IFI = .94 ; TLI = .94 ; RMSEA = .06)* indiquant que le modèle théorique rencontre les données. Tous les items ont des coefficients structurels standardisés largement élevés (Kennedy *et al*, 2002). Les t-values relatives à chaque item sont largement supérieures à 1.96 (Anderson et Gerbing, 1988). Ces deux résultats prouvent

1. De plus amples informations sur les dimensions et items théoriques peuvent être consultées à l'annexe…de la présente thèse.

2. De plus amples informations sur le processus de purification de l'échelle peuvent être trouvées dans le premier chapitre de cette thèse.

3. Ces valeurs sont élevées et vont de 11, 22 pour la première dimension à 1.1 pour la dernière.

que l'échelle exhibe les propriétés de la validité convergente. La validité discriminante a été prouvée en estimant quatre autres modèles structurels qui s'évertuaient à lier les 43 items à moins de 10 dimensions. Tous les quatre modèles présentent des indices d'ajustement d'une qualité inférieure à ceux du modèle de base (Lings et Greenly, 2005). Après avoir confirmé que chaque item était lié à son construit latent, nous avons additionné et divisé les items (Veira, 2011 ; Parasuraman *et al*, 1988 ; Bahia et Nantel, 2000 ; Lings et Greenly, 2005, Karapete *et al*, 2005 ; Spector, 1985 ; Tsui *et al*, 1997 ; Bruck *et al*, 2002 ; Akhtar *et al*, 2008) se rapportant à chaque dimension afin de trouver des index moyens relatifs à chaque dimension.

Le diagramme ci-contre nous donne de plus amples informations sur les dimensions et les items de la satisfaction des employés.

En vue de nous rassurer de la fiabilité et de la validité des deux construits utilisés, nous avons estimé un modèle de mesure comprenant les 10 dimensions de la satisfaction des employés et les trois items mesurant l'intention de départ. Les indices d'ajustements résultant de ce modèle (*CFI = .94 ; IFI = .94 ; TLI = .93 ; RMSEA = .08*) montrent que ce dernier décrit convenablement les données. Les résultats confirment que chaque variable est liée au construit latent auquel elle était censée être liée avec des coefficients structurels standardisés élevés. Tous les t-values sont élevées et sont significatives au seuil de .000. Les autres mesures se rapportant à la fiabilité et à la validité peuvent être visionnées dans le tableau ci-après.

TABLEAU 1
Informations se rapportant aux mesures des variables sous analyse

Construit	Dimension	Nombre d'Items	Coefficient Alpha de Cronbach (α)	Fiabilité de construit (rho)	Variance moyenne extraite
Satisfaction des employés	10	43	.83	.84	.51
Intention de départ	1	3	.80	.80	.58

Source. Compilations sur base des résultats de l'analyse factorielle exploratoire et confirmatoire

SCHÉMA 2

Dimensions et attributs de la satisfaction des employés

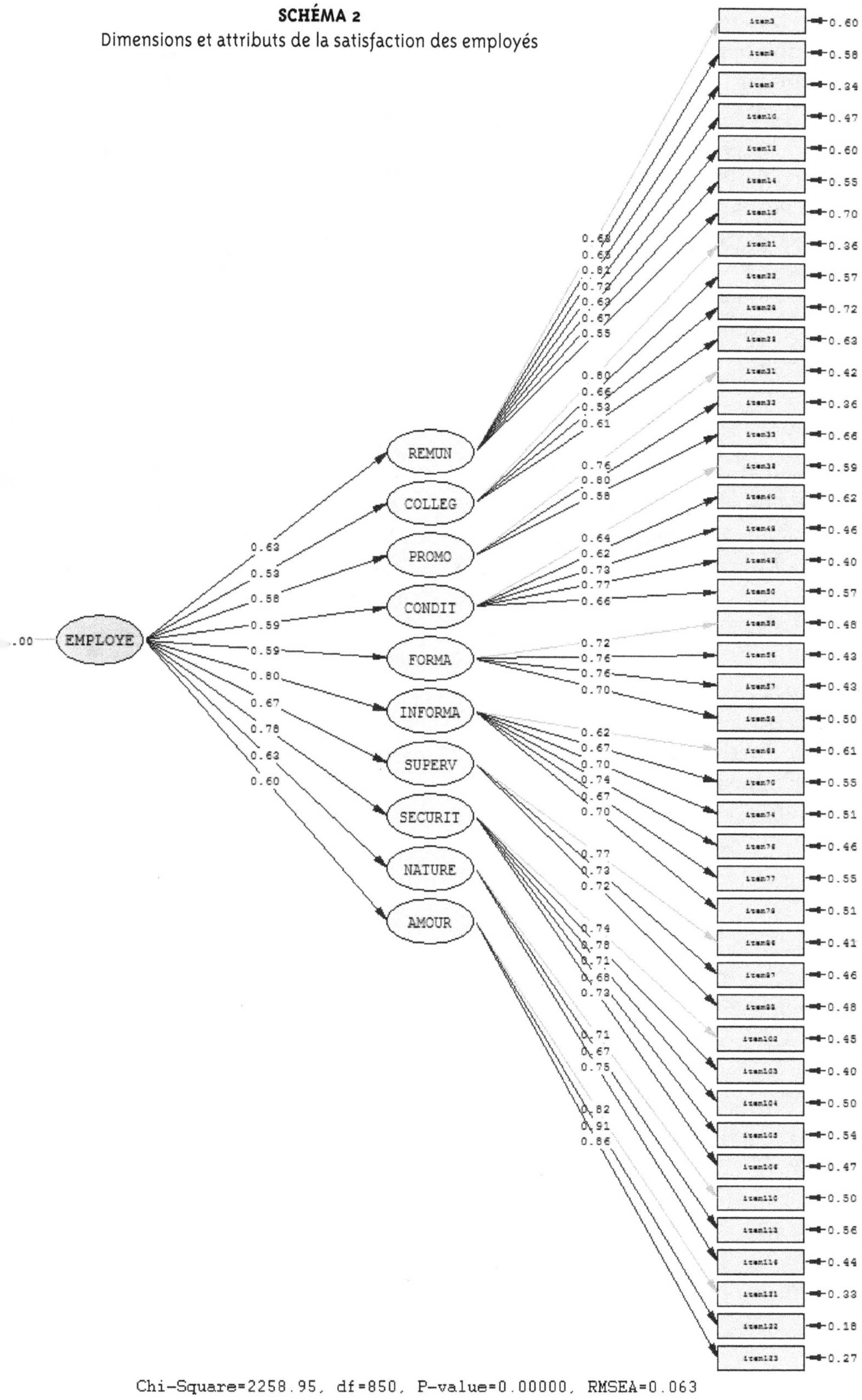

Les résultats issus du tableau1 montrent que les deux construits présentent des coefficients alpha de Cronbach supérieurs à la norme de .7 soit α =. 83 pour la satisfaction des employés, α =. 80 pour l'intention de départ. Toutes les valeurs de la fiabilité des construits (CR) sont élevées et sont supérieures à la norme de .7 pour les deux construits, soit .82 pour la satisfaction des employés et .81 pour l'intention de départ. Les valeurs relatives à la variance moyenne extraite se rapportant à chaque construit sont élevées soit .51 pour la satisfaction des employés et .58 pour l'intention de départ. Les informations ci-haut confirment que les deux construits exhibent les propriétés de la validité convergente. La validité discriminante a été prouvée à partir de la matrice de corrélation entre les deux concepts (Fornell et Larcker, 1981). Le tableau suivant nous en donne de plus amples informations.

Les résultats issus du tableau 2 montrent que le carré de la corrélation entre les deux construits est inférieur à la variance moyenne partagée. Pareils résultats prouvent donc que les mesures de différents construits sont bien différentes les unes des autres. Cela donne la certitude que le modèle remplit les conditions de la validité discriminante.

Les variables sociodémographiques

Cinq variables ont été considérées : l'âge, l'ancienneté, le niveau d'études, le sexe et la relation de parenté avec les dirigeants des IMFs. Toutes les variables ont été saisies sous formes nominales (en classes d'intervalles) en vue de nous permettre d'effectuer une analyse préliminaire (ANOVA et Test T) sur leurs liens probables avec les index moyens de la satisfaction des employés et leurs intentions de quitter les IMFs.

TABLE 2

Matrice de corrélation entre les construits

Construits	1	2	Variance Moyenne Extraite (AVE)
Intention de départ des employés	1		.58
Satisfaction des employés	-.32** (.10)	1	.51

Source. Compilations sur base des résultats de la corrélation sous SPSS 16.0 ; ** p .05 ; () = Carrés de la corrélation entre construits.

3.3. Techniques de traitement des données

Le traitement des données a été effectué en recourant respectivement aux équations structurelles[1] et à la régression hiérarchique. Les équations structurelles ont été utilisées pour tester la relation entre la satisfaction des employés et leurs intentions de départ. Un modèle simplifié comprenant les index moyens des dix dimensions de la satisfaction des employés ainsi que les trois items mesurant les intentions de départ a été testé. En utilisant l'analyse factorielle confirmatoire sous LISREL9.1, nous avons testé le modèle de mesure en vue de nous assurer que chaque variable était significativement liée à la variable latente à laquelle elle était censée être attachée. Cette condition a été vérifiée par la taille et l'importance des coefficients structurels standardisés et par les t-values relatives à chaque variable.

Le modèle structurel permettait, quant à lui, de juger de la qualité et de la force d'association entre les deux variables latentes (satisfaction et intention) en observant leurs coefficients standardisés et leurs t-values (> 1.96). Pour confirmer que le modèle était conforme aux données et qu'il témoignait de bonnes propriétés psychométriques, nous avons recouru aux différents indices renseignant sur la qualité des modèles structurels (RMSEA ≤ .08 ; IFI ≥ .90, CFI ≥ .90 ; TLI ≥ .90) (Hu et Bentler, 1999 cités par Matzler et Renzl, 2007).

La régression hiérarchique a été utilisée pour tester si les variables sociodémographiques affectaient la nature de la relation entre la satisfaction des employés et leurs intentions de départ (Baron et Kenny, 1986 ; Mackinnon et Luechen, 2011). Sur base des recommandations des auteurs ci-contre, nous avons testé séparément trois modèles. Le premier modèle comprend uniquement la satisfaction des employés, le deuxième adjoint la satisfaction des employés aux variables sociodémographiques. Le troisième modèle intègre à la fois la satisfaction des employés, les variables sociodémographiques ainsi que les variables d'interaction, c'est-à-dire le produit de chacune des variables sociodémographiques avec la satisfaction des employés. La qualité globale de chaque modèle était jugée par le *F* de Ficher alors que la qualité de l'ajustement était jugée par le R^2. L'importance de chaque variable était liée directement à son t-value ainsi qu'à la probabilité y relative. Nous avons recouru au test de Durbin–Wu–Hausman (Davidson et MacKinnon, 1993) pour tester l'endogénéité des variables âge et ancienneté dans le modèle de l'intention de départ. Ainsi avons-nous régressé chacune de ces deux variables sur l'ensemble des autres variables exogènes. Nous avons ensuite sauvegardé les résidus issus de ces régressions que nous avons, par la suite, intégrés dans l'équation de l'intention de départ. La présence

1. La méthode d'estimation choisie est le maximum de vraisemblance (Chi et Cursoy, 2009 ; Brown, 2006).

de l'endogénéité était testée par la significativité des résidus.

4. Résultats et discussions

Nous offrons d'abord un aperçu sur les dimensions de la satisfaction des employés, ensuite nous testons les liens entre la satisfaction et les intentions de départ via un modèle structurel et enfin nous apprécions l'effet interactif des variables socio-démographiques sur la relation entre satisfaction et intention de départ.

4.1. Dimensions de la satisfaction des employés des IMFs et nature de sa relation avec l'intention de départ des employés

Les résultats issus du modèle de mesure et du modèle structurel révèlent que le modèle ainsi spécifié reflète assez bien les données (*CFI = .93 ; IFI = .93, TLI = 0.91 ; RMSEA = .06*). En effet, tous les indices d'ajustements exhibent des valeurs satisfaisantes (Brown, 2006 ; Malhotra *et al*, 2010). Le tableau ci-contre nous donne de plus amples informations.

Les résultats issus du modèle de mesure montrent que chaque variable est statistiquement liée au construit latent auquel elle était censée être rattachée. Toutes les dimensions se rapportant à la satisfaction des employés présentent des coefficients structurels standardisés largement supérieurs à .5 ainsi que des t-values largement supérieures à 1.96. Le pourcentage de variance expliquée par chaque dimension est élevé et varie entre 27 % (relations entre collègues et nature du travail) à 49 % (pour circulation de l'information). Les mêmes conclusions peuvent être tirées pour les variables qui mesurent l'intention de quitter les IMFs. Ces dernières exhibent des coefficients structurels et t-values élevées avec des pourcentages de variance expliquée individuels allant de 53 % (intention 5) à 67 % (intention1). Ces quelques résultats montrent que le modèle estimé exhibe des propriétés de validité convergente et discriminante (Vieira, 2011 ; Lings et Greenly, 2005 ; Fornell et Larcher, 1981 ; Anderson et Gerbing, 1988). Ces résultats peuvent être visualisés sur le diagramme 3.

Les résultats issus des diagrammes 2 et 3 et ceux du tableau ci-avant montrent que la satisfaction des employés dans les IMFs du Kivu est un construit multidimensionnel constitué de 43 items.[1] Ces derniers sont subdivisés en dix dimensions principales (voir diagramme 5) : la rémunération, les relations avec les collègues de même rang, la promotion, les conditions de travail, la formation, la circulation de l'information, les relations avec le superviseur, la sécurité de l'emploi, la nature du travail ainsi que l'amour du travail. La contribution de chaque dimension à l'explication des sentiments de satisfaction est appréciée par son coefficient structurel, les

1. De plus amples informations sur les libellés des items sont fournies à l'annexe 1 de la présente thèse.

TABLEAU 4

Dimensions de la satisfaction des employés et relation entre la satisfaction des employés et intention de départ

Paramètres	Estimateurs	Erreur standard	T-Value	R^2
Rémunération ← Satisfaction des employés	0.57	0.06	11.23	0.33
Relations avec collègues ← Satisfaction des employés	0.52	0.05	10.58	0.27
Promotion ← Satisfaction des employés	0.56	0.07	11.50	0.31
Conditions de travail ← Satisfaction des employés	0.57	0.07	11.87	0.33
Formation ← Satisfaction des employés	0.61	0.07	12.72	0.37
Circulation information ← Satisfaction des employés	0.70	0.06	11.36	0.49
Relation avec superviseur ← Satisfaction des employés	0.58	0.07	12.04	0.34
Sécurité du travail ← Satisfaction des employés	0.68	0.06	14.75	0 .46
Nature du Travail ← Satisfaction des employés	0.53	0.06	10.76	0.27
Amour du travail ← Satisfaction des employés	0.52	0.07	10.71	0.28
INT1 ← Intention de départ	0.82	0.01	7.26	0.67
INT3 ← Intention de départ	0.74	0.09	13.23	0.55
INT5 ← Intention de départ	0.72	0.09	13.08	0.53
SATISFACTION ← INTENTION DEPART	-0.32	0.06	-5.51	0.10

Source : Résultats de l'enquête à partir de LISREL 9.1

dimensions présentant des coefficients structurels élevés étant aussi les plus importantes (Karapate *et al*, 2005).

La circulation et le partage de l'information se positionne comme étant la première (ƛ= *.80)* dimension de la satisfaction des employés des IMFs du Kivu. Cette dimension se rapporte à l'existence et au recours à des canaux formels pour communiquer les informations. Elle se rapporte aussi à la possibilité des employés de donner leurs avis sur la gestion de leur IMF. Cette dimension renseigne aussi sur le fait que tout le monde est bien informé sur tout ce qui se passe dans l'organisation. Cette dimension souligne aussi l'importance des réunions régulières entre les départements. Les arguments ci-avant rappellent aux IMFs de favoriser le partage des informations pour que les décisions

DIAGRAMME 3

Relation en la satisfaction des employés et leurs intentions de départ

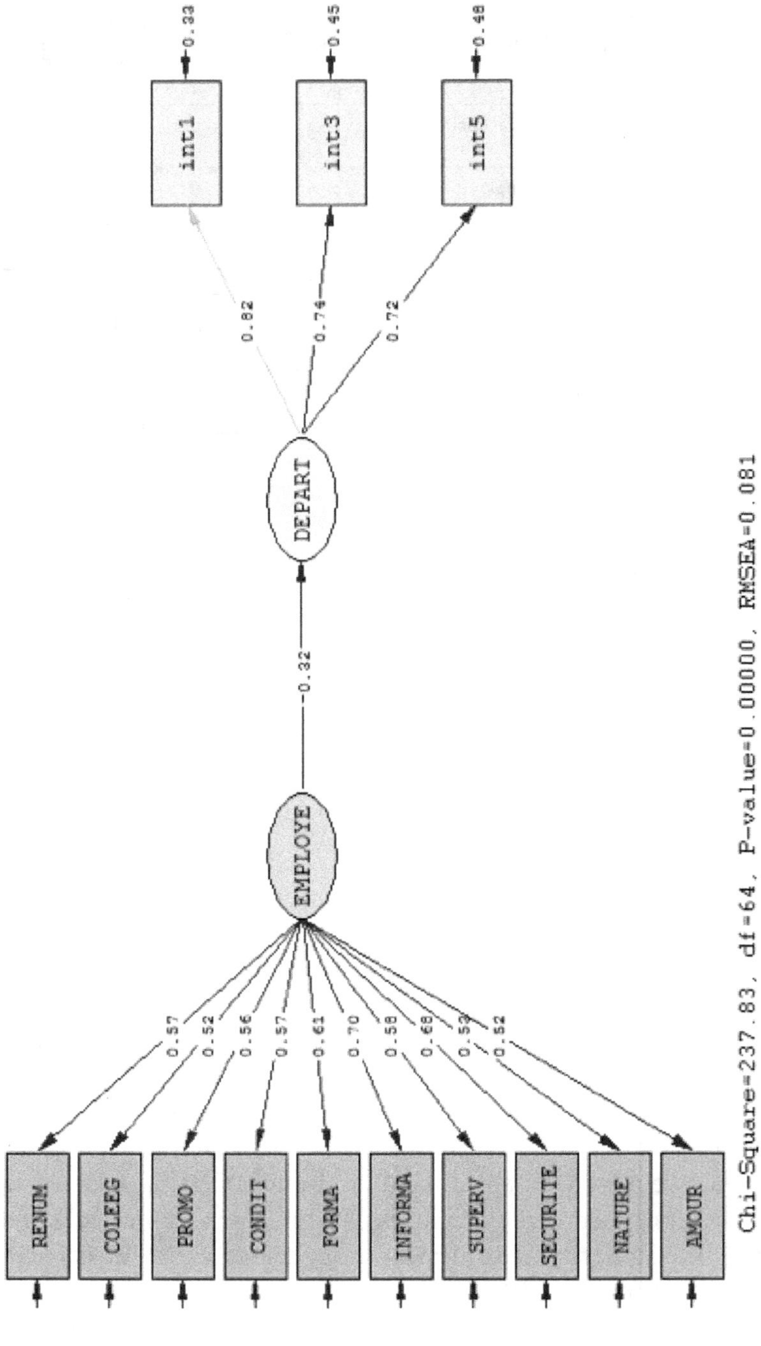

importantes se prennent à temps opportun. Les réunions régulières inter et intra départements sont une bonne occasion pour mettre tout le monde au courant de la bonne marche ou non de l'organisation. Ces réunions sont une occasion offerte aux managers pour rendre compte et dévoiler les plans futurs de développement des IMFs. Les employés peuvent aussi profiter de ces réunions pour donner leur avis et propositions. Ils peuvent aussi profiter de l'occasion pour faire un état des lieux des prérogatives qui leur incombent, exposer les difficultés auxquelles ils sont soumis dans la réalisation de leur travail ainsi que des avancées majeures auxquelles ils sont parvenus.

L'accès de tout le monde à l'information est la meilleure voie qui permet à chaque employé d'être sensibilisé sur tout ce qui se passe dans son IMF, de comprendre les grands enjeux et surtout se comporter en conséquence. Cette dimension sensibilise donc les IMFs à adopter « l'orientation marché » pour survivre dans l'environnement concurrentiel. Dans cette perspective, les IMFs se doivent de collecter l'information sur le marché pour identifier les besoins et les préférences des clients, identifier les actions probables des concurrents, partager ces informations à l'intérieur de l'organisation pour que des actions soient prises (Kohli et Jaworski, 1990). Les arguments ci-avant sensibilisent les IMFs pour qu'elles promeuvent le dialogue, la transparence et une communication efficace à l'intérieur de leurs institutions (Sarker, 2013). La circulation de l'information revêt une importance capitale pour les IMFs du Kivu qui partagent peu ou pas d'informations aux autres parties prenantes de leur environnement immédiat.

En effet, certaines IMFs du Kivu sont comparables à des « boîtes noires » où l'information n'est disponible qu'auprès de la direction générale ; les autres employés étant considérés comme des exécutants qui sont souvent sous informés sur la gestion de leur entreprise. En effet, certaines IMFs hésitent de partager des informations avec leurs employés ou avec d'autres parties prenantes externes (chercheurs, auditeurs, entre autres). Certaines IMFs croient même que l'employé moyen ne comprend rien de l'organisation, qu'il n'a rien à ajouter ou à modifier par rapport aux procédures existantes. Une telle conception peut avoir des répercussions négatives sur l'IMF. En effet, l'absence de transparence et des informations utiles peut réduire la possibilité des employés à s'attacher à leur IMF. Cela est justifié par le fait que des employés mal informés auraient difficile à faire un lien entre leurs propres efforts et l'atteinte des objectifs de leur institution (Ross et Denzer, 2011). Cette conception négative devrait donc être abandonnée en cette période où la microfinance a entamé une forte phase de commercialisation. Cette dernière repose en effet sur la diffusion des informations à l'intérieur comme à l'extérieur des IMFs qui se doivent d'attirer les investisseurs privés en vue de continuer à octroyer les produits financiers et non financiers aux personnes exclues de la finance formelle.

La sécurité du travail et la conformité à la loi se positionnent comme étant la deuxième dimension (λ = *.78)* de la satisfaction des employés des IMFs du Kivu. Cette dimension se rapporte notamment au respect des engagements assignés aux employeurs dans le code du travail, la signature du contrat à durée indéterminée par les employés ainsi qu'à la stabilité de leur emploi. La primauté de la sécurité de l'emploi est expliquée par l'insécurité qui caractérise presque tous les secteurs d'emplois en RDC. Les résultats de l'étude de Makabu ma Nkenda, Mba et Torelli (2005) portant sur l'emploi en RDC montrent que "la précarité des emplois se manifeste par la faible contractualisation des relations de travail. Un employé sur deux n'a aucun contrat écrit vis-à-vis de son employeur et quatre sur dix ne possèdent pas de bulletin de paie....dans le secteur privé, 62 % des salariés sont détenteurs de contrat de travail et 59,3 % d'un bulletin de paie".

L'importance de la sécurité de l'emploi avait déjà été mise en exergue dans l'explication de la satisfaction des employés dans quelques études antérieures. Les résultats de l'enquête du Programme Social International (1989) ainsi que ceux de l'étude de Moguerou (2002) repris par Theodossiou et Vasileio (2007) révèlent tous que la sécurité au travail est le déterminant le plus important de la satisfaction des employés dans plusieurs secteurs d'activités. L'importance de la sécurité du travail tient au fait qu'elle permet aux employés de parer contre l'incertitude du futur, de planifier et d'entrevoir des projets d'investissement à long terme. L'importance de la stabilité de l'emploi en RDC tient au fait que les ONG internationales et celles du système des Nations Unies qui paient de gros salaires n'octroient pas de contrats à durée indéterminée. Dans ce cas, les employés peuvent accepter des salaires plus ou moins faibles en espérant les gagner sur une longue période.

Les relations que les employés entretiennent avec leurs superviseurs (λ= *.67)* constituent la troisième dimension de la satisfaction des employés des IMFs au Kivu. Cette dimension se rapporte à la considération que les chefs hiérarchiques ont pour leurs subalternes ainsi qu'au niveau de coopération et de collaboration qui existe entre les chefs à tous les niveaux et les autres employés se situant au bas de l'échelle. L'importance de cette dimension est liée à la fois à l'importance des employés de contact dans les IMFs ainsi qu'à la conception médiévale du pouvoir qui continue à caractériser les relations de travail au Kivu. Les employés de contact occupent une place stratégique dans la relation de crédit. Ils accèdent à une masse d'informations portant sur la qualité des clients (honnêteté, capacité de remboursement, entre autres) auxquelles les managers n'accèdent préalablement pas. La nature et la qualité des relations que ces employés entretiennent avec leurs superviseurs pourraient les pousser à divulguer ou pas ces informations. Par conséquent, les superviseurs qui favorisent et créent un bon climat de travail et une ambiance fraternelle entre eux et leurs subalternes distillent la confiance dans les chefs de leurs employés.

Un tel climat est susceptible de favoriser le dialogue et permettre aux employés de communiquer toutes les informations qu'ils détiennent à travers des canaux formels et informels disponibles pour ce fait (Kumar Jha et Singh, 2015). L'intérêt placé dans la coopération et la collaboration entre les employés et leurs superviseurs montre que les relations de travail ne devraient pas être analysées seulement en termes d'avantages matériels et économiques. En effet, sans enfreindre aux règles de la hiérarchie et de la subordination, les relations de travail devraient être fondées sur une interaction humaine caractérisée par la compréhension, l'entente et la confiance mutuelle. Ainsi, en créant une culture et des attitudes favorables à l'écoute et à la compréhension mutuelle, les superviseurs accroissent la motivation, la satisfaction ainsi que l'appartenance de ces derniers à leurs IMFs (Sarker, 2013 ; Herzberg, Mausser et Snyderman, 1959). En mettant le cap sur ces motivations psychologiques, les IMFs se prédisposeraient donc à satisfaire leurs employés, à les motiver pour qu'ils travaillent et développent peu ou pas d'intentions de départ (Sarker, 2013). L'étude conduite au Nigéria par Ibok et Umana (2013) sur les liens entre la supervision et la performance de la force de vente dans les IMFs corroborent ces faits en démontrant qu'il existe une relation positive entre le comportement de supervision et la performance de la force de vente.

Ainsi, les IMFs qui créent un climat favorable au dialogue et relations apaisées entre la direction et les employés seront capables d'identifier les problèmes auxquels les employés sont confrontés et d'y apporter facilement des solutions adéquates parce que préalablement négociées. L'existence d'une bonne coopération entre les managers et les employés finira par créer une ambiance fraternelle qui est susceptible d'encourager la rétention des employés (Kumar Jha et Singh, 2015). Les relations ainsi créées favorisent l'ouverture et l'échange entre employés et superviseurs. Elles conduisent en définitive **à** une certaine banalisation de l'autorité, de la bureaucratie ainsi que des rapports hiérarchiques rigides qui frustrent les employés, les contraignent à la résignation et inhibent leur créativité.

La rémunération et les autres avantages se positionnent ex aequo avec l'amour du travail comme la quatrième dimension (λ = *.63)* de la satisfaction des employés des

IMFs du Kivu. Cette dimension se rapporte à une politique salariale qui respecte la procédure et les règlements, à un salaire qui s'ajuste en fonction du niveau d'études et qui s'aligne au salaire interprofessionnel minimum garanti. Cette dimension décrit aussi la possibilité pour les employés de recevoir des avantages dus à leur rang et qui soient supérieurs à ceux offerts dans d'autres IMFs ainsi qu'à la possibilité de recevoir un treizième mois à la fin de l'année. Le salaire et les différentes récompenses accordées aux employés jouent un rôle capital au sein des IMFs. Ces éléments exercent un impact positif sur le moral des employés et accroissent intuitivement la satisfaction et la productivité des employés. Le salaire et les autres avantages accordés aux employés reflètent la disposition des IMFs à se conformer à la justice et à l'équité à l'intérieur comme à l'extérieur de l'entreprise.

En effet, les employés qui sentent qu'ils ne sont pas bien rémunérés par leurs IMFs seraient peu enclins à travailler avec attention. Par conséquent, ils sont vulnérables à la fraude, spécialement dans des pays où des sommes qui passent entre leurs mains sont plus importantes que leurs salaires annuels (Pityn et Hemuth, 2007). Les bas salaires et la faible reconnaissance accordée aux employés peuvent expliquer en partie les comportements malveillants de fraude et de détournement des fonds qui se vivent actuellement dans quelques IMFs du Kivu. La coopérative d'épargne et de crédit de Nyawera a dû chasser deux de ses gérants pour détournement de plus de 40.000 USD. Les coopératives d'épargne et de crédit "Kawa" et "Tulinde Azina" sont aussi régulièrement confrontées aux comportements opportunistes des collecteurs qui ne déposent souvent pas l'argent qu'ils ont collecté auprès des clients dans la caisse centrale. Plus de 30 cas de fraude ont été rapportés à la coopérative Kawa en moins de deux ans pour un montant total de 11.500 USD[1].

Même si ces comportements peuvent être expliqués par la recherche des gains faciles et rapides dans le chef des employés, ils devraient aussi interpeller les responsables des IMFs pour qu'ils modifient et adaptent leur structure salariale aux besoins de leurs employés. En effet, un bon salaire et des récompenses régulières sont un moyen efficace pour stimuler la performance des employés et rendre l'IMF plus attractive pour eux et les autres employés potentiels. La forte concurrence qui gagne peu à peu le secteur de la microfinance au Kivu invite les IMFs à motiver les employés en vue d'accroître leur rétention et contribuer ainsi à renforcer la compétitivité des IMFs (Ismawan, nd). Des efforts devraient être fournis en termes de rémunération pour que le secteur de la microfinance

1. Ces données sont glanées sur base des entretiens que nous avons réalisés avec les responsables de la collecte des fonds de ces coopératives ainsi qu'avec le directeur adjoint de la coopérative NYAWERA.

devienne plus attractif en offrant une bonne structure salariale, de bonnes conditions de travail, entre autres.

La nature du travail (λ = *.63)* se positionne aussi à la quatrième place comme la rémunération. Cette dimension renvoie à la possibilité que les employés ont d'apprécier les résultats de leur propre travail. Elle se réfère aussi au fait que les employés soient affectés dans des postes pour lesquels ils ont de grandes prédisposions et des compétences ; c'est-à-dire le travail qu'ils font mieux. Cette dimension montre l'importance que les employés accordent à l'évaluation de leur travail par eux-mêmes. En effet, les employés des IMFs veulent se rendre utiles à leurs IMFs par le biais d'un travail bien fait. Ils veulent ainsi participer à la performance de leur institution. Cela n'est possible que si les employés sont commis à des fonctions et à des tâches qu'ils font le mieux possible.

Ceci démontre donc que la répartition des tâches dans les IMFs devrait normalement tenir compte des prédispositions et des compétences des employés avant de les affecter. Ceci indique donc que les managers devraient requérir l'avis des employés avant de les affecter et de les changer de poste. En effet, lorsqu'un employé exprime un attachement particulier pour un travail et qu'il a les compétences voulues, il aura tendance à investir tout son effort pour s'affirmer et produire ainsi le résultat voulu. Le travail d'un agent de crédit est par exemple très stressant et demande un niveau d'engagement élevé. Seuls les agents de crédit qui aiment réellement leur travail peuvent le trouver agréable, l'amour du travail servant de tampons aux périodes de stress et d'anxiété.

L'amour du travail (λ = *.60)* se positionne à la cinquième position des dimensions de la satisfaction des employés des IMF du Kivu. L'amour du travail se réfère au fait que les employés trouvent ou non leur travail intéressant et qu'ils en sont donc fiers. Un travail est intéressant pour l'employé s'il lui permet de mettre en évidence ses talents, ses connaissances et son expertise. L'amour du travail prédispose l'employé à donner le meilleur de lui-même. Cette caractéristique est importante pour le secteur de la microfinance pour lequel plusieurs fonctions revêtent un caractère routinier conduisant souvent à l'ennui et au stress. Comme les employés travaillent sous pression, il arrive qu'ils se découragent et quittent leurs IMFs. Seuls l'amour et l'attachement qu'ils ont envers leur poste de travail peuvent réduire significativement ces imperfections.

La fierté que les employés tirent du travail peut aussi contribuer à renforcer l'amour du travail. Certaines IMFs ont par exemple institué une forme de reconnaissance publique de leurs employés qu'elles priment comme "meilleure caissière, meilleur agent de crédit de l'année". Même si ces récompenses peuvent ne pas avoir une incidence financière significative, elles contribuent toutefois à renforcer l'image et la réputation personnelle des employés concernés. Cette reconnaissance pourrait être utilisée, les cas échéants, lors des promotions futures. Elle peut aussi servir de signal de compétence à l'endroit des autres IMFs et autres organisations qui sont à la recherche d'une main-d'œuvre qualifiée.

La formation et le développement du personnel constituent la sixième dimension (ƛ = *.59)* de la satisfaction des employés des IMFs du Kivu. Cette dimension se rapporte à l'accès à des formations qui confèrent de nouvelles connaissances aux employés, connaissances qui les préparent à occuper des postes futurs plus élevés. Cette dimension met aussi en exergue le fait que les employeurs prodiguent des conseils aux employés en rapport avec le développement de leur carrière. L'importance de ces formations est justifiée par le fait qu'il n'existe à présent que quelques universités et instituts supérieurs qui forment particulièrement en microfinance en RDC et au Kivu. La plupart des employés des IMFs ont des connaissances générales en gestion et en économie. Les formations qu'ils reçoivent devraient renforcer leurs capacités et leur permettre de faire carrière dans un secteur de microfinance qui est aujourd'hui à la recherche d'un personnel qualifié (Mubarik, 2008).

La formation accroît donc l'efficacité des employés, augmente leur adaptabilité et leur permet d'adopter facilement les nouvelles technologies. La formation du personnel encourage la satisfaction et la rétention des employés. En effet, les diverses formations reçues au sein d'une IMF permettent aux employés de mieux s'imprégner de la culture organisationnelle de leurs IMFs, de construire une histoire avec l'IMF et d'exprimer peu ou pas d'intentions à les quitter. Par conséquent, les employés formés sont aussi les plus compétents car ils comprennent mieux leurs tâches. Ces formations les préparent à assumer de grandes responsabilités dans le futur et les prédisposent à ne pas quitter leurs IMFs. En effet, il existe une relation positive entre les formations reçues et l'accroissement de l'estime en soi dans le chef des employés (Pityn et Helmuth, 2007).

Les conditions de travail constituent la sixième dimension (ƛ = *.59)* de la satisfaction des employés des IMFs du Kivu au même titre que la formation. Cette dimension se rapporte à la présence d'une gestion informatisée au sein des IMFs, à la disponibilité des outils et équipements de travail, à une bonne répartition des tâches ainsi qu'à l'état des bâtiments abritant les IMFs. L'importance de la gestion informatisée est due au fait qu'elle facilite le travail des employés en leur permettant de gagner du temps. L'informatisation de la gestion favorise la rapidité des opérations tout en évitant aux employés de commettre des erreurs. La présence des outils de travail et autres équipements contribue aussi à améliorer le rendement des employés. En effet, comme le travail des agents de crédit se déroule sur le terrain, ils devraient disposer de motos, de véhicules et autres éléments logistiques qui leur facilitent la tâche. Ces moyens logistiques rappellent que les employés des IMFs ne sont ni des machines ni des robots infatigables (Sarker, 2013).

Certaines IMFs du Kivu comme PAIDEK octroient une moto à crédit à chaque agent pour l'aider à atteindre facilement les clients. D'autres encore accordent un crédit voiture pour favoriser la mobilité des agents. Ces initiatives ont pour objectif d'introduire une petite dose d'ergonomie et tenter de soulager la fatigue et le stress auxquels les agents des IMFs sont quotidiennement soumis. L'importance de la répartition des tâches tient au fait que les employés des IMFs sont souvent surchargés, submergés car ils sont appelés à exécuter plusieurs tâches à la fois. Une description claire des tâches les empêcherait de se disperser et se consacrer ainsi aux tâches essentielles se rapportant à leur mission principale. La répartition claire des responsabilités (job description) est sans nul doute le remède parfait qui libèrerait les employés de leur pression quotidienne et qui les prédisposerait à exprimer un niveau élevé de satisfaction envers leur IMF (Sarker, 2013).

La promotion constitue la septième dimension (λ = *.58)* de la satisfaction des employés des IMFs du Kivu. Cette dimension se rapporte à la rapidité avec laquelle les employés sont promus, au respect du critère de compétence des employés dans l'octroi des promotions ainsi qu'au respect des critères décrits dans le guide des promotions. La rapidité du processus de promotion est un remède au découragement et à l'insatisfaction des employés compétents qui occupent des postes inférieurs. En effet, la promotion peut encourager la satisfaction, la fidélité et l'attachement des employés ainsi promus. Dans le chef des employés, la promotion est perçue comme la reconnaissance du travail rendu. Elle est aussi perçue comme un motif de fierté et un symbole de réussite professionnelle et sociale.

L'accent placé sur les compétences des agents met en évidence l'intégrité, l'impartialité ainsi que la rigueur qui doivent accompagner tout le processus de promotion. En effet, ne devraient être promus que les employés qui ont fait preuve des compétences avérées dans l'exercice de leur travail ou ayant excellé dans un domaine particulier. L'application des critères définis dans le document de promotion permet d'éviter l'arbitraire en favorisant par exemple des personnes qui sont proches de la direction. Ceci est d'autant plus important dans le contexte du Kivu où les relations sociales et claniques peuvent parfois l'emporter sur tous les autres critères objectifs.

Les managers devraient donc comprendre que des promotions mal distribuées peuvent entraîner le découragement des employés compétents, entraîner leur insatisfaction ainsi que leur départ de l'institution et inversement. Ceci laisse entendre qu'un bon système de promotion permet aux IMFs de se doter progressivement des ressources humaines compétentes pouvant assurer la continuité de l'organisation même en l'absence des fondateurs. En effet, il est "beau d'avoir un fondateur charismatique mais aussi il faut avoir un réservoir de main-d'œuvre compétente prêt à assurer". Tout cela ne peut être possible que grâce à un bon système de promotion.

La dimension *relations et respect envers les collègues de même niveau* se positionne comme la dernière dimension (λ= *.53)* de la satisfaction des employés des IMFs du Kivu. Cette dimension se rapporte à la qualité des relations existant entre employés, au respect mutuel qui caractérise ces relations, à la prédisposition qu'ils ont pour construire des liens d'amitié solides entre eux ainsi qu'à l'appréciation qu'ils se font les uns les autres. Le travail dans une IMF se fait en chaîne. Si le processus de demande d'un crédit par exemple commence et se termine entre les mains des agents de crédit, il semble que d'autres personnes interviennent directement ou indirectement dans une ou plusieurs étapes du processus. Le chargé du contentieux juridique va se rassurer de la conformité du contrat à la loi, le caissier va libérer l'argent et le comptable va passer les écritures. Le concours de toutes ces personnes est nécessaire pour que l'opération se déroule parfaitement.

Tout cela n'est possible que si les employés cultivent de bonnes relations entre eux. Autrement, ils vont se tendre des pièges, multiplier les tracasseries, nuire à la rapidité des opérations et bloquer le système et la performance de l'institution. La complémentarité entre les différentes personnes œuvrant dans cette chaine est nécessaire. Ceci implique que la performance d'une IMF implique une forte coopération entre les employés. Les managers des IMFs devraient s'efforcer de développer des relations de collaboration entre les employés. Il s'agit donc de faire émerger un esprit de corps entre les employés, de les pousser à travailler ensemble en constituant par exemple des groupes de travail par départements et créer des occasions festives en dehors des heures de travail pour favoriser plus de familiarité entre les employés. L'objectif est de faire en sorte que l'IMF devienne une seconde famille pour chaque employé. Ce dernier doit sentir qu'il y a autour de lui des personnes, des collègues et des amis sur lesquels il peut compter à chaque fois qu'il est confronté à un élément heureux ou malheureux. Ces arguments peuvent expliquer la création des caisses d'assistance mutuelle existant dans certaines IMFs du Kivu (PAIDEK). Chaque employé accepte de verser une cotisation mensuelle d'un montant défini de façon consensuelle et dont une partie est versée à un collègue qui a été frappé par le sinistre. Ces initiatives peuvent émaner soit des employés eux-mêmes ou de l'IMF.

Plusieurs autres initiatives existent (sorties collectives, visites à domicile). Leur objectif principal est d'encourager les employés à tisser des liens amicaux, à mieux se connaître en vue de les pousser à plus de coopération. Pareilles initiatives ont aussi pour rôle de renforcer l'attachement des employés à leur organisation et à les persuader à passer une plus grande partie de leur carrière professionnelle au sein de cette organisation. L'expérience montre que les relations d'amitié construites au cours d'une relation d'emploi peuvent devenir des barrières psychologiques empêchant les employés de changer d'organisation. Les employés craignent de perdre les avantages que procurent les relations amicales qu'ils considèrent d'ores et déjà comme un investissement à long terme.

Les résultats issus du modèle structurel montrent que la satisfaction des employés influence négativement et statistiquement les intentions de départ des employés des IMFs au Kivu ($\gamma = = -.32$, $t = -5.51$, $p = .000$). Ces résultats confirment ainsi notre première hypothèse en attestant que plus les employés seront satisfaits de leur travail et moins ils seront enclins à quitter leurs IMFs (Arndt *et al*, 2006 ; Muchinsky et Tuttle, 1979 ; Porter, Steers *et al*, 1974 ; Wei et Tian-Foreman, 2009 ; Jange et George, 2012). Ces résultats sont conformes aux conclusions de plusieurs études antérieures qui affirment que la satisfaction des employés exerce une influence significativement grande sur les intentions de départ des employés (Griffeth *et al*, 2000 ; Egan, Yang *et al*, 2004 ; MacIntosh et Doherty, 2009 ; Leisanyane et Khaola, 2013). Les résultats de cette étude sont en lien direct avec les conclusions issues de la méta-analyse de Muchinsky et Tuttle (1979) qui ont montré que la satisfaction des employés joue un rôle de premier plan dans l'explication des intentions de départ ainsi que des départs effectifs des employés.

En effet, lorsque les employés deviennent insatisfaits de leur travail, ils nourrissent des intentions de quitter, lesquelles sont souvent suivies par des départs effectifs (Hom *et al*, 1992 ; Lyons et O'Brien, 2006 ; Koch et Steers, 1978). Cheng-Ping Chang et Wei-Chen Chang (2008) corroborent l'argument ci-haut en montrant, sur base des résultats d'une étude conduite par Watson Wyatt Worldwide, que « 58 % des employés quittent leur entreprise parce qu'ils sont insatisfaits de leur salaire alors que 48 % des employés abdiquent car ils sont insatisfaits du système de gestion de leur institution et du manque des opportunités de promotion … ». Alfonso Sousa-Poza et Andres Sousa-Poza (2007) et Clark (2001) soutiennent que la satisfaction des employés est le meilleur déterminant du comportement des départs futurs dans les entreprises. Le même argument est repris par Lambert *et al* (2001) qui démontrent que la satisfaction des employés exerce l'impact le plus significatif sur les intentions de départ des employés.

Les auteurs prouvent que l'effet de la satisfaction des employés est deux fois plus grand que celui produit par les autres variables explicatives. Les résultats de l'étude de Chan Yin-Fah *et al* (2010) vont dans le même sens en prouvant que 20 % de la variance totale des intentions de départ des employés sont expliqués par de faibles niveaux de satisfaction des employés … L'étude de Vidal *et al* (2007) aboutit au même résultat en démontrant que la satisfaction des employés expatriés constituait l'un des déterminants majeurs de leurs intentions de départ. Ryan et Sagas (2009) corroborent l'argument ci-avant en prouvant que les intentions et les départs effectifs des managers et agents marketing dans le secteur sportif sont principalement expliqués par leur salaire. Kautonen, Hytti *et al* (2012) démontrent que les employés satisfaits de leur travail pourraient retarder leur période de retraite et prolonger ainsi leur carrière car ils trouvent leur travail plaisant et attrayant.

Les résultats de Hanish et Hulin (1991) indiquent que des employés insatisfaits et qui sentent que leur travail n'est pas important sont plus prédisposés à quitter leur travail en utilisant tous les moyens nécessaires. Bref, les employés doivent être traités correctement en termes de salaire, de promotion … Dans cette perspective, il faut se rassurer de leur satisfaction en vue d'éviter qu'ils ne soient mécontents et qu'ils ne désertent les IMFs.

4.2. Effets interactifs des variables sociodémographiques

L'effet des variables sociodémographiques sur la relation entre la satisfaction des employés et leurs intentions de départ est testé par trois modèles. Les résultats de ces trois modèles peuvent être visualisés dans le tableau ci-contre.

Les résultats issus du tableau cidessus présentent trois modèles différents. Les R^2 ajustés pour ces modèles sont respectivement de .04 pour le premier et respectivement de .09 et .11 pour les deuxième et troisième modèles. En utilisant le R^2 ajusté comme critère d'ajustement pour ces trois modèles, nous constatons que le modèle (3) présente le R^2 ajusté le plus élevé comparativement aux deux autres. Cela étant, ce modèle est plus ajusté que les autres. Par conséquent, nous le préférons aux deux autres et nous fondons donc toutes les interprétations sur ce modèle. Les résultats montrent que les variables indépendantes expliquent 11 % de la variance des intentions de départ. Le modèle est globalement bon ($F = 6.04$, $p = .000$).

Les résultats montrent que le niveau d'études des employés influence positivement et significativement les intentions de turnover ($ß = .33$; $t = 2.04$; $p = .04$). Pareils résultats indiquent que les employés ayant un niveau d'études élevé sont plus prédisposés à quitter leur emploi (Bright, 2008 ; Hersch, 1991).

TABLEAU 4
Test de la modération des variables sociodémographiques

Variables indépendantes	Intentions de départ comme variable dépendante		
	Modèle (1)	Modèle (2)	Modèle (3)
Constant	4.94 (11.16)***	5.12 (6.83)***	3.06 (2.69) ***
Satisfaction des employés	-.33 (3.21) ***	-.31 (3.19)***	.23 (.96)
Sexe de l'employé		.13 (.97)	.59 (.91)
Age de l'employé		-.19 (1.90) **	- .19 (.68)
Ancienneté au sein de l'IMF		-.23 (3.16) ***	-.14 (.68)
Niveau d'études de l'employé		.09 (.77)	.33 (2.04) **
Parenté avec le directeur		.12 (1.30)	.29 (1.54)
Sexe * Satisfaction de l'employé			-.12 (.76)
Age * Satisfaction de l'employé			-.005 (.07)
Ancienneté * Satisfaction de l'employé			-.03 (.40)
Niveau d'études * Satisfaction de l'employé			-.06 (2.20) **
Parenté * Satisfaction de l'employé			-.05 (1.18)
F-Ficher	10.29	7.96	6.04
R^2 ajusté	.04	.09	.11

***, p .001 ; **, p .05. Les termes entre parenthèses représentent les t-values

Ces résultats sont en contradiction avec ceux de Borkowski, Amann *et al*, 2007) qui ont trouvé qu'il n'existait aucune relation statistiquement significative entre les intentions de départ des infirmiers et leur niveau d'études. Les résultats de la présente étude corroborent toutefois ceux qui ont été trouvés par Clark-Rayner et Harcourt (2000) dans une étude consacrée aux déterminants du comportement de turnover dans le secteur bancaire en Nouvelle Zélande. Les auteurs montrent que les employés ayant un niveau d'études élevé sont parfois engagés dans des postes de niveau inférieur (agent de crédit, caissier, agent de marketing). Ces employés sont obligés d'exécuter des tâches routinières et simples à telle enseigne qu'ils finissent par trouver leur travail comme ennuyant et peu stimulant. Poussés par le chômage, ils acceptent, malgré eux, ce travail qu'ils considèrent comme un emploi temporaire, transitoire, le temps qu'ils trouvent un travail compatible avec leurs qualifications dans d'autres secteurs d'activité.

Même si ces résultats ont été trouvés dans un environnement sociologiquement différent du contexte de cette étude, ils sont toutefois compatibles avec certaines caractéristiques du marché du travail de la RDC et du secteur de la microfinance au Kivu. En effet, les IMFs recrutent souvent des employés ayant un niveau d'études relativement élevé (graduat, licence) et les placent dans des positions d'emploi inférieures (agents de crédit, caissiers ...) pour une charge de travail ample et récurrente (visites sur le terrain, montage des dossiers ...) avec des salaires souvent faibles. Dans un contexte du Kivu marqué par la rareté et la précarité des emplois mieux rémunérés, la majorité des employés acceptent, malgré eux, de prendre ce travail par manque d'alternative.

Comme l'ont bien démontré Clark-Rayner et Harcourt (2000), on peut donc imaginer que ces employés se trouvent dans une étape transitoire et ne tarderaient pas à quitter leurs IMFs s'ils trouvaient une meilleure offre d'emploi. L'avènement des nouvelles banques commerciales au Kivu et les différentes initiatives étatiques visant à recruter les jeunes diplômés dans la fonction publique tendent **à** confirmer cette forte prédisposition des employés des IMFs ayant un niveau d'études élevé à quitter leurs institutions. En effet, presque toutes les nouvelles banques implantées au Kivu ont trouvé l'essentiel de leur personnel auprès des IMFs par un débauchage volontaire. Pour les banques, ces types d'employés sont intéressants car ils engendrent moins de coûts de transaction en termes de formation ; ils sont en effet presque prêts pour la tâche comme ils étaient déjà presque dans la profession bancaire. Pour les employés, les banques offrent de meilleures perspectives en termes de rémunération, d'avancement en grade et valorisent plus leurs employés auprès de leur entourage (en termes d'image). En effet, la société valoriserait plus le statut du banquier que celui d'un agent de crédit simple d'une IMF.

Les arguments ci-dessus expliquent aussi en partie les démissions qu'on a enregistrées à Bukavu ces derniers mois dans certaines IMFs au profit d'un emploi dans la fonction publique[1]. FINCA Bukavu a perdu, à elle seule huit employés en trois mois. Ces derniers ont quitté leur IMF pour travailler comme conseillers ou consultants auprès des communes, des territoires et ministères étatiques. Ces employés détiennent en majorité une licence en sciences économiques et de gestion, en sciences politiques et juridiques et exerçaient tous comme agents de crédit. Les interviews non structurées que nous avons eues avec quatre d'entre eux révèlent qu'ils en avaient marre de subir des pressions de leur hiérarchie en vue d'atteindre les objectifs de performance. Ils n'en pouvaient plus d'occuper des postes qui ne rimaient pas avec leur niveau d'études ; ils réalisaient un travail ingrat pour lequel ils n'étaient pas assez bien payés et ils n'avaient aucun espoir de promotion.

1. L'un de ces programmes gouvernementaux s'appelle : "Services de consultants (145 individus) Experts en développement capables d'élaborer et de suivre la mise en œuvre des stratégies de développement au niveau des territoires."

Pareilles révélations corroborent les conclusions de Sarker (2013) sur le travail des agents de crédit lorsqu'il soutient que les agents de crédit des IMFs sont soumis à de grosses pressions dans l'exercice de leur travail. L'auteur révèle que "ces pressions réduisent la productivité du personnel, entraînent l'insatisfaction... et poussent les agents de crédit à nourrir des fortes intentions de quitter leurs IMFs". Ces révélations sont compatibles avec les sentiments que certains employés des IMFs en Inde expriment par rapport à leur emploi : "les possibilités de promotion sont quasiment impossibles. Le travail routinier que nous exécutons est fatiguant. Les salaires ne peuvent pas être ajustés à la hausse pour tenir compte de l'inflation et ne sont pas comparables à ceux offerts dans d'autres secteurs. Les aspirations personnelles ne sont pas rencontrées ...

Les employés les plus expérimentés quittent le secteur" (Report on Human Resource Management in Microfinance Institutions : The State of Practice in India). Tous les arguments ci-dessus tendent à confirmer la théorie de la surqualification (over-education, educational mismatch) des employés dans le secteur de la microfinance au Kivu. En effet, on peut conclure que les agents de crédit, les chargés de clientèle et les autres agents des IMFs du Kivu occupent actuellement des emplois qui probablement ne sont pas compatibles avec leur niveau d'études. Ces emplois conduisent par conséquent à des salaires bas, à un faible niveau de satisfaction et à des intentions élevées de turnover (Bender et Roche, 2013 ; Kucel, Molina *et al*, nd).

Les résultats montrent aussi que la satisfaction des employés en interaction avec le niveau d'études influence négativement et significativement leurs intentions de départ au sein des IMFs du Kivu (ß = -.06 ; t = 2.20 ; p= .02). Ces résultats révèlent que si les employés sont plus satisfaits, ils ont d'autant moins tendance à quitter leur IMF qu'ils sont de niveau d'étudess plus élevé. Pareil résultat confirme que le niveau d'études tempère l'intensité de la relation entre la satisfaction des employés et leurs intentions de quitter les IMFs. En effet, des employés ayant un niveau d'études élevé et qui sont satisfaits des conditions actuelles de leur travail manifestent peu ou pas d'intentions de départ comparativement à ceux qui ont un niveau d'études bas. Ce résultat confirme partiellement notre deuxième hypothèse (H2b). Pareils résultats peuvent être expliqués à la lumière de la théorie de l'équité.

Les employés qui jouissent d'un niveau d'études élevé sont susceptibles d'occuper des postes de grande responsabilité et toucher des salaires élevés comparativement aux autres (Hersch, 1991). Par conséquent, ils exhibent intuitivement des taux de satisfaction élevés (Theodossiou et Vasileio, 2007) ainsi que de faibles intentions de départ (Borkowski, Amann *et al*, 2007) comparativement aux autres catégories de travailleurs. L'expérience montre que dans certaines IMFs de la RDC, ces types d'employés peuvent gagner des salaires largement supérieurs à ceux payés par les ONGs internationales et les organismes du système des Nations Unies. Par conséquent, ils répondront favorablement aux récompenses offertes par leur IMF en attachant une grande importance à leur emploi et en démontrant des attitudes positives envers leur organisation (Hanisch et Hulin, 1991). Les résultats de cette étude confirment cette thèse en montrant par exemple que le niveau de satisfaction des gérants des IMFs sous étude était supérieur à toutes les autres catégories d'employés enquêtés. Koch et Steers (1978) corroborent l'argument ci-dessus en montrant que les employés ayant un niveau d'études élevé accèdent facilement aux meilleurs postes d'emploi et sont grandement satisfaits de leur institution. Ainsi, seront-ils peu ou pas motivés de quitter l'IMF dans laquelle ils gagnent correctement leur vie.

Ces résultats sont conformes au contexte de la microfinance et aux réalités socioéconomiques du contexte de cette étude. En effet, la majorité des IMFs octroient les promotions en fonction de l'ancienneté résultant d'un travail dur réalisé au sein d'une IMF particulière. Si un agent hautement qualifié et qui occupe de hautes responsabilités quitte son IMF actuelle pour une autre, il est rare qu'il retrouve un poste hiérarchiquement plus élevé que celui qu'il avait. Il risque donc d'être soumis au même critérium de promotion, c'est-à-dire trimer quelques années, réussir une période probatoire et attendre d'obtenir un poste qui rime avec ses aspirations. Non seulement il perd les avantages qu'il avait déjà acquis par son niveau d'études élevé mais surtout il perd le statut et le prestige qui en résultaient. Tous ces faits l'entraînent à se résigner et à rester plutôt fidèle à son organisation.

La RDC en général et le Kivu en particulier sont des régions caractérisées par un chômage massif des cadres (FMI, 2013 ; Ministère du Plan, 2011 ; PNUD, 2009). Makabu ma Nkenda, Mba et Torelli (2005) notent que " dans la capitale, le taux de chômage des personnes non scolarisées est de 8 % contre 16 % pour celles ayant suivi des études secondaires ou supérieures". On comprend donc que les opportunités d'emploi sont rares dans ce contexte et chaque personne qualifiée qui trouve un emploi répondant à son profil tend à s'y accrocher (Balogun et Olowodunoye, 2012 ; Hellman, 1997).

5. Conclusions, implications, limites et recherches futures

Cette étude s'est fixé deux objectifs complémentaires : développer préalablement une échelle pour mesurer la satisfaction des employés dans les IMFs et identifier les liens existant entre la satisfaction des employés et leurs intentions de départ (1) et tester si les variables sociodémographiques sont susceptibles de modérer cette relation (2).

Les résultats montrent que la satisfaction des employés a un impact d'autant plus important sur les intentions de départ que le niveau d'étudess est élevé. Ainsi, plus un employé est satisfait de son travail, moins il va développer des intentions de quitter son emploi. Les résultats confirment que le niveau de scolarisation des employés modère la relation entre la satisfaction des employés et leurs intentions de départ. En effet, plus les employés jouissent d'un niveau de scolarisation élevé, plus ils s'attachent à cette dernière et développent peu ou pas d'intentions de départ en fonction des postes de responsabilité qu'ils occupent et donc du salaire élevé qu'ils perçoivent.

Les résultats de cette étude offrent aux gestionnaires des IMFs un outil managérial qui leur permet d'identifier les besoins et les préférences des employés et d'y répondre de façon adéquate. Les résultats se rapportant à la satisfaction des employés rappellent aux gestionnaires des IMFs qu'ils devraient en premier lieu renforcer la sécurité au travail. Cela passe par l'octroi des contrats à durée indéterminée aux employés. Ce qui évitera le favoritisme et l'arbitraire. Les dirigeants des IMFs devraient aussi investir dans la formation de leurs employés. Cette formation peut prendre la forme des séminaires modulaires ou des formations diplomantes. Une telle initiative a l'avantage de doter les IMFs des cadres bien formés qui font convenablement leur travail et qui confèrent ainsi aux IMFs un avantage compétitif dans un secteur de microfinance voué désormais à la concurrence.

Les gestionnaires des IMFs devraient aussi associer leurs employés à la prise de décisions et leur donner des informations se rapportant à la vie de leur IMF. Il s'agit là d'un début de management par objectifs, où les employés connaissent les objectifs de leur IMF, participent à leur définition et sont motivés à les réaliser. Dans le même ordre d'idée, les dirigeants devraient promouvoir les employés méritants et améliorer l'environnement du travail ainsi que les conditions salariales. Bref, les IMFs sont donc invitées à investir dans leurs employés. Ces investissements pourront réduire l'écart entre les avantages que les employés obtiennent et les efforts qu'ils investissent dans le travail ; ce qui pourrait progressivement renforcer leur attachement à leur IMF. La satisfaction et l'attachement des employés ainsi obtenus réduiront sensiblement les intentions de départ et les autres comportements opportunistes à même d'entraîner une détérioration de la qualité des services et influencer négativement la rétention et la loyauté des clients (Huey-Ming Tzeng, 2002).

La capacité du niveau d'études à influencer la relation entre la satisfaction des employés et leurs intentions de départ est à la fois une opportunité et une interpellation pour les IMFs dans la mise en œuvre de leurs politiques de promotion et de gestion de carrière des employés. Les employés qui ont des niveaux de scolarisation élevés devraient être valorisés et promus car ils constituent des actifs intangibles permettant à l'organisation d'atteindre ses objectifs. Par hypothèse, ces employés seraient plus qualifiés et leur niveau de satisfaction permettrait de les maintenir le plus longtemps au sein de l'entreprise. De tels employés devraient donc recevoir un traitement spécifique. Ainsi, lorsqu'ils sont promus et reçoivent d'autres avantages monétaires et non monétaires, ce n'est que justice qui est faite. En retour, ils s'attacheront à leur IMF et seront peu ou pas tentés d'aller vers les concurrents. Les responsables des IMFs devraient réfléchir aussi sur la nature et le type de promotions qui correspondent aux besoins des employés moins scolarisés (formation, rémunération, crédit) et leur permettre de se réaliser et de développer leur carrière (Enzi Chang *et al*, 1999 cités par Khan *et al*, 2013).

La contribution de cette étude à la littérature est de deux ordres : premièrement, elle confirme que le niveau d'études influence positivement les intentions de départ des employés ; cette même variable tempère la relation entre l'intention de départ et la satisfaction des employés. Les résultats sensibilisent donc les IMFs à recruter les employés en fonction de leur niveau d'études et de les placer dans des postes qui leur plaisent. Cela pourrait se traduire par un attachement exclusif à leurs IMFs avec des répercussions positives sur la performance des IMFs. Deuxièmement, cette étude analyse ces liens dans un secteur de microfinance où les études portant sur les employés en général, la satisfaction et les intentions de turnover en particulier, sont pour ainsi dire inexistantes. Les résultats confirment donc l'importance capitale des ressources humaines dans le secteur de la microfinance et invitent ainsi les IMFs à la valorisation de leur personnel.

La présente étude comporte toutefois quelques limites. Elle ne teste que l'effet interactif des variables sociodémographiques sur la relation entre la satisfaction des employés et leur intention de départ. Une étude globale tenant compte des autres variables organisationnelles comme l'attachement organisationnel et la loyauté des employés viendrait enrichir et compléter les présents résultats. Cette étude n'analyse pas non plus l'influence directe du comportement des gérants des IMFs sur la satisfaction des employés. Une étude portant sur le style de management et la satisfaction des employés pourrait aussi permettre de comprendre comment le comportement des gérants ou des directeurs (manager autocrate versus manager démocratique) peut influencer le niveau de satisfaction des employés des IMFs. La présente étude utilise des données collectées auprès des employés des IMFs à une période fixée dans le temps (données en coupes instantanées).

On peut donc envisager de reproduire cette étude (mais avec les mêmes variables mesurées) dans une perspective longitudinale. Ainsi, on pourrait obtenir des données à différentes années (données de panels), ce qui permettrait l'application des techniques économétriques plus sophistiquées permettant de tenir compte d'éventuels biais d'estimation résultant d'hétérogénéité inobservée entre différentes IMFs, d'endogénéité des variables explicatives ou encore de dépendance des variables expliquées dans la durée.

Bibliographie

Abbing M (2011), Loan officers of Pro Mujer México, An explorative case study on field workers' issues in a non-profit microfinance institution in Mexico, Master Thesis of Science International Development Studies, Wageningen University.

Ahmad B, Shahid M, Zill-E-Huma et al (2012), Turnover Intention : An HRM Issue in Textile Sector, Interdisciplinary Journal of contemporary Research in Business, 3 (12) : 125-130.

Alexandrov A , Babakus E et Yavas U(2007), The Effects of Perceived Management Concern for Frontline Employees and Customers on Turnover Intentions Moderating Role of Employment Status, Journal of Service Research, 9 (4) : 356-371.

Alniacik, Cigerim, Akcin et al (2011) , Independent and joint effects of perceived corporate reputation, affective commitment and job satisfaction on turnover intentions, Procedia Social and Behavioral Sciences, 24 (2011) : 1177-1189.

Arndt A, Arnold T et Landry T (2006), The effects of polychronic-orientation upon retailemployee satisfaction and turnover, Journal of Retailing, 82 (4) : 319-330.

Athanassopoulos A, Gounaris S and Stathakopoulos V (2001), Behavioural responses to customer satisfaction: an empirical study. European Journal of Marketing, 35 (5/6) : 687-707.

Aubert C, Janvry A et Sadoulet E (2009), Designing credit agent incentives to prevent mission drift in pro-poor microfinance institutions, Journal of Development Economics, 90 (2009): 153–162.

Aziri B (2011), Satisfaction: a literature review, Management Research and Practice, 3 (4): 77-86.

Bajpai N et Srivastava D (2011), Sectorial Comparison of Factors Influencing Job Satisfaction in Indian Banking Sector, Singapore Management Review, 26 (2): 89-99.

Balogun A and Olowodunoye S (2012), Psychological factors as predictors of turnover intention among employees of post-consolidation banks in Nigeria, European Scientific Journal, 8 (20) : 81-95.

Bashir M, Ghazanfar F and Mahroof Khan M (2011), Role of Demographic Factors in the Relationship between High Performance Work System and Job Satisfaction: A Multidimensional

Approach, International Journal of Business and Social Science, 2 (18): 207-218.

Beck T, Behr P et Madestam A (2011), Sex and Credit: Is There a Gender Bias in Microfinance?, p. 1-35.

Bedeian A, Ferris G et Kacmar M (1992), Age, Tenure, and Job Satisfaction: A Tale of Two Perspectives, Journal of Vocational Behavior, 40 (1992) : 33-48.

Bender K and Heywood J (2006), Job satisfaction of the highly educated: the role of gender, academic tenure, and earnings, Scottish Journal of Political Economy, 53 (2) : 253-279.

Bettencourt L et Brown S (1997), Contact Employees: Relationships Among Workplace Fairness, Job Satisfaction and Pro social Service Behaviors, Journal of Retailing, 73 (l): 39-61.

Canales R (2010), Rule bending, sociological citizenship andorganizational contestation in microfinance, Regulation & Governance (2010) doi:10.1111/j.1748-5991.2010.01095.x, 1-28.

Canales R (nd), The Stranger as Friend: Loan Officers and Positive Deviance in Microfinance.

Chan Yin-Fah B , Yeoh Sok Foon, Lim Chee-Leong et al (2010), An Exploratory Study on Turnover Intention among private Sector Employees, International Journal of Business and Management, 5 (8) : 57-64.

Cheng-Ping Chang et Wei-Chen Chang (2008), Internal Marketing Practices and Employees' Turnover Intentions in Tourism and Leisure Hotels, *The Journal of Human Resource and Adult Learning*, 4 (2) *:* 161-172.

Clark A, Oswald A et Warr P (1996), Is job satisfaction U-shaped in age? Journal of Occupational and Organtzational Psychology, V (9G) : 57-81.

Cossette M et Gosselin A (2012), Quitter, rester ou progresser ? Les profils d'intentions des agents en centre d'appels, Relations industrielles / Industrial relations, 67 (4) : 703-725.

Currivan D (1999), The causal order of job satisfaction and organizational commitment in models of employee turnover, Human Resource Management Review, 9 (4) : 495-524.

Drexler A et Schoar A (nd), Do relationships matter? Evidence from loan officer turnover, Dixon R, Ritchie J et Siwale J (2007), Loan officers and loan 'delinquency' in microfinance : a Zambian case. Accounting forum, 31 (1) : 47-71.

George J et Jones G (1996), The Experience of Work and Turnover Intentions: Interactive Effects of Value Attainment, Job Satisfaction, and Positive Mood, Journal of Applied Psychology, 81(3) : 318-325.

Gibson S (2000), The People Part Common Sense Advice in Motivating Microfinance Clients and Staff, Catholic Relief Services Microfinance.

Gil I , Berenguer G et Cervera A (2008), The roles of service encounters, service value, and job satisfaction in achieving customer satisfaction in business relationships, Industrial Marketing Management, 37 (2008) : 921-939.

Griffeth R, Hom P et Gaertner S (2000), A Meta-Analysis of Antecedents and Correlates of Employee Turnover : Update, Moderator Tests, and Research Implications for the Next Millennium, Journal of Management, 26 (3), p. 463-488.

Hanisch K et Hulin C (1991), General Attitudes and Organizational Withdrawal: An Evaluation of a Causal Model, Journal of Vocational Behavior, 39 (1991) : 110-128.

Harvey P , Harris K et Martinko M (2008) , The Mediated Influence of Hostile Attributional Style on Turnover Intentions, J Bus Psychol, 22 (2008): 333-343.

Hellman C (1997), Job Satisfaction and Intent to Leave, The Journal of Social Psychology, 137 (6) : 677-689.

Herzberg F, Mausser B et Snyderman (1959), The motivation to work, Transaction Publishers: New Brunswick(U.S.A.) and London(U.K.).

Hoppock R (1935), Job satisfaction, New York : Harper and Brothers.

Huey-Ming Tzeng (2002), The influence of nurses' working motivation and job satisfaction on intention to quit: an empirical investigation in Taiwan, International Journal of Nursing Studies, 39 (2002): 867-878.

Irshad Z et Khalid S (2010), Job Satisfaction Among Bank Employees in Punjab, Pakistan: A Comparative Study, European Journal of Social Sciences, 17(4) : 570-577.

Jang J et George R (2012), Understanding the influence of polychronicity on job satisfaction and turnover intention: A study of non-supervisory hotel employees, International Journal of Hospitality Management, 31 (2012): 588-595.

Jaramillo F, Grisaffe D , Chonko L et al (2009), Examining the impact of servant leadership on salesperson's turnover intention,Journal of Personal Selling & Sales Management, XXIX (4) : 351-365.

Jaworski B et Kohli A (1993), Market Orientation: antecedents and consequences, Journal of Marketing, 57 (1993) : 53-70.

Kabungaidze T, Mahlatshana N et Ngirande H (2013), The Impact of Job Satisfaction and Some Demographic Variables on Employee Turnover Intentions, International Journal of Business Administration, 4 (1): 53-65.

Kamal R et Sengupta D (2008), A Study of Job Satisfaction of Bank Officers, Prajnan, XXXVII (3): 230-240.

Kankaanranta T, Nummi T, Vainiom J et al (2007), The role of job satisfaction, job dissatisfaction and demographic factors on physicians' intentions to switch work sector from public to private, Health Policy, 83 (2007) : 50-64.

Kanwar, Singh et Kodwani (2012), A Study of Job Satisfaction, Organizational Commitment and Turnover Intent among the IT and ITES Sector Employees, Vision, 16(1) : 27-35.

Karatepe O, Uludag O (2007), Conflict, exhaustion, and motivation: A study of frontline employees in Northern Cyprus hotels, Hospitality Management, 26 (2007) : 645-665.

Karatepe O, Uludag O, Menevis I et al (2006), The effects of selected individual characteristics on frontline employee performance and job satisfaction, Tourism Management, 27 (2006) : 547-560.

Kautonen T, Hytti U, Bogenhold D et al (2012), Job satisfaction and retirement age intentions in Finland Self-employed versus salary earners, International Journal of Manpower, 33 (4) : 424-440/

Khiljia S et Xiaoyun Wang (2007), New evidence in an old debate: Investigating the relationship between HR satisfaction and turnover, International Business Review, 16 (2007): 377-395.

Koch J et Steers R (1978), Job Attachment, Satisfaction, and Turnover among Public Sector Employees, Journal of Vocational Behavior, 12(1978) : 119-128.

Koch J et Rhodes S (1981), Predictors of Turnover of Female Factory Workers, Journal of Vocational Behavior, 18 (1981) : 145-161.

Koh W and Keow Yer L (2002), The impact of the employee organization relationship on temporary employees' performance and attitude: testing aSingaporean sample, International Journal of Human Resource Management, 11 (2) : 366-387.

Labie M, Méon P-G et Szafarz A (2009), Discrimination in Microfinance : The Role of Credit Officers, CEB Working Paper N° 09/017, Université Libre de Bruxelles - Solvay Brussels School of Economics and Management.

Lambert E, Hogan L , Barton S (2001), The impact of job satisfaction on turnover intent: a test of a structural measurement model using a national sample of workers, The Social Science Journal, 38 (2001) : 233-250.

Leisanyane K et Khaola P (2013), The influence of organizational culture and job satisfaction on intentions to leave: the case of clay brick manufacturing company in Lesotho, EASSRR, XXIX (1) : 60-75.

Lew Tek Yew (2007), Job satisfaction and affective commitment : a study of employees in the tourism industry in Sarawak, Malaysia, Sunway Academic Journal , (4) : 27-43.

Lumley E, Coetzee M, Tladinyane R et al (2011), Exploring the job satisfaction and organizational commitment of employees in the information technology environment, Southern African Business Review, 15 (1) : 100-118.

Lyons H et O'Brien K (2006), The Role of Person-Environment Fit in the Job Satisfaction and Tenure Intentions of African American Employees, Journal of Counseling Psychology , 53 (4) : 387-396.

Maghrabi A et Johnson D (1995), An Arabic version of the Revised Job Descriptive Index, Current Psychology: development, learning, personality and Social, 14(1): 47-53.

Malhotra N , Mavondo F , Mukherjee A et al (2012), Service

quality of frontline employees: A profile deviation analysis, Journal of Business Research, 66 (2013): 1338-1344.

Mansor N, Mohd Noor J et Nik Hassan N (2012), Job Satisfaction among the Bankers: An investigation on Islamic Financial Institution in Eastern Region of Malaysia, Asian Social Science, 8 (10): 186-197.

Matzler K et Renzl B (2006), The Relationship between Interpersonal Trust, Employee Satisfaction, and Employee Loyalty, Total Quality Management, 17(10): 1261-1271.

Matzler K et Renzl B (2007), Assessing asymmetric effects in the formation of employee satisfaction, Tourism Management, 28 (2007):1093-1103.

McKim A et Hughart M (2005), Staff Incentive Schemes in Practice: Findings from a Global Survey of Microfinance Institutions.

Mitchell T, Holtom B, Lee T et al (2001), Why people stay using job embeddedness to predict voluntary turnover, Academy of Management Journal , 44 (6) : 1102-1121.

Mohsina A, Lenglerb J et Kumar B (2013), Exploring the antecedents of intentions to leave the job : The case of luxury hotel staff, International Journal of Hospitality Management, 35 (2013) : 48-58.

Moutte J (2010), L'influence de la satisfaction au travail du personnel en contact sur la satisfaction du client dans les services, W.P. n° 872, Communication publiée dans les actes de la 9th International Marketing Trends Conference, Venice, January 21th-23rd 2010.

Muchinsky P et Tuttle M (1979), Employee Turnover: An Empirical and Methodological Assessment, Journal of Vocational Behavior, 14 (1979): 43-77.

Natarajan C and Nagar D (2011), Effects of Service Tenure and Nature of Occupation on Organizational Commitment and Job Satisfaction, Journal of Management Research, 11 (1) : 59-64.

Newaz M, Ali T et Akhter I (2007), Employee perception regarding turnoverdecision in context of bangladesh bankingsector, BRAC University Journal, IV (2) : 67-74.

Norris D et Niebuhr R (1984), Organization Tenure as a Moderator of the Job Satisfaction-Job Performance Relationship, Journal of Vocational Behavior, 24(1984) : 169-178.

Parasuraman S (1982), Predicting Turnover Intentions and Turnover Behavior: A Multivariate Analysis, Journal of Vocational Behavior, 21(1982): 111-121.

Raddaha A , Alasad J, Albikawi Z et al (2012), Jordanian nurses' job satisfaction and intention to quit, Leadership in Health Services, 25 (3) : 216-231.

Rania S, Kamalanabhanb et Selvarania (2011), Work / life balance reflections on employee satisfaction, Serbian Journal of Management, 6 (1) : 85-96.

Rose J et Hulin C (1985), Adaptation to Work : An Analysis of Employee Health, Withdrawal, and Change, Organizational Behavior and Human Decision Processes, 36 (1985) : 324-341.

Rouleau D , Fournier P, Philibert A et al (2012), The effects of midwives' job satisfaction on burnout, intention to quit and turnover : a longitudinal study in Senegal, Human Resources for Health, 10 (9) : 2-14.

Ryan T et Sagas M (2009), Relationships between pay satisfaction, work-family conflict, and coaching turnover intention, Team Performance Management, 15 (3/4): 128-140.

Saba I (2011), Measuring the Job Satisfaction Level of the Academic Staff in Bahawalpur Colleges, International Journal of Academic Research in Business and Social Sciences, 1(1): 1-8

Sagamba et Shchetinin (2013), Do Microloan Officers Want to Lend to the Less Advantaged? Evidence from a Choice Experiment, World Development, 42 (2013) : 182-198.

Sarwar S , Mirza E , Ehsan N et al (2013) , Determining the impact of age and LOS on job satisfaction: a case study of Pakistan automotive industry, The International Journal of Human Resource Management, 24 (2) : 415-435.

Servin R, Lensink R et Van den Berg M (2011), The Impact of Loan Officers on Relationship Lending in Microfinance: Empirical evidence from PROMUJER-Mexico.

Seston E , Hassell, K , Ferguson J *et al* (2009) , Exploring the relationship between pharmacists' job satisfaction, intention to quit the profession, and actual quitting, *Research in Social and Administrative Pharmacy*, 5 (2009) : 121-132.

Shankar Man Shrestha (nd), Role of Field Officer and Robust HR Policy, Rural Microfinance Development Centre Ltd, Kathmandu, Nepal.

Singh P et Loncar N (2010), Pay Satisfaction, Job Satisfaction and Turnover Intent, *relations industrielles / industrial relations*, 65 (3) : 470-490.

Sousa-Poza A, Andres A. Sousa-Poza (2007), The effect of job satisfaction on labor turnover by gender: An analysis for Switzerland, *The Journal of Socio-Economics*, 36 (2007) : 895-913.

Sowmya K et Panchanatham N (2011), Factors influencing job satisfaction of banking sector employees in Chennai, India, *Journal of Law and Conflict Resolution* , 3 (5): 76-79.

Spagnoli P , Caetano A et Santos S (2012), Satisfaction with job aspects: Do patterns change over time? *Journal of Business Research, Journal of Business Research*, 65 (2012): 609-616.

Spector P (1997), Job satisfaction: application , Assessment , causes and consequences, Advanced Topics in Organizational Behavior , Sage Publications, International Educational and Professional Publisher, California, USA.

Uchida H, Udell G et Yamori N (2012), Loan officers and relationship lending to SMEs, *J. Finan. Intermediation*, 21 (2012): 97-122.

Tsui A, Pearce J et Porter L *et al* (1997), Alternative approaches to the employee-organization relationship: does investment in employees pay off ? *Academy of Management Jaurnal*, 40 (5) : 1089-1121.

Valentine S, Godkin L, Fleischman G *et al* (2011), Corporate Ethical Values, Group Creativity, Job Satisfaction and Turnover Intention: The Impact of Work Context on Work Response, *Journal of Business Ethics* , (98) : 353-372.

Valle M, Harris K and Andrews M (2004), An Examination of Tenure in Negative Organizational Environments, *Journal of Management Research*, 4 (2) : 113-119.

Vidal M, Valle S, Aragón B (2007), Antecedents of repatriates' job satisfaction and its influence on turnover intentions: Evidence from Spanish repatriated managers, *Journal of Business Research* , 60 (2007) : 1272-1281.

Vroom V (1995), Work and Motivation, Jossey-Bass Publishers: San Francisco (U.S.A.).

Wallace E, Chernatony L et Buil I (2013), Building bank brands: How leadership behavior influences employee commitment, *Journal of Business Research*, 66 (2013): 165-171.

Wang G, Yu-Je Lee et Chuan-Chih Ho (2012), The Effects of Job Satisfaction, Organizational Commitment and Turnover intention on Organizational operating performance: as Exemplified with Employees of Listed Property Insurance Companies in Taiwan, *Research in Business and Management*, 1(2): 41-53.

Wayne SJ, Shore LM, Liden RC (1997), Perceived organizational support and leader–member exchange: a social exchange perspective, *Academy Management Journal* , 40 (1) : 82-111.

Wei (Amy) Tian-Foreman (2009), Job satisfaction and turnover in the Chinese retail industry, *Chinese Management Studies*, 3 (4) : 356-378.

Yang J (2010), Antecedents and consequences of job satisfaction in the hotel industry, *International Journal of Hospitality Management*, 29 (2010): 609-619.

Yıldız Z, Ayhan S et , Erdoğmuş S (2009), The impact of nurses' motivation to work, job satisfaction, and sociodemographic characteristics on intention to quit their current job: An empirical study in Turkey, *Applied Nursing Research* , 22 (2009) : 113-118.

Yucel I et Bektas C (2012), Job satisfaction, organizational commitment and demographic characteristics among teachers in Turkey : Younger is better? *Procedia - Social and Behavioral Sciences*, 46 (2012) : 1598-1608.

Déterminants des inégalités de revenu à Burhale au Sud-Kivu

Batano Kusimwa Godelive, Bucekuderhwa Bashige Célestin & Jean Baptiste Ntagoma Kushinganine

RÉSUMÉ/ABSTRACT

Objectif : Déterminer le niveau de pauvreté et d'inégalité de revenu dans un milieu rural du Sud Kivu, ainsi que les déterminants des inégalités.

Méthodologie : La méthodologie s'inscrit dans les modèles de ménages de non séparabilité des décisions de production et de consommation. Dans un premier temps, la variable endogène est le niveau de vie du ménage déterminée par les variables exogènes telles que les dotations en capital physique et humain ; les caractéristiques du ménage et celles du chef. Dans un deuxième temps, pour lier inégalités et risque, la variable endogène devient l'utilité, le revenu par tête devient ainsi exogène de même que l'attitude face au risque et le niveau d'inégalité. Le traitement des données a été rendu possible en recourant respectivement au MCO et au logit multinomial ordonnée.

Résultats : Les résultats montrent que 82% des ménages sont en situation de pauvreté et vivent avec moins de 1 800 CDF par jour et par équivalent adulte, aussi les ménages dirigés par les femmes sont plus pauvres que ceux dirigés par les hommes. En décomposant l'inégalité totale par source, la contribution la plus élevée provient du commerce et des activités minières soit 56%, en deuxième position les métiers contribuent à 15% à l'inégalité totale. La hausse des revenus issus du commerce et des activités minières augmente les inégalités tandis qu'une telle hausse du revenu agricole, du salariat, des métiers ou des transferts diminue les inégalités.

Limite et perspective : Une limite de ce travail est l'utilisation des données en coupe instantanée, plusieurs variables d'intérêt seraient plus pertinentes avec les données de panel. Une deuxième limite est d'avoir négligé les inégalités au sein du ménage. En effet, Sen (1984) cité par Peluso et Tranoy (2005) souligne que les discriminations (par exemple en défaveur des femmes) pourraient conduire aux inégalités intra-ménages, notre étude n'a pas circonscrit cet aspect.

Mots-clés : pauvreté, inégalité, revenu, dépenses par équivalent adulte, Burhale.

JEL classifications: Q01, Q12, Q16, Q18.

1. Introduction

Le monde actuel se caractérise par un contraste frappant dans la répartition des ressources : 20% de la population mondiale s'arrogent plus de 80% des richesses (Ortiz et Cummins, 2012). Cette répartition laisse une majeure partie de la population dans des situations d'extrême privation. Une telle révélation a milité pour la définition, du premier objectif du millénaire : la réduction, d'ici 2015, de l'extrême pauvreté avec une diminution de moitié de la proportion des individus vivant avec moins d'un dollar par jour et souffrant de la faim. Entre 1990 et 2008, des avancées significatives ont été observées. La proportion d'individus vivant avec moins de 1,25$ par jour est passée de 43,1% à 22,2% (Banque Mondiale, 2012). Ainsi, plusieurs régions du monde ont vu l'extrême pauvreté reculer significativement.

Néanmoins, cela n'est pas le cas pour l'Afrique subsaharienne où la part de la population concernée par l'extrême pauvreté n'a régressé que faiblement, passant de 56,5% en 1990 à 47,5% en 2008. A la base de cette défaillance se trouve la croissance démographique (Banque mondiale, 2012) mais surtout **les inégalités** (Guénard et Dubois, 2001 ; Cogneau *et al*, 2006 et BAD, 2012). En RDC, les études sur la pauvreté mettent en exergue la mauvaise situation du pays. L'analyse de Moummi (2010) aboutit aux résultats selon lesquels le taux de pauvreté avoisine 70% au niveau national, il est de 72% en milieu rural contre 59% en milieu urbain. Kodila (2010) situe le taux de pauvreté à 80% ; il insiste sur le fait qu'en RDC, les questions d'inégalités sont étroitement liées à celles de pauvreté. L'indice de Gini est de 42%, les provinces des deux Kasaï et celle du Katanga accusent de fortes inégalités alors qu'au Bas-Congo et au Sud-Kivu les inégalités sont relativement faibles. Aussi, les individus sont exposés aux risques[1] et cela les fragilisent encore plus.

La littérature sur les inégalités est vaste. Une optique traitée est celle des relations entre inégalités, pauvreté et croissance économique (Mourji *et al*, 2006). Partant des travaux pionniers de Kuznets (1955), les tendances actuelles divergent fortement. L'effet de la croissance sur la pauvreté et les inégalités est loin d'être univoque, les idées se retrouvent chez Dollar et Kraay (2002), Sala-i-Martin (2002), Bourguignon (2002) et Atkinson et Brandolini (2004). L'inégalité sous la lumière de la justice est l'apanage des travaux de Rawls (1987). Pour cet auteur, la justice s'identifie à la répartition équitable des ressources. Dans le même ordre d'idée, l'approche des capacités développée par Sen (1999) propose d'aller au-delà des moyens d'accomplir les actions, pour centrer la réflexion sur les libertés de choix ainsi que les opportunités offertes à l'individu.

1. Les risques majeurs en RDC sont politiques, économiques, sanitaires etc. (cf. Harley *et al* (2003).

Selon Diamond *et al* (1990), l'analyse de la distribution des revenus poursuit deux buts : le premier est la description à l'aide des indices et le second est la recherche des déterminants de cette distribution. Les indices d'inégalité (Gini, Theil, Atkinson, ...) sont des mesures synthétiques qui offrent l'information sur l'ensemble de la distribution du revenu. Ils considèrent que la population est réduite à un agent représentatif. Ceci n'est pas toujours le cas. La décomposition de ces mesures, par sous-populations ou par sources de revenu, offre plus d'information. Ainsi, les déterminants des inégalités sont recherchés dans les caractéristiques des ménages telles que l'éducation, la santé, l'accès aux ressources etc. Plusieurs études se sont intéressées aux déterminants des inégalités en Afrique, il s'agit entre autres de Lachaud (2003) et Montaud (2002) pour le Burkina Faso, de Babatunde (2008) pour le Nigeria, de House (1991) pour le Soudan, etc. Les éléments significatifs sont la démographie du ménage, l'instruction du chef de ménage ainsi que son statut sur le marché de l'emploi (Lachaud, 2003). Les transferts de revenu diminuent les inégalités pour Babatunde (2008) et les augmentent pour Montaud (2002).

L'angle de vue pertinent est celui de la relation entre *inégalité et attitude face au risque*. L'article pionnier dans ce domaine est celui de Friedman (1953) qui va au-delà de la répartition fonctionnelle classique pour s'intéresser à la répartition personnelle[1]. Selon cet auteur, les alternatives offertes aux individus diffèrent les unes des autres par les probabilités des distributions de revenu qu'elles promettent. Le choix entre diverses alternatives dépend du goût du risque de l'individu. Il sera différent suivant que l'agent aime ou est hostile au risque. Ainsi, dans une société hostile au risque, les inégalités tendent à être plus faibles que dans celle aimant le risque. Atkinson (1970) établit un parallèle entre la comparaison des distributions de revenus et la théorie de la décision en incertitude dans le classement des distributions de revenu. L'aversion au risque de l'individu joue un rôle central. Pour Hoogeveen *et al* (2005), l'étude de la pauvreté et de la distribution de revenu en Afrique doit nécessairement prendre en compte les risques auxquels les individus sont exposés.

De ce qui précède, il ressort qu'il existe un lien entre répartition des revenus et attitude face au risque. Mais, à notre connaissance, aucune étude n'a tenté de le vérifier dans la province du Sud-Kivu, moins encore en RDC. Cette étude veut pallier à cette lacune et se veut innovante. Nous nous intéressons à la répartition des revenus à Burhale,

1. La répartition des revenus peut s'entendre de deux manières : la *répartition fonctionnelle* (qui s'applique, au sens de Ricardo, à la répartition entre les propriétaires des principaux facteurs de production ou encore qui s'applique à l'analyse des salaires, des profits et des rentes) et la *répartition personnelle* qui désigne la répartition des revenus entre des personnes suivant la place qu'elles occupent dans l'échelle des revenus.

territoire de Walungu, au Sud-Kivu, en RDC.

L'objectif de l'étude est de ressortir les principales sources de revenus, les déterminants des inégalités observées dans ledit milieu ainsi que le lien entre niveau de revenu et attitude des chefs de ménage face au risque. Une observation exploratoire du milieu permet d'avancer l'hypothèse selon laquelle les éléments comme le capital physique, humain et financier sont autant d'éléments qui placent les individus à divers échelons ou niveaux de bien-être. Une telle approche est similaire à celle de Lachaud (2003), House (1991) et Diamond *et al* (1990). Deux aspects seraient significatifs : le capital humain et le capital physique (à travers la « *possession des terres cultivables* » étant donné que le milieu est essentiellement rural et tourné vers les activités agro-pastorales). Et à la suite de Friedman (1953), l'amour du risque entraine des niveaux de revenu élevé.

L'intérêt porté à ce sujet est double. D'un côté, l'acception générale admet que des disparités excessives entre riches et pauvres vont à l'encontre d'une certaine perception de justice sociale. Elles peuvent être un frein à une croissance économique durable et à une réduction efficace de la pauvreté (Bourguignon, 2004 ; Mestre *et al*, 2009, Dubois *et al*, 2002). Ainsi, une attention particulière à l'ampleur des inégalités peut permettre d'identifier les causes profondes de la pauvreté et agir en conséquence (Mestre *et al*, 2009). D'un autre côté, l'attitude des agents face au risque détermine leur dynamisme économique. Ce dernier permet la création de la valeur et l'amélioration du bien-être.

Au vu du problème des disponibilités des données de panel, la présente étude est statique. L'unité d'analyse est le ménage rural. La méthodologie s'inscrit dans les modèles de ménages de non séparabilité des décisions de production et de consommation. Dans un premier temps, sur les pas de Naschold (2009) et Lachaud (2000b), la variable endogène est le niveau de vie du ménage déterminé par les variables exogènes telles que les dotations en capital physique et humain, les caractéristiques du ménage et celles du chef. Dans un deuxième temps, pour lier inégalités et risque, la variable endogène devient l'utilité, le revenu par tête devient ainsi exogène de même que l'attitude face au risque et le niveau d'inégalité. Une telle procédure est proche de celle utilisée par Ferrer-i-Carbonell et Ramos (2010).

Hormis cette introduction, la deuxième section présente les concepts d'inégalité, la troisième décrit la méthodologie du travail, la quatrième expose les résultats empiriques et la cinquième rapporte les conclusions et les implications de l'étude.

2. Cadre conceptuel

L'inégalité peut être entendue comme la différence de positionnement de chaque personne par rapport aux différentes dimensions de la pauvreté. Elle ne peut donc se réduire aux seules formes monétaires du revenu, de consommation ou de capital selon Mestre *et al* (2009). D'après Picketty (2002), « l'inégalité mesure une différence relative de situation entre individus au regard, soit de la dotation d'un facteur (le capital physique, le capital humain), soit du revenu, soit de l'accès à certaines prestations (qu'elles soient allouées par le marché ou par le secteur public) ».

Les inégalités peuvent revêtir diverses formes (Mestre *et al*, 2009). Les premières sont les inégalités spatiales (entre pays, entre milieu rural et urbain, etc). Une deuxième classification distingue les inégalités monétaires et non monétaires. Ces dernières sont celles des conditions de vie, d'accès aux ressources productrices, les inégalités des chances et de genre, etc. Francis Stewart distingue les inégalités horizontales de celles verticales (Stewart *et al*, 2005). Les inégalités horizontales s'intéressent à la répartition des ressources entre groupes donnés tandis que les inégalités verticales traitent de la répartition des ressources entre individus. Ainsi, les inégalités reposent sur des déterminants sociaux, économiques, politiques, culturels et peuvent être liées à l'histoire ou aux trajectoires individuelles.

L'inégalité s'appréhende selon deux approches : l'approche normative et l'approche descriptive. L'approche normative (fonction de bien-être social) s'intéresse à la manière dont les revenus devraient être distribués dans la population tandis que l'approche descriptive (mesure des inégalités) étudie la manière dont les revenus sont effectivement distribués dans la population. Plusieurs mesures peuvent être utilisées pour mesurer le degré d'inégalité d'une série statistique. Il s'agit notamment de l'écart type, du coefficient de Gini et de la courbe de Lorenz, de l'indice de Theil, de l'indice d'Atkinson. Le coefficient de Gini, dérivé de la courbe de Lorenz est la mesure de l'inégalité la plus couramment utilisée. Il varie entre 0 et 1 ; 0 traduit une égalité complète et 1 indique une inégalité totale.

Plusieurs études se sont intéressées à l'analyse des inégalités. Lachaud (2000a), en s'appuyant sur 2 enquêtes nationales auprès des ménages mauritaniens, examine les facteurs micro économiques de la réduction de la pauvreté et des inégalités. La décomposition de l'indice de Gini s'effectue par milieu rural et urbain. Pour la décomposition des écarts de bien-être, la variable dépendante retenue est le logarithme du ratio de bien-être (le ratio de bien-être est le rapport entre la consommation nominale par tête et le seuil de pauvreté), tandis que les variables indépendantes incluent le niveau d'instruction du chef de ménage, la démographie du ménage, la proportion des personnes employées dans le ménage, ainsi que le statut du chef de ménage sur le marché de l'emploi. A l'aide d'estimations économétriques, l'étude montre que la consommation par tête des ménages ruraux et urbains est influencée par l'instruction du chef de ménage, l'accès à l'emploi, la localisation spatiale et la démographie des groupes.

De même, Babatunde (2008) s'intéresse aux inégalités en milieu rural. Elle utilise les données des enquêtes ménages sur les revenus et les dépenses menées dans une région du nord du Nigeria en 2006. L'usage de la décomposition du coefficient de Gini permet de ressortir les contributions marginales des différentes sources de revenus dans l'inégalité totale. Les résultats montrent que le coefficient de Gini est de 0,4 et le revenu agricole diminue les inégalités tandis que les revenus non agricoles augmentent les inégalités. Dans le même ordre d'idée, Lawson *et al.* (2006), en adoptant une approche non monétaire de la pauvreté, aboutit à la construction d'un indicateur composite de niveau de vie et un indice composite de la pauvreté. Aussi, la décomposition de l'inégalité s'effectue par milieu de résidence (rural ou urbain). L'étude montre que la pauvreté non monétaire est une réalité au Togo : la proportion est de 74% en 1988 et de 59,8% en 1998.

Parmi les composantes du bien-être, l'habitat et la communication possèdent les plus fortes contributions. Les composantes à faible contribution sont l'éducation, l'accès à l'eau et les moyens de transport. House (1991) en explorant la nature et les déterminants des inégalités socio-économiques entre les ménages du Sud-Soudan part d'une analyse des modèles de ménage et s'intéresse au revenu par équivalent adulte comme mesure de bien-être. Elle aboutit au résultat selon lequel les ménages qui sont capables de diversifier leurs principales sources de revenu, dans des activités génératrices de revenus non agricoles, et dans le secteur formel d'emploi salarié, sont susceptibles d'atteindre des niveaux de vie élevés. Naschold (2009) analyse les déterminants microéconomiques des inégalités de revenus au Pakistan rural en se fondant sur une décomposition des inégalités basée sur la régression telle que proposée par Fields (2003). La variable dépendante est le logarithme du revenu par équivalent adulte. Les variables explicatives se regroupent en quatre catégories : la démographie du ménage, l'éducation, les actifs physiques et la localisation du ménage. L'étude aboutit au résultat selon lequel la possession des champs explique significativement le niveau des inégalités. L'étude de Binswanger (1980) s'intéresse à la mesure des attitudes envers le risque à travers des expériences de loteries et d'équivalent certain. Les résultats indiquent qu'à des niveaux de rentabilité faible, l'attitude face au risque est pratiquement distribuée entre le niveau intermédiaire et la neutralité.

L'étude de Chang (2012) évalue les disparités de consommation qui existent entre les ménages agricoles et non agricoles. En utilisant des données d'une enquête auprès des ménages représentatifs au niveau national de Taiwan, Chang (2012) applique une méthode basée sur la régression quantile inconditionnelle de décomposition pour désagréger les différences dans la répartition des dépenses des ménages entre les ménages agricoles et non agricoles. Les résultats indiquent que les différences dans les caractéristiques observées entre ces deux types de ménages expliquent en grande partie l'inégalité de consommation. En outre, la différence dans le niveau d'éducation de l'exploitant agricole, les revenus des ménages et le degré d'urbanisation sont particulièrement importants.

3. Méthodologie

3.1. Données

Les données sont issues d'une enquête réalisée en mai 2013. La pré-enquête s'est déroulée du 1er au 5 mai 2013 à l'aide des interviews, des focus groups et des entretiens de profondeur. Nous avons recouru à une stratification au second degré. Au premier degré, les villages ont été sélectionnés et au second degré les ménages. La population étant de 44 232, répartie en 48 localités durant l'année 2013, avec une taille de ménage moyenne de 7 personnes, le nombre des ménages a été estimé à 6319.

L'échantillon de 300 ménages a été subdivisé en 10 strates (les strates sont les divers villages tirés aléatoirement) grâce à l'allocation proportionnelle[1]. La répartition par village est donnée dans le tableau ci-dessous :

L'enquête s'est déroulée du 13 au 29 mai 2013. Elle s'effectuait par entretien personnel avec le chef de ménage ou son conjoint. Afin de s'assurer d'un tirage aléatoire et au vu de la non disponibilité des listes des ménages constitutifs des villages, nous avons opté pour un tirage probabiliste plus pratique. Les enquêteurs, au nombre de 4, prenaient un point cardinal chacun à partir de la résidence du chef de ménage, il fallait ainsi effectuer un pas de 3 maisons après chaque enquête.

L'administration du questionnaire s'effectuait avec le chef de ménage ou son conjoint au lieu d'habitation. Les questions portaient sur l'identification de l'interviewé, les caractéristiques sociodémographiques des membres du ménage, l'accès à l'éducation et à la santé, les actifs possédés par le ménage, l'agriculture et l'élevage, les risques majeurs auxquels a été exposé le ménage.

Pour traiter les données recueillies, nous avons recouru à la statistique descriptive, ainsi qu'à la régression en utilisant les logiciels SPSS et STATA. Une épuration préalable a été nécessaire : il s'agissait d'harmoniser les échelles de mesures (par exemple pour l'estimation des quantités semées et récoltées) et d'identifier les erreurs de saisie des données avec le cas par exemple des données

1. Elle utilisait la proportion ou le poids de la population dudit village dans la population totale des villages sélectionnés.

aberrantes. Les données aberrantes étaient constituées des données manquantes et des données fortement éloignées de la moyenne. Ces types d'éléments étaient remplacés par la moyenne de la série dans le village concerné en suivant les recommandations de Neuman (2011), Tabachnick et Fidell (2012). De même, il fallait harmoniser les échelles monétaires. Les dépenses étant estimées en franc congolais pour certaines et en dollar pour d'autres, nous avons choisi la parité de 1$ = 1000 CDF pour les facilités de calcul. La couverture de l'échantillon était de 100%. La taille totale initiale de l'échantillon a été effectivement couverte, par contre la répartition par village s'est légèrement modifiée. Tous les villages ont été explorés à l'exception de NShimbi[1]. La population effectivement enquêtée se répartit par village selon la quatrième colonne du tableau (annexe 1).

3.2. Choix et définition des variables

3.2.1. Les variables dépendantes

Les variables à expliquer incluses dans le modèle ci-dessous ont été choisies à partir de la littérature sur les déterminants de l'inégalité de revenu et dans le même ordre d'idée que les éléments contenus dans le questionnaire. Ainsi, le niveau de bien-être est retenu comme variable en utilisant l'optique « dépenses » pour plusieurs raisons. D'une part, les flux des dépenses sont plus réguliers et plus facilement saisissables que ceux des revenus. Etant donné que l'étude s'effectue dans une zone rurale essentiellement tournée vers les activités agricoles, le revenu est très fluctuant au cours de l'année ; les dépenses sont supposées plus stables. D'autre part, certains ménages pauvres affirment avoir un revenu nul ; les dépenses de consommation permettent de les prendre en compte. Pour une variable pertinente, il sied de considérer l'existence d'économie d'échelle en matière de consommation et les disparités internes au ménage. Pour ce faire, nous appliquons l'échelle d'équivalence proposée par l'OCDE. L'adulte de référence (le chef de ménage) reçoit un poids équivalent à 1, les autres adultes un poids de 0,7 et les enfants (individus avec moins de 14 ans) 0,5. L'unité de référence, à savoir l'équivalent adulte, est ainsi obtenue. Les dépenses du ménage sont divisées par le nombre d'équivalent adulte pour obtenir les dépenses par équivalent adulte. C'est l'indicateur de bien-être utilisé dans notre étude. Cette approche a été utilisée aussi par Naschold (2009) et Babatunde (2008).

Nous avons aussi recouru à la variable utilité du ménage. Cette dernière est appréhendée de manière

1. Il nous a été impossible d'atteindre ce village non seulement par son éloignement mais surtout à cause de l'insécurité qui y régnait suite au système « Kabanga ». Etant le dernier village sur notre liste, et nous retrouvant avec 261 enquêtés, nous avons jugé bon de réallouer proportionnellement 39 enquêtés restants aux villages accessibles pour couvrir la taille totale de l'échantillon prévu initialement.

subjective sur une échelle directe allant de 0 (complètement insatisfait) à 10 (complètement satisfait). Le ménage devait se positionner selon qu'il était satisfait par la vie ou pas.

3.2.3. Les variables indépendantes

1. Variables ayant trait au chef de ménage

Les caractéristiques du chef de ménage ne peuvent être sans effet sur le ménage. Il est en effet la personne qui apporte plus en termes de revenu, mais aussi possède la clé de la décision d'allocation de plusieurs ressources du ménage. L'âge du chefs de ménage capture l'expérience du chef de ménage ainsi que le cycle de vie. La variable dichotomique du sexe du chef de ménage est de taille car en milieu rural, les rares femmes chef de ménage sont souvent des veuves et souffrent d'un manque d'accès à un revenu diversifié. Ainsi, l'activité exercée par le chef de ménage détermine le niveau de revenu du chef, son bien-être et celui de son ménage, les chefs ayant un travail salarié ou exerçant une activité minière sont supposés avoir des niveaux de vie élevés.

2. Variables ayant trait aux caractéristiques socio-économiques du ménage dans son ensemble

La théorie du capital humain renseigne sur l'importance des qualifications individuelles dans la détermination des rémunérations et par ricochet des revenus. Il en découle la rétention des variables éducation primaire, secondaire et supérieure par équivalent adulte. Les caractéristiques démographiques telles que la taille du ménage déterminent aussi dans quelle mesure le ménage supporte un poids quelconque afin de se nourrir ainsi que le nombre des personnes qui apportent une contribution au revenu. Le degré de promiscuité qui règne au sein du ménage serait aussi important dans la mesure du bien-être. Les ménages aux dépenses élevées rechercheraient plus un certain degré de confort dans l'habitat. Aussi, l'accès à l'emploi non agricole indique que le ménage possède des sources de revenus diversifiés et permet d'améliorer le bien-être selon House (1991). De même, les dotations constituent un aspect important du bien-être du ménage. La possession des actifs permet au ménage d'accéder à certaines facilités en termes de confort (radio, meubles, matelas, ...) et de facteur de production (hache, houe, machette, ...). Ainsi nous utilisons la variable index des actifs comme étant la sommation des actifs que possède le ménage à l'exemple de House (1991). Les actifs retenus sont au nombre de 21. La terre est le principal facteur de production des biens agricoles dans le milieu étudié. Elle permet l'accès à la nourriture mais aussi au revenu issu de la vente des récoltes. Les individus possédant des superficies des terres considérables sont perçus comme nantis.

3. Variables du risque

Le risque peut être perçu comme une menace ou comme une

opportunité. Comme menace, il développe la littérature sur la vulnérabilité des ménages. Le ménage rural est soumis à plusieurs aléas (naturels, sociaux, économiques...). Ces derniers affectent négativement son bien-être.

L'exposition au risque peut être vue comme une dimension de la pauvreté et possède un effet direct sur le bien-être (Hoogeveen *et al*, 2005, Bucekuderhwa *et al*, 2012). Les risques retenus étaient regroupés en trois catégories :

TABLEAU 1
Différents risques auxquels les ménages ruraux sont exposés

a. Risques naturels (agricoles)	b. Risques sociaux et politiques	C. Risques économiques
Inondation/Pluie abondante	Discrimination sociale	Chômage
Sécheresse	Attaque des groupes armés	Crise actuelle
Maladie des plantes	Soulèvement populaire	Tracasseries (multiplicité des taxes)
Maladie des animaux	Guerre	Faillite (pertes considérables en commerce)
Déforestation	Sorcellerie	Bas prix en vendant les produits agricoles /faible rentabilité
Glissement de terrain	Conflit foncier	
	Vol	

Si le ménage a été exposé à plus de la moitie des risques retenus, il est qualifié de vulnérable. La variable exposition au risque ou vulnérabilité a été ainsi élaborée. Le risque comme opportunité rejoint la littérature de l'attitude face au risque. Afin d'appréhender au niveau empirique l'attitude des individus face au risque, trois méthodes peuvent être utilisées. Il s'agit du jeu de loterie [voire Barsky *et al* (1997) cité par Arrondel et *al* (2004)), de la mesure directe de l'aversion au risque (Ferrer-i-Carbonell et Ramos (2010)) et de la méthode de score (Arrondel *et al* (2004). Chacune de ces approches possédant aussi bien des limites que des avantages, nous avons mesuré l'attitude face au risque selon les deux dernières approches. La première demande plus d'attention de la part de l'enquêté, cela occasionne des cas élevés de non réponse. Ainsi, nous avons défini deux variables. La première est le score global d'attitude face au risque.

A l'aide de diverses questions relatives au risque (module 7 du questionnaire), nous avons construit un indicateur synthétique de l'information recherchée. La formation de cet indicateur utilise une méthode de scoring. En s'inspirant de Arrondel *et al* (2004), les réponses des individus ont été codées sous forme trois modalités : +1 = risquophilie, 0= neutre ou non applicable, et -1= risquophobie. Le score est alors la somme des notes obtenues à différentes questions. La seconde variable est l'attitude subjective face au risque : le chef de ménage était amené à répondre à la question sur son attitude globale vis-à-vis du risque (au vu des divers domaines tels que l'agriculture, la consommation, le travail). La variable ainsi définie est le niveau subjectif d'attitude de l'individu face au risque. Elle varie de 0 (risquophobie) à 10 (risquophilie).

3.3. Décomposition des inégalités de revenu par source

L'approche par décomposition a été utilisée dans plusieurs travaux sur l'inégalité notamment celui de Zhu (2001) et de Babatunde (2008). Nous utilisons la méthode de décomposition du coefficient de GINI tel que développé par Lopez-Feldman (2006) inspirés de Shorrocks (1982) et Lerman et Yitzhaki (1985). Cette méthode permet d'élaborer un indice de GINI qui peut être décomposé selon les différentes sources de revenu. Soit y le revenu total provenant des k sources des revenus, $y = \Sigma_1^K yk$; le coefficient de Gini *Go* peut s'écrire de la manière suivante $Go = \Sigma^k_{k=1} S_k G_k R_k$, S_k est la part du revenu de la source *k* dans le revenu total *Y*, G_k est le coefficient de Gini du revenu yk et Rk est la corrélation de Gini entre yk et y et définie par

$$yk, F\,(y0)/cov\,(yk, F(yk))$$
$$Rk = cov$$

où *F(yo)* et *F(yk)* sont les fonctions cumulatives des revenus respectivement du total de revenu et du revenu de la source *k*. Si la composante de revenu *j* s'accroît partant d'un facteur *e*, (et ce pour tous les ménages) l'effet marginal de ce pourcentage sur l'inégalité total est

$$\frac{\partial G_0}{\partial e_j} = Sj(RjGj - G_0)$$

En divisant cette équation par G_0, nous obtenons

$$\frac{\frac{\partial G_0}{\partial e_j}}{G_0} = (SjRjGj)/G_0 - sj.$$

Le membre de droite de l'équation ci-dessus est l'élasticité de l'inégalité totale par rapport à la source de revenu j.

3.4. Modèles économétriques

Les auteurs qui nous ont inspirés dans la spécification de modèles sont Naschold (2009), Ferrer-i-Carbonell et Ramos (2010), Lachaud (2000b) et Diamond *et al.* (1990). Les modèles suivants seront utilisés :

Modèle 1 : Quels sont les déterminants des dépenses par équivalent adulte ? Les déterminants des dépenses par *EA* sont recherchés dans les caractéristiques du ménage, ceux du chef. La forme implicite du modèle est :

$$Y = \alpha_0 + \alpha_i X \text{ (1)}$$

Avec i allant de 1 à k (*k* est le nombre des variables explicatives), *Y* la variable expliquée (ici le logarithme des dépenses par *EA*) et *X* l'ensemble des variables explicatives.

Modèle 2 : l'Utilité du ménage dépend-t-elle des inégalités et du risque ? Le modèle **1** sera légèrement modifié. La variable endogène devient « *U* » et « *EP/EA* » se modifie pour s'ajouter aux variables exogènes. L'hypothèse est que l'utilité dépend du niveau des inégalités dans le village et de l'attitude de l'individu face au risque. Pour vérifier la relation entre les inégalités et l'attitude face au risque, nous utilisons la spécification en s'inspirant de Ferrer-i-Carbonell et Ramos (2010).

$$Uih = \alpha + \beta_1 Ih + \beta_2 Rih + \beta_3 Xih + \beta_4 yih \text{ (2)}$$

Avec : utilité du ménage, : indice d'inégalité dans le village : le score global de risque du ménage i situé dans le village : caractéristiques socio-économiques du chef ménage i situé dans le village h, : logarithme des dépenses par équivalent adulte ménage i situé dans le village h. Cette dernière devra subir un test d'homogénéité au vu du modèle 1 précédent.

Modèle 3 : Quelles sont les caractéristiques affectant la probabilité d'être dans un quintile donné ? Il serait intéressant de déterminer la probabilité qu'un ménage ayant des caractéristiques spécifiques puisse être localisé dans un certain quintile de distribution de niveau de bien-être. Pour ce faire, un modèle logistique ordonné sera utilisé en s'inspirant de Lachaud (2000b). Soit *Q* la variable de sélection qui identifie les quintiles de la distribution de la dépense par *EA* des ménages *Di. Q prend lesvaleurs 0,1, ..., j avec j = 4*. Le modèle déterminant est :

$$Prob[Qi = j] = exp(\propto_j' Xj) / \sum_{j=1}^{J} exp(\propto_j' Xj) \quad \textbf{(3)}$$

4. Résultats et discussions

4.1. Anatomie des dépenses des ménages

Les dépenses globales annuelles du ménage peuvent être scindées en deux sous-composantes : les dépenses alimentaires et non alimentaires. Les dépenses alimentaires regroupent les dépenses pour l'achat des aliments tels que la farine, les légumes, les fruits, le lait, le pain, l'huile, le haricot, le sucre, le poulet, la viande rouge, les œufs, les poissons, et autres mais aussi les frais de constitution du stock

GRAPHIQUE 1

DA annuelles moyennes par EA et par village

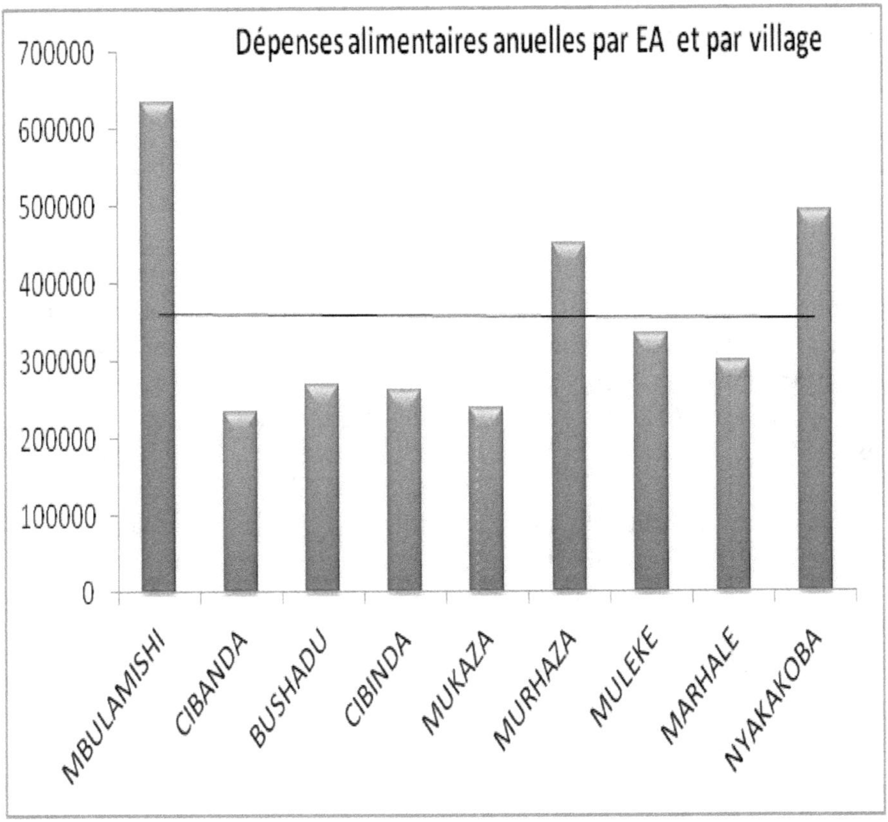

alimentaire. La moyenne de ces dépenses alimentaires s'élève à 361 473,65 CDF par an et par EA. Elles se répartissent par village suivant le graphique ci-dessous.

Les villages de Mbulamishi, de Murhaza et de Nyakakoba présentent des moyennes supérieures à celles des autres villages en termes de montant destiné aux dépenses alimentaires. Cela peut se justifier par les niveaux de vie de ces villages qui sont légèrement au-dessus des autres. Le graphique ci-dessous montre que la proportion des dépenses pour l'achat de la farine de manioc (et quelques fois de maïs) est la plus importante[1]. En deuxième lieu, viennent les dépenses pour les légumes. Ce graphique ne valorise pas les aliments auxquels les ménages ont accès par

1. Le manioc est l'aliment de base de la population de Burhale. Selon les participants aux focus groups, depuis les années 1998, le manioc est devenu rare dans la région. Cette raréfaction s'est prononcée avec la présence de la mosaïque de manioc qui fait des ravages considérables.

GRAPHIQUE 2

Poids des différents produits dans les dépenses alimentaires

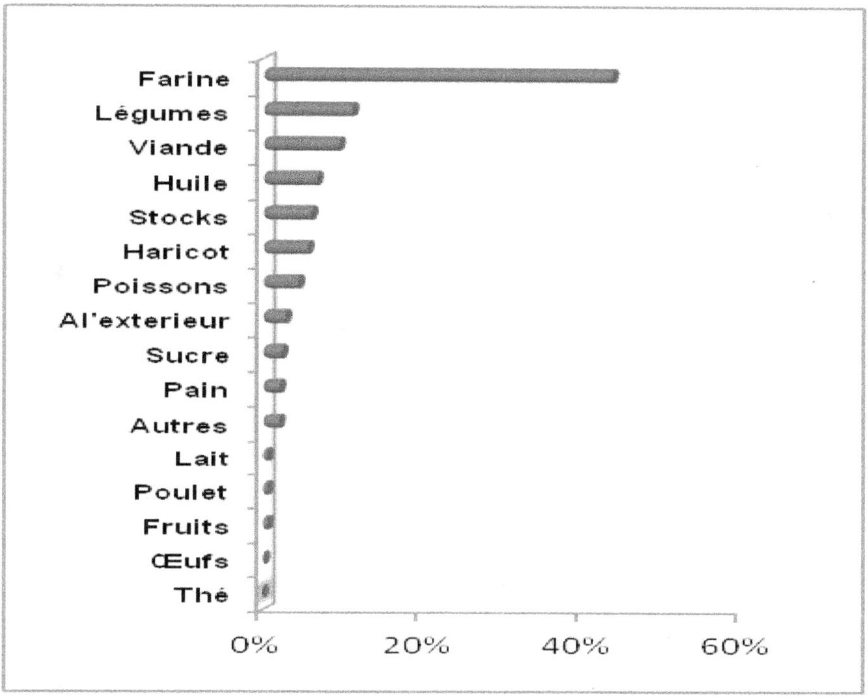

autoconsommation, il s'agit de la patate douce et de la banane. Ces deux aliments viennent après le manioc en ordre d'importance dans le régime alimentaire du milieu.

Les dépenses pour l'achat de la viande viennent en troisième lieu : les ménages consomment de la viande en moyenne une fois par mois. Le prix élevé de cette dernière rend l'accès difficile. Les ménages ne constituent pas de stocks alimentaires, sur 245 ménages, 46 soit 18% constituent des stocks alimentaires composés essentiellement de la farine de manioc pour un montant mensuel moyen de 12 444 CDF.

Les dépenses non alimentaires, quant à elles, sont constituées des dépenses mensuelles et annuelles. Les dépenses mensuelles portent sur l'accès à l'eau ; l'achat des piles et des torches, du charbon, des produits de beauté et des cigarettes ; les dépenses de communication, les frais de santé, le remboursement du crédit, l'aumône, les loisirs et les transports. Les dépenses annuelles portent sur les frais scolaires, l'habillement, les frais de construction et des voyages, les dons et transferts ; les dépenses liées à la naissance, à la circoncision, au mariage, au deuil et aux dommages ayant affecté la maison.

GRAPHIQUE 3

DNA annuelles moyennes par EA et par village

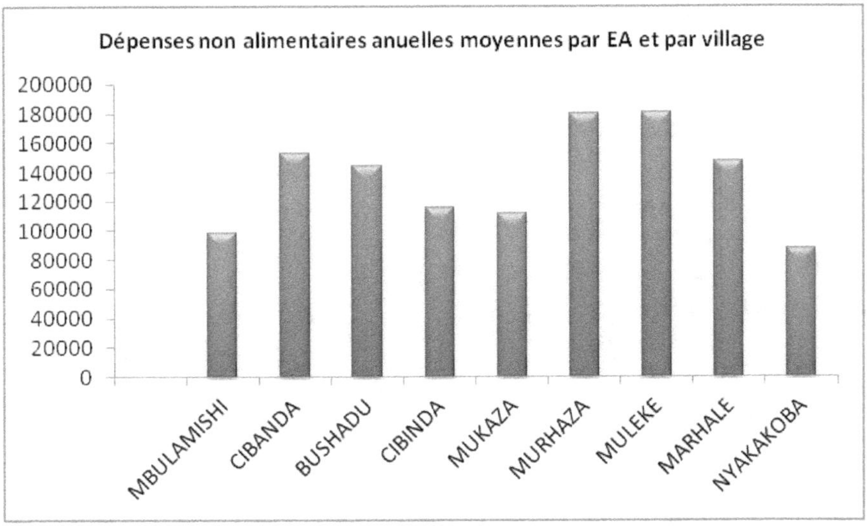

La moyenne de ces dépenses s'élève à 13 8495,30 CDF par EA par an (soit 38% des dépenses alimentaires) avec un écart type de 159 154 ; les DNA sont au-dessus de la moyenne pour les villages de CIBINDA, BUSHADU, MURHAZA, MULEKE ET MARHALE. En s'intéressant au rapport entre les dépenses alimentaires et non alimentaires, la structure des dépenses argumente en faveur de la pauvreté des ménages vu que les DA constituent plus de 50% des dépenses totales. Le graphique 4.a montre les proportions des dépenses totales par village et le graphique 4.b. montre ces proportions pour l'ensemble des ménages. Il en ressort que les DA constituent 73% des dépenses totales du ménage. Cette proportion est légèrement supérieure à celle rapportée dans le DSRCP 2 de la RDC qui est de 62,3% (Ministère du Plan, 2011, p.15).

4.2. Exposition aux risques

Parmi les risques retenus, les individus se sentent plus exposés aux risques naturels et agricoles. Ces derniers constituent 47% des risques. En deuxième position, viennent les risques économiques avec 39% et en dernier lieu, les risques sociaux et politiques avec 14%.

Parmi les risques naturels et agricoles, les maladies des plantes

GRAPHIQUE 4. A
Structure des dépenses totales

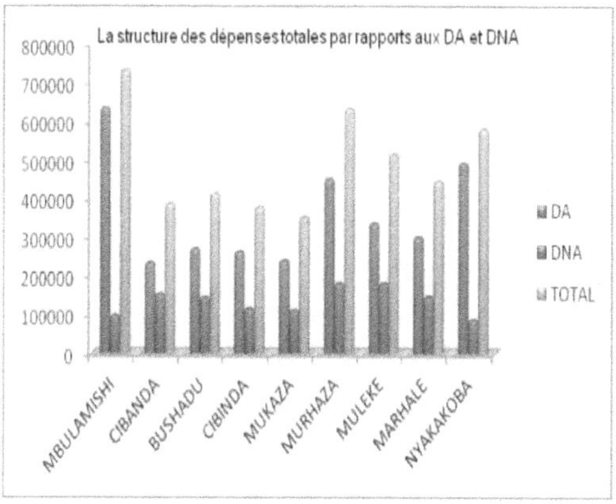

GRAPHIQUE 4.B

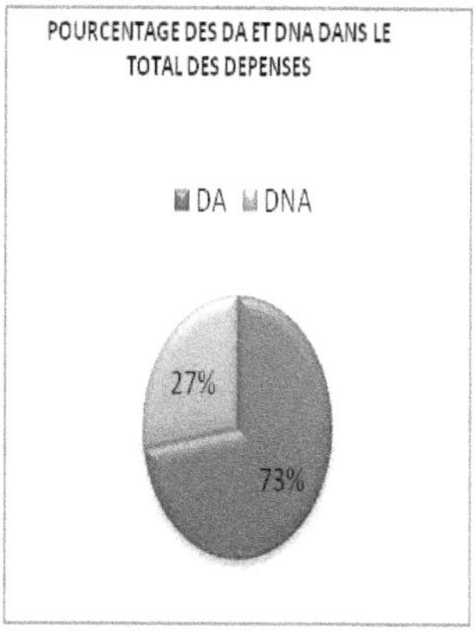

battent le record et ont affecté 80% des ménages durant l'année d'étude. Il s'agit essentiellement de la maladie du manioc (mosaïque) et de banane (wilt banana). Parmi les risques sociaux et politiques, les ménages sont peu exposés au risque de guerre. En effet, à Burhale il s'observe une accalmie par rapport aux autres contrées du milieu telles que Nzibira. De tous les risques économiques, les bas prix sont les moins perçus. Les ménages ne sont pas exposés aux bas prix agricoles lors de la vente de leurs produits tout simplement parce qu'ils ont un comportement orienté vers la subsistance plutôt que de participer au marché. La grande part de la production sert à l'autoconsommation et le petit surplus est alors écoulé. Il y a lieu de mentionner que les routes de desserte agricole posent énormément problème. Elles sont impraticables après la pluie.

4.3. Seuil de pauvreté et incidence de la pauvreté

Pour déterminer le seuil de pauvreté, nous avons procédé en deux étapes : dans une première étape nous avons tout d'abord déterminé le seuil de pauvreté alimentaire (SPA), ensuite le seuil de pauvreté non alimentaire (SPNA). A la suite du PNUD (2006), le SPA correspond à la dépense minimale nécessaire à un individu ou un ménage pour se procurer un panier de biens alimentaires qui respecte à la fois les normes nutritives d'un régime alimentaire équilibré (2400 Kcal/jour par équivalent adulte) et les habitudes de consommation de la population. Le SPNA est équivalent à la dépense minimale nécessaire à l'acquisition des biens non alimentaires et les services publics essentiels à la population. Il est estimé (i) en calculant l'importance relative

GRAPHIQUE 5
Risques naturels, sociaux et économiques

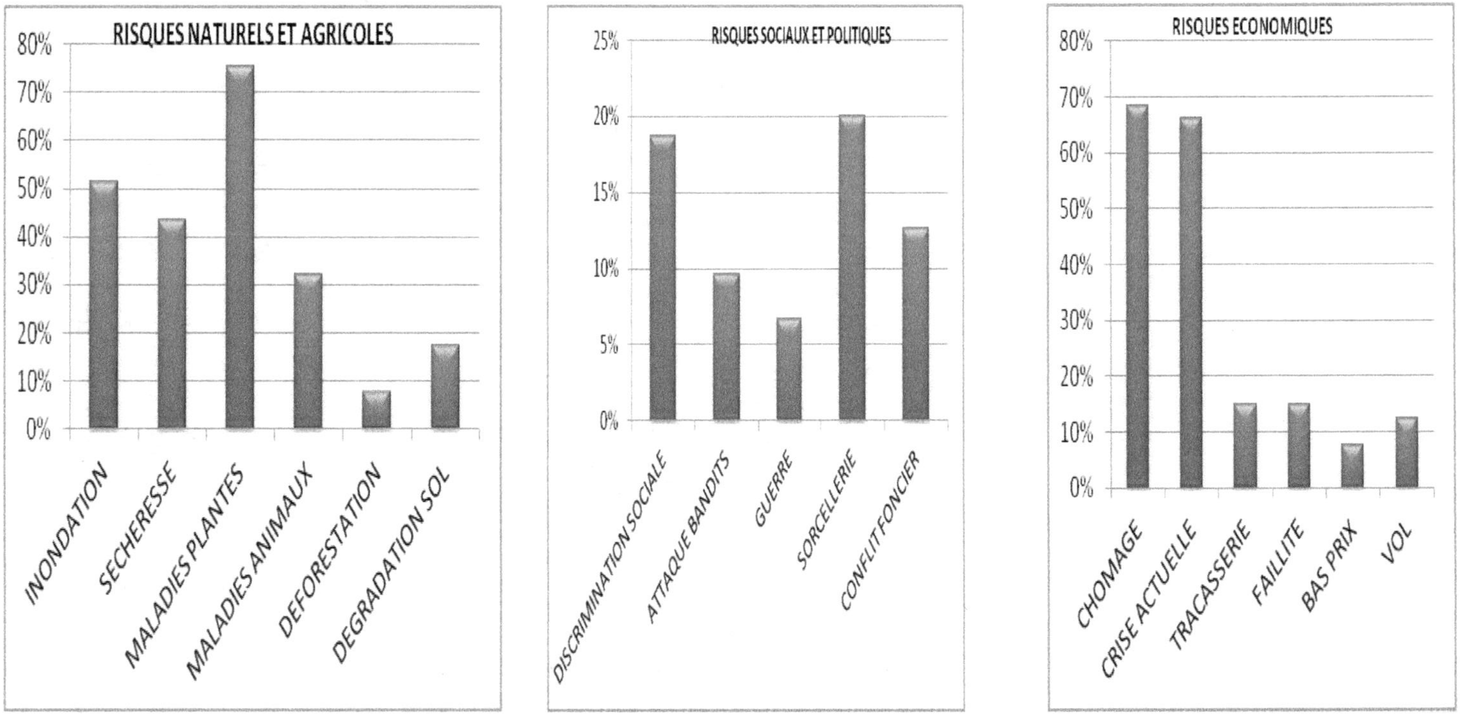

TABLEAU 2
Profil de pauvreté selon le sexe du chef de ménage

SEXE	PROPORTIONS MENAGES	INCIDENCE	PROFONDEUR	SÉVÉRITÉ
HOMME	79%	81%	38%	27%
FEMME	21%	88%	52%	32%

des dépenses non alimentaires par rapport aux dépenses alimentaires pour l'ensemble des ménages et (ii) en multipliant le seuil de pauvreté alimentaire déterminé par le ratio calculé précédemment. Le seuil de pauvreté global est la somme des seuils de pauvreté alimentaire et non alimentaire (SPA et SPNA).

Pour la présente étude, le seuil de pauvreté alimentaire est de 474 500 CDF par EA et par an (soit de 1 300 CDF par équivalent adulte et par jour), en y adjoignant le seuil non alimentaire de 184 100 CDF par EA et par an (obtenu en multipliant le seuil alimentaire par le coefficient 0,388 qui représente l'importance relative des dépenses non alimentaires par rapport aux dépenses alimentaires) ; le seuil global devient 658 600 CDF par EA et par an (soit 1 800 CDF par EA par jour). L'incidence de la pauvreté est ainsi de 82,6%. La profondeur est de 48% et la sévérité est de 28%.

En s'intéressant aux ménages selon que le chef est homme ou femme, nous remarquons que l'incidence de la pauvreté est légèrement plus élevée pour les ménages dirigés par les femmes que pour ceux dirigés par les hommes.

4.4. Profil d'inégalité

Nous rapportons les indices d'inégalités pour deux variables : le revenu et le patrimoine. Ce dernier comprend 3 principaux éléments : tous les actifs (inclus dans le calcul de l'index des actifs et valorisés à leur valeur actuelle), la maison en valeur ainsi que les terres en valeur. Les revenus sont les dépenses par EA.

En s'intéressant au revenu, le coefficient de Gini est de 41 % ; il est plus élevé que celui trouvé par le DSCRP (2006) pour le milieu rural (soit 36%) et celui trouvé par le PNUD (2009) pour le Sud Kivu (33%). Ainsi, les inégalités à Burhale tendent à être légèrement plus élevées que ne l'ont souligné les études antérieures. En s'intéressant aux pauvres et aux non pauvres, l'indice de Gini est plus élevé entre les non pauvres qu'entre les pauvres. A la lecture de tous les coefficients, la distribution des revenus est moins inégalitaire entre les pauvres, qu'entre les non pauvres.

Le patrimoine (richesse) est plus inégalitaire que le revenu. Son coefficient de Gini est de 74% pour l'ensemble, il est de 71% pour les pauvres contre 83% pour les

TABLEAU 3

Principaux indices d'inégalité pour l'ensemble et pour les sous-groupes pauvres et non pauvres

INDICES POUR TOUTE LA DISTRIBUTION DES REVENUS				
VARIABLES	GINI	ATKINSON (ε=0,5)	ENTROPIE	(CV)
REVENU	0, 41	0,14	0,33	1,05
PATRIMOINE	0,74	0, 48	1 ,27	2,81

INDICES D'INÉGALITÉ POUR LES PAUVRES				
VARIABLES	GINI	ATKINSON (ε =0,5)	ENTROPIE	CV
REVENU	0,25	0,05	0,99	0,4
PATRIMOINE	0,71	0, 45	1,16	2,6

INDICES D'INÉGALITÉ POUR LES NON PAUVRES				
VARIABLES	GINI	ATKINSON (ε=0,5)	ENTROPIE	CV
REVENU	0,30	0,07	0,17	0,69
PATRIMOINE	0,83	0,63	1,8	3,6

GRAPHIQUE 6
Courbe de Lorenz de Burhale

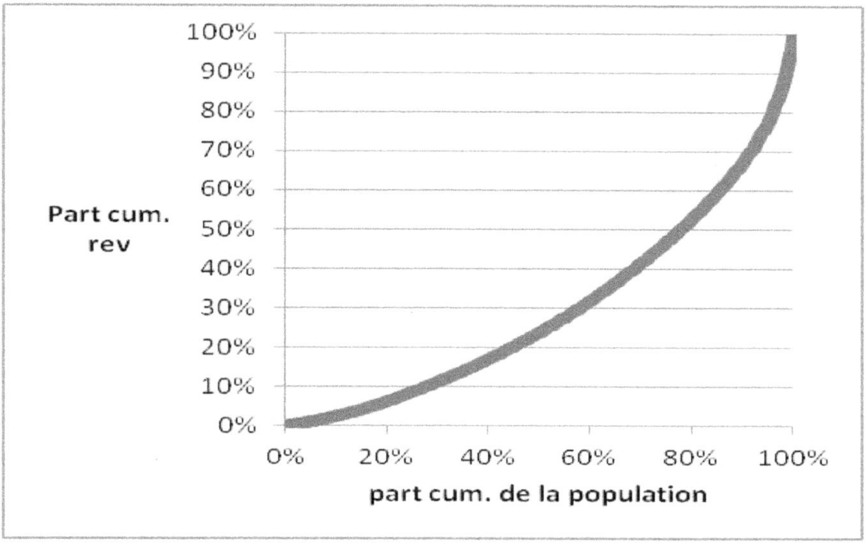

non pauvres. A la lecture de tous les coefficients, la distribution du patrimoine est moins inégalitaire entre les pauvres, qu'entre les non pauvres. Le graphique IV.8 illustre la distribution des revenus pour Burhale.

D'un autre angle, en s'intéressant aux ménages selon que le chef est homme ou femme, nous remarquons que les inégalités sont plus élevées pour les ménages dirigés par les femmes (le Gini est de 44%) que pour ceux dirigés par les hommes (avec un Gini de 39%).

4.5. Décomposition des inégalités par source

Pour la rétention de la variable revenu par EA, nous avons buté sur un problème pratique : la variable de bien-être retenue étant les dépenses par EA, il était difficile de la désagréger par source de revenu. Alors, nous avons jugé bon de corriger tous les montants de différentes sources de revenu en les pondérant par le coefficient de l'importance relative des dépenses par rapport aux revenus. Les résultats de la décomposition demeurent inchangés. Les principales sources de revenu retenues sont :

- **Le revenu agricole**, il comprend le revenu provenant de la vente des récoltes de même que le revenu reçu du travail journalier en agriculture.
- **Le revenu salarié non agricole** : il regroupe principalement les employés ou fonctionnaires de l'Etat, entre autres enseignants des écoles primaires et secondaires, les soldats, les greffiers, les autorités administratives et leaders locaux tels que le chef de groupement ou de localité. Du point de vue de la

TABLEAU 4
Composition du revenu des ménages

	Part en % dans le revenu total	Moyenne	Écart- type	Min	Max
Revenu total par EA	100%	541839,8	587728,5	47941,18	5522667
Agriculture	28%	152538	244611,2	0	2041177
Salariat	12%	62974,49	155480	0	1009556
Métiers	16%	84944,52	354935,3	0	5522667
Commerce et activités minières	38%	203198,2	457620,2	0	3330364
Transferts	3%	16039,75	66841,16	0	704896,6
Autres revenus	4%	22144,83	150249	0	1909091

perception de la population, cette classe est plus vue comme riche et aisée car disposant d'un revenu plus ou moins fixe au cours de l'année, ce qui est différent pour le revenu agricole.

– **Les métiers** : cette catégorie regroupe les revenus issus des métiers tels que la scierie, la couture, la maçonnerie, la menuiserie, la fabrication de charbon de bois etc. Nous avons jugé bon d'exclure les creuseurs artisanaux de cette catégorie pour mieux appréhender l'apport de leur activité[1].

– **Commerce et activité minière** : cette catégorie regroupe les revenus issus du commerce (nous n'avons pas distingué le petit commerce du grand) ainsi que ceux issus de l'activité minière.

– **Les transferts** : cette classe est constituée des transferts que reçoit le ménage des autres membres de la famille élargie ou autres.

– **Autres revenus** : cette catégorie comprend les revenus issus des transferts de quelques ONG œuvrant dans le milieu, le revenu de la vente des biens du ménage et tout autre revenu ne pouvant se classer parmi les cinq précédents.

La part du commerce et des activités minières dans le revenu total est la plus élevée, ceci provient du fait que ces activités génèrent des excédents élevés par rapport aux autres secteurs d'activité ; en deuxième position vient le revenu agricole avec une contribution de 28%, ensuite les métiers pour 16%, le revenu salarié non agricole qui contribue pour 12%, les transferts

1. Les revenus des creuseurs artisanaux étaient significativement élevés par rapport à ceux d'autres métiers. Pour parvenir à isoler cet effet, nous l'avons inclus dans le sous-groupe « commerce et activités minières ».

TABLEAU 5

Décomposition du coefficient de Gini par source de revenu

Source	Part du revenu de la source k dans le revenu total **Sk**	Le coefficient de Gini du revenu yk **Gk**	Corrélation de Gini **Rk**	contribution relative à l'inégalité totale (sKGkRk/G)	Elasticité de l'inégalité totale à la source k
Agriculture	0,282	0,67	0,265	0,118	-0,163
Salariat	0,116	0,864	0,376	0,089	-0,027
Métiers	0,157	0,888	0,472	0,155	-0,002
Commerce et act. minières	0,375	0,821	0,765	0,556	0,181
Transferts	0,03	0,934	0,223	0,015	-0,015
Autres revenus	0,041	0,977	0,712	0,067	0,026
Revenu total		0,424			

TABLEAU 6
Statistiques descriptives des principales variables

Variable	Obs	Mean	Std. Dev.	Min	Max
Agechef	300	44.25333	14.07633	20	84
Sexechef	300	.7933333	.4055908	0	1
Educchef	300	300	.7	.4590232	0
Statutmatr	300	.7066667	.4560506	0	1
Activitéchef	300	.57	.4959029	0	1
Educprimaire	300	.4312743	.3488075	0	1.25
Educsecondaire	300	.1390961	.2354226	0	1.111111
Educsupérieure	300	.0098564	.064709	0	.7843137
Tailleménage	300	4.016667	1.563138	1	9.8
Promiscuité	300	9.402966	8.185324	1.139241	67.11864
Emploinonagr	300	.3266667	.4697778	0	1
Indexactifs	300	7.283333	2.087482	3	13
Terre	300	1546.66	3702.854	0	33573.33
Vulnérabilité	300	.1333333	.3405026	0	1
Risqueobj	300	-1.756667	4.223377	-13	13
Risquesubj	300	4.615	2.100153	0	10
Log (DEP/EA)	300	5.576995	.3059468	4.680709	6.742149

pour 3% et enfin les autres revenus pour 4%.

Le tableau ci-dessus présente les résultats de la décomposition de Gini par sources de revenu retenues. Le coefficient de Gini global est de 42% légèrement supérieur à celui trouvé précédemment car il prend en compte les faibles épargnes. Le coefficient de Gini des « autres revenus » est le plus élevé (soit 97%). Il est suivi par celui des transferts (93%) : plusieurs ménages ne bénéficient pas de transferts (que ce soit provenant des membres de famille ou de quelques organisations). En troisième position, viennent les revenus du commerce et de l'activité minière (89%) suivis du salariat (86%). En dernière position, viennentt les revenus agricoles (67%). De manière générale, les revenus de différentes sources sont inégalement distribués.

La contribution à l'inégalité totale est la plus élevée pour le commerce et les activités minières soit 56%, en deuxième position les métiers contribuent à 15% à l'inégalité totale. La hausse des revenus issus du commerce et activités minières augmente les inégalités tandis qu'une telle hausse du revenu agricole, du salariat, des métiers ou des transferts diminue les inégalités. Le résultat selon lequel le revenu agricole diminue les inégalités a été obtenu aussi par Babatunde (2008). Par contre, affirmer que les transferts diminuent les inégalités est contraire à l'étude de Montaud (2002).

4.6. Résultats des régressions des dépenses par équivalent adulte

Les statistiques descriptives des variables utilisées sont reprises dans le tableau ci-dessous.

Le chef de ménage est âgé en moyenne de 44 ans. Il s'agit en majeure partie des hommes du niveau secondaire : 70% d'entre eux sont monogames et 57% possèdent pour activité principale l'agriculture. La taille du ménage est de 4 EA. Pour un ménage représentatif, 43% de ses membres sont de niveau primaire, 13% de niveau secondaire et 1% de niveau supérieur. Pour ce qui est de la promiscuité, une personne occupe en moyenne 9 mètres carrés ; 32% de ménages accèdent à l'emploi non agricole. Les actifs sont au nombre de 7 par ménage et chaque EA possède 1546 mètres carrés de terres cultivables. Selon l'approche d'exposition au risque, 13% des ménages sont vulnérables, le chef de ménage affiche une faible tendance à l'aversion au risque avec un score moyen de -1,75.

4.6.1. Estimation du modèle 1

La matrice de variance-covariance rapporte une faible corrélation entre toutes les paires des variables explicatives (le coefficient de corrélation tend vers zéro), sauf pour la paire risqueobj-risquesubj. Ainsi, la variable risquesubj a été omise de la régression finale. Le test de « robust » d'hétéroscédasticité ainsi que celui de Breusch-Pagan rapportent la présence des erreurs hétéroscédatiques. La correction est mise en œuvre à l'aide de l'estimation consistante de White. Les résultats de la régression sont donnés dans le tableau ci-dessous.

La première colonne reprend les variables, la seconde donne les valeurs des coefficients et la troisième présente les « t » statistiques. La variable Risquesubj a été enlevée du modèle au vu de sa forte corrélation avec la variable Risqueobj. Toutes les variables ont les signes attendus sauf l'âge du chef, la promiscuité et la terre. Les variables significatives au seuil de 5% sont l'âge du chef de ménage, la taille du ménage, l'index des actifs et l'attitude face au risque.

L'âge du chef a un effet sur sa capacité à saisir les opportunités en termes d'activités artisanales par exemple. Les chefs des ménages jeunes sont assez vigoureux pour accéder à des revenus élevés non agricoles. Le résultat est différent avec celui de Naschold (2009) pour le signe et la significativité. Cette contradiction peut être due aux milieux d'études qui sont différents.

La taille du ménage explique significativement le niveau de dépenses du ménage : plus la taille est élevée, plus les dépenses par EA sont faibles. Ceci s'explique par le

TABLEAU 7

Résultat de la régression MCO du log des dépenses par EA, modèle 1

Variable dépendante =Log (DEP/EA)	Coef.	t
Log Age du chef du ménage	-.1351271	-2.55**
Sexe du chef ménage	.0078554	0.17
Education du chef ménage	.0317177	0.80
Statut matrimonial	.0308307	0.80
Activité chef du ménage	-.0385389	-0.99
Education primaire	.0137312	0.29
Education secondaire	.0137199	0.19
Education supérieure	.5645724	1.37
Log Taille du ménage	-.2737347	-6.38**
Log Promiscuité	-.0294806	-1.21
Emploi non agricole	.0543455	1.39
Index actifs	.0443517	4.55**
Log Terre	-.0159555	-1.48
Vulnérabilité	-.0424436	-0.93
Risqueobj	.0154068	3.82**
_cons		

**= significatif à 5%, N= 300, F(15, 283) = 7.46 , Prob" F = 0.000, R-squared = 0.2926 , Root MSE = .26437

fait qu'avec plusieurs membres, la pression sur les ressources est forte. Le revenu du chef de ménage est alloué à plusieurs rubriques telles que l'alimentation, l'éducation ou autres de manière significative. A Burhale, un ménage est constitué en moyenne de 6,2 personnes soit 4 EA. La taille du ménage est légèrement supérieure par rapport à la moyenne du pays qui se situe à 5,4 personnes par ménage selon le DSCRP 2 (Ministère du Plan, 2011, p. 86). Les ménages larges tendent à être plus pauvres que les petits ménages. Ce résultat est conforme à celui du Ministère du Plan (2011).

L'index des actifs est significatif. Il traduit la possession par les ménages d'un certain nombre d'actifs. Plus l'index est élevé, mieux le ménage s'en porte. L'attitude face au risque est significative à 5%. Cette variable a un effet positif sur les dépenses, ce qui atteste notre deuxième hypothèse de recherche, à savoir le lien positif entre amour du risque et niveau de revenu.

TABLEAU 8
Déterminants de l'utilité, modèle 2

Variable dépendante=Utilité	Coeff.	t
Gini par village	3.425853	2.57**
Log risque subjectif	1.844755	3.44**
Log age chef du ménage	.3562819	0.90
Sexe chef de ménage	-.187361	-0.50
Education chef de ménage	.4795987	1.68*
Statut matrimonial	.49857	1.50
Activité chef du ménage	-.3626398	-1.35
LogDEP/EA	.2707465	1.46
_constante	-3.615793	-1.16

*= significatif à 10%, **= significatif à 5%, N =300, F(8, 291) = 4.92 , Prob" F= 0.0000, R-squared = 0.1192, Adj R-squared = 0.0950, Root MSE = 2.1002

Le niveau d'instruction du chef de ménage n'est pas significatif mais possède le signe attendu, si le chef de ménage est de niveau secondaire ou de niveau plus élevé, le revenu est aussi élevé. Ce résultat est conforme à celui de Petemoya (2006). Pour cet auteur le niveau d'éducation diminue la probabilité d'être pauvre à Kabare mais pas de manière significative.

4.6.2. Estimation du modèle 2

L'estimation du deuxième modèle est rapportée dans le tableau ci-dessous. Le test de Nakamura a été utilisé pour vérifier l'endogénéité de la variable logDEP/EA. Les résultats, rapportés en annexe, ont montré que cette variable ne souffre pas d'endogénéité. Pour rappel, ce modèle explique l'utilité en fonction des caractéristiques du chef de ménage, de l'inégalité et de l'attitude face au risque. La matrice variance-covariance rapporte de faibles corrélations entre les paires des variables explicatives et l'hétéroscédasticité est une seconde fois corrigée grâce à l'estimation des écarts-types robustes. L'utilité dépend significativement de 3 variables : le coefficient de Gini par village, le risque subjectif et le niveau d'éducation du chef de ménage.

Le niveau des inégalités (à travers le Gini) a un effet positif sur la satisfaction qu'a l'individu de sa vie. Ce constat est contraire à plusieurs études qui ont testé ce lien. L'étude de Ferrer-i-Carbonell et Ramos (2010) et celle d'Alesina *et al* (2004) rapportent un lien négatif entre inégalités et satisfaction des individus par la vie. Cette incohérence de notre résultat avec ceux d'autres études peut provenir de deux aspects : le premier est la taille de l'échantillon (les deux études ont utilisé des échantillons de plus de 24000). Le deuxième aspect est la différence des contextes. Le milieu dans lequel nous avons mené la recherche présente un taux de pauvreté de 83%, typique des pays en développement ; l'étude d'Alesina s'est déroulée aux Etats-Unis et en Europe où les standards de niveaux de vie sont très élevés par rapport à ceux de l'Afrique. Les individus riches se préoccupent plus des inégalités ; une hausse de ces inégalités diminue leur satisfaction tandis que pour notre cas, si pour un village donné le coefficient de Gini est élevé, cela suppose la présence des individus non pauvres et plus ou moins satisfaits. La satisfaction et les inégalités évoluent donc dans le même sens.

L'éducation du chef de ménage joue en faveur de la satisfaction. La catégorie de base étant le niveau primaire et l'analphabétisme, les individus qui ont ces niveaux d'éducation sont limités en termes d'opportunité d'emploi (surtout salarié). Le revenu n'est pas significatif mais possède le signe attendu, ceci laisse entendre que la satisfaction des individus ne provient pas uniquement du revenu mais aussi d'autres aspects tels que l'accès aux soins de santé, à l'éducation etc. Les individus les plus « risquophiles » sont aussi les plus satisfaits de la vie. Cette conclusion est proche de celle trouvée dans le premier modèle.

4.6.3. Estimation du logit multinomial ordonné

A ce niveau de notre analyse, nous avons généré une variable Q = Quintile. Elle catégorise chaque ménage selon la classe à laquelle il appartient dans l'ordre croissant des revenus par EA. La limite inférieure du cinquième quintile est proche du seuil de pauvreté retenu de 658 600 CDF. Ce quintile est donc celui des non pauvres. A la lumière du tableau ci-dessous, les ménages qui se situent dans les quintiles les plus élevés sont les plus satisfaits de la vie. La moyenne de la satisfaction passe de 3,5 dans le premier quintile à 4,4 pour le cinquième quintile.

L'allure de la moyenne de l'âge du chef de ménage confirme les résultats obtenus ci-haut. En évoluant dans des quintiles aux niveaux de vie élevés, l'âge diminue légèrement. Les autres variables ont des moyennes à évolution très contrastée suivant les quintiles. Ceci renvoie à la limite de la statistique « moyenne » de par sa sensibilité aux valeurs extrêmes.

La régression logistique utilise alors pour variable dépendante les quintiles de niveau de vie. La catégorie de base est celle de non pauvres (quintile 5), à l'exemple de Lachaud (2000b). Les coefficients apportent peu en termes d'interprétation de nos résultats. Pour ce faire, nous recourons aux effets marginaux. L'analyse des effets marginaux aboutit aux conclusions plus ou moins similaires à celles du modèle 1 et 2.

TABLEAU 9

Indicateurs de bien-être des ménages selon la distribution par quintile

Quintile	1	2	3	4	5	Total
U	3.583333	3.566667	4.016667	4.05	4.4	3.923333
DEP/EA	155083	269578.2	366859.7	521860.7	1186465	499969.3
Agechef	48.65	46.9	44.31667	44.33333	37.06667	44.25333
Sexechef	.7333333	.7833333	.7666667	.8	.8833333	.7933333
Educchef	.6	.65	.6333333	.8166667	.8	.7
Statutmatr	.7166667	.6166667	.6333333	.7333333	.8333333	.7066667
Activitéchef	.7166667	.6166667	.65	.5166667	.35	.57
Educprimaire	.4932553	.4378227	.4085164	.4717901	.3449872	.4312743
Educsecondaire	.159369	.104257	.1510379	.1872955	.0935211	.1390961
Educsupérieure	.0208506	.0025641	0	.0059524	.0199147	.0098564
Tailleménage	4.588333	4.028333	3.846667	4.035	3.585	4.016667
Promiscuité	7.791415	11.477	8.870864	9.667471	9.20808	9.402966
Emploinonagr	.25	.3166667	.3333333	.3833333	.35	.3266667
Indexactifs	6.783333	7.316667	6.883333	7.683333	7.75	7.283333
Terre	1335.8	1760.511	1984.061	1416.429	1391.167	1577.594
Vulnérabilité	.1	.1666667	.1166667	.1833333	.1	.1333333
Risqueobj	-3.85	-2.55	-1.666667	-.5166667	-.2	-1.756667

TABLEAU II

Effets marginaux du modèle logit multinomial

Quintiles	1		2		3		4	
	variable dy/dx	Z	variable dy/dx	Z	variable dy/dx	Z	variable dy/dx	Z
Log Agechef	.0893334	0.98	.1560335	1.49	-.0216848	-0.37	-.0770095	-0.71
Sexechef	-.0970758	-1.04	.0964482	1.15	.0075694	0.15	-.0135558	-0.15
Educchef	-.0787443	-1.20	-.0812785	-1.11	-.0210179	-0.51	.1325417	2.02**
Statutmatr	.0591575	0.95	-.1172265	-1.36	-.0326069	-0.72	.0070718	0.09
Activitéchef	.043522	0.75	.0071275	0.11	.0421521	0.94	.0141765	0.23
Educprimaire	.0383874	0.50	-.0435002	-0.50	-.0493962	-0.80	.0686364	0.71
Educsecondaire	.0575749	0.46	-.2310098	-1.65*	.0903277	1.10	.2363588	1.61*
Educsupérieure	2.416963	3.39**	1.588895	1.46	-9.103628	-7.56**	2.34239	1.94*
LogTailleménage	.3555932	4.97**	.1246003	1.38	.0293115	0.59	-.1709732	-1.88*
Log Promiscuité	.0151245	0.42	.0951422	1.76*	-.0004905	-0.02	-.0397947	-0.75
Emploinonagr	-.0515873	-0.93	.0086845	0.11	.0447542	0.94	.0557255	0.78
Indexactifs	-.0461025	-3.36**	.003506	0.24	-.0151106	-1.44	.010035	0.58
LogTerre	-.0045389	-0.28	.0084947	0.46	.009526	0.95	.0151292	0.91
Vulnérabilité	.0736797	0.70	.0296203	0.32	-.041711	-0.99	-.0010875	-0.01
Risqueobj	-.0235427	-3.85**	-.0140767	-1.88*	.0016744	0.34	.0184231	2.33**

Les variables significatives dans au moins un des quintiles sont : l'éducation du chef, l'éducation secondaire, l'éducation supérieure, la taille du ménage, la promiscuité, l'index des actifs et le score de risque objectif.

L'éducation du chef de ménage diminue les probabilités de se retrouver dans les quintiles très pauvres, mais de manière significative pour le deuxième quintile seulement. Ainsi, si l'éducation passe de 0 (aucune et primaire) à 1 (secondaire et plus), les probabilités d'être très pauvres diminuent. Aussi, la présence des membres de niveau secondaire au sein du ménage diminue la probabilité de se retrouver dans le deuxième quintile et augmente celle de se situer au quatrième quintile et échapper ainsi à la pauvreté. A ce niveau, l'importance du capital humain jaillit dans toute son intensité.

L'effet de l'éducation supérieure sur la probabilité de se situer dans le premier quintile (2,41) et le quatrième quintile (2,34) est élevé et significatif. Cela parait contradictoire aux premiers abords. Les résultats montrent que la présence des membres ayant le niveau supérieur peut ou ne peut pas aider à sortir de la pauvreté. A ce niveau, l'importance de la conscientisation des intellectuels ruraux ressort de manière pertinente. Il ne suffit pas de disposer en son sein des personnes ayant étudié, il faudrait aussi que ces personnes aident effectivement le ménage. Il est possible que certains interviewés aient inclus les membres absents dans cette catégorie. En effet, il s'observe une importante fuite des cerveaux en défaveur de Burhale : les intellectuels ne veulent pas rester au village et ce, pour plusieurs raisons comme le manque de fourniture de certains services de base, tels que l'électricité, l'eau courante etc.

La taille du ménage est significative pour le premier et le quatrième quintiles. Il renchérit le résultat trouvé dans le modèle 1. La taille élevée augmente la probabilité (de 0,35) d'être très pauvre. En évoluant vers les quintiles au niveau de vie plus élevé, l'effet marginal de la taille diminue, et la tendance se renverse dans le quatrième quintile (dans celui-ci, la probabilité de s'y retrouver avec une taille de ménage élevée est faible). La promiscuité est significative pour le deuxième quintile seulement ; aussi, l'index des actifs diminue significativement la probabilité d'être dans le premier quintile, sa tendance dans les autres quintiles est contrastée. La « risquophilie » diminue significativement la possiblilité de se situer dans le quintile le plus pauvre, et augmente celle d'être dans le quintile le moins pauvre de manière significative. Cette conclusion corrobore celle du modèle 1.

Bref, relativement au cinquième quintile, la probabilité d'être très pauvre augmente avec le niveau bas d'éducation du chef de ménage, la taille du ménage élevé, le faible index des actifs et l'aversion au risque. Elle diminue avec la présence des membres ayant le niveau secondaire, l'index des actifs et la faible aversion au risque.

4.6.4. Discussions

A la lumière de nos résultats, nous pouvons développer quelques arguments. Les inégalités de revenu ne sont pas très élevées (car en-dessous de 50%), les individus ont tendance à être pauvres de la même façon en prenant le revenu comme référence. Avec la décomposition des inégalités, les activités minières et celles du commerce contribuent plus à l'inégalité (56%) que toutes les autres sources de revenu. Les zones minières proches de Burhale (vers le territoire de Mwenga) attirent plusieurs jeunes. L'activité minière est non soutenue pour le long terme, car elle puise des ressources non renouvelables. Ainsi, il ne s'agit pas d'un secteur cible pour une visée de développement.

Le commerce est essentiellement constitué du négoce : les commerçants s'approvisionnent en biens manufacturés *et ali*mentaires à Bukavu et les vendent à Burhale à un prix double voire triple. Ceci réduit le bien-être du consommateur plus que proportionnellement au surplus réalisé par le vendeur. Les consommateurs étant plus nombreux, le bien-être global diminue. Une intervention axée sur la dynamisation du commerce doit être d'abord tributaire de l'agriculture. En promouvant le commerce des biens agricoles en provenance de Burhale, l'agriculteur est plus à même d'en bénéficier. Cela suppose des interventions en amont et en aval.

En amont, nous retrouvons l'agriculture avec tous ses maux. Le premier est l'infertilité du sol, issue de la qualité même du sol. Le deuxième est la présence des maladies qui ravagent les cultures. La culture du manioc est gravement touchée tandis que celle de la banane ne l'est pas encore (même si dans certains villages tels que Muleke la maladie du Wilt bactérien est présente). Il est grand temps de repenser l'agriculture. Une intervention pour la hausse de la productivité et le ciblage des biens agricoles commercialisables aideraient la population. Dans le même ordre d'idée, une diversification des produits agricoles peut améliorer la sécurité alimentaire (la culture du soja, peu répandue), pourrait constituer un puissant moteur de lutte contre la malnutrition.

Le changement de culture alimentaire n'est pas aisé mais il serait aussi indiqué. La terre, facteur de production essentielle se lie négativement au revenu. Elle ne permet pas de dégager des surplus considérables lors de la vente des produits agricoles. Le mode de tenure de terre par le « bwassa » ne favorise pas un engagement de l'agriculteur. Des comportements d'agence peuvent en résulter et mettre en mal la productivité. En aval, la dégradation des infrastructures enfreint l'écoulement des produits vers les centres de consommation tels que Bukavu. L'inexistence des coopératives agricoles ou commerciales n'encourage pas les agriculteurs.

Les inégalités patrimoniales sont très élevées (le Gini est de 74%). Certains privés s'approprient des étendues des terres « fertiles » dans la région et y instaurent des plantations et des fermes. Une telle pratique est fortement encouragée si elle profite à la population environnante. Ceci est loin d'être le cas : les plantations en semi activité (Cibeke et Gombo) ne peuvent pas engager des employés de manière permanente au cours de l'année[1]. Toutefois, les politiques de redistribution ne seraient pas adaptées au stade actuel. Le fait de ravir les terres pour les redistribuer par des pratiques prédatrices n'a pas toutes les chances de réussir. De plus, les inégalités élevées se lient aussi aux revenus plus ou moins significatifs ainsi qu'à des niveaux élevés de satisfaction tel que montré par le modèle 2. En d'autres termes, il faudrait d'abord accumuler avant de penser à redistribuer, car ce sont les non pauvres qui sont à la base de la hausse des inégalités patrimoniales.

A l'inverse des inégalités de revenu, le taux de pauvreté est élevé (82,6%). La lutte contre la pauvreté s'impose avec acuité. Un premier axe serait l'élevage. Au vu de l'infertilité du sol, l'élevage offre une alternative pragmatique. Les ménages pourront ainsi accéder au fumier et au revenu provenant de la vente du bétail. Actuellement, l'élevage souffre énormément de diverses épidémies et d'une absence physique ou économique des vétérinaires. Certaines ONGD offrent le bétail sous forme de crédit rotatif. Après que la chèvre ait mis bas, un des chevreaux est donné à un autre membre du groupe. De telles pratiques ont des chances de réussir à atténuer un tant soit peu la pauvreté.

Les soins de santé sont un casse-tête pour une majeure partie de la population. La mise en place en 2012 d'une mutuelle de santé n'a pas amélioré la situation. Sur 300 ménages, seulement 15% sont dans la mutuelle de santé. Les raisons de non adhésion sont notamment le manque d'information, le manque d'argent et l'anticipation adaptative selon laquelle la maladie ne se présentera pas au cours de l'année vu qu'elle ne s'est pas présentée l'année précédente.

Le capital humain demeure important pour la hausse du niveau de revenu des ménages à Burhale. Ceci plaide en faveur des interventions pour faciliter l'accès à l'éducation telles que les bourses scolaires, l'appui des écoles en fournitures, etc. L'essentiel n'est pas la construction des écoles mais plutôt leurs équipements. L'investissement dans des structures d'enseignement supérieur (université et institut

1. Cependant, une pratique qui a réussi (et est à encourager) est celle de la plantation Boukina. Le propriétaire de cette plantation a mis ses terres en location durant la saison culturale B de l'année 2012. Un espace de 600 mètres carrés était loué à 30 000 CDF la saison. La population s'est dite satisfaite de cette manière de procéder, puisque la terre était fertile. En effet, la plantation finissait une période longue (plus de 30 ans) de jachère durant laquelle elle servait de pâturage. Malheureusement, l'expérience ne s'est pas renouvelée.

supérieur) serait indiqué car la présence au sein des ménages des personnes ayant une éducation supérieure diminuent sensiblement la probabilité que le ménage soit pauvre mais il faudrait penser à la lutte contre la fuite des cerveaux.

Le taux de pauvreté est élevé pour les ménages dirigés par les femmes comparativement à ceux dirigés par les hommes. La promotion de la femme par l'accès aux sources génératrices de revenu serait un outil de choix. Les structures coopératives telles que les regroupements des femmes dans les « majambere » sont un facteur important de lutte contre la pauvreté. Le petit groupe offre à l'individu la protection et le poids qu'il n'aurait pas s'il était isolé. A ce stade, la place doit être accordée au capital social.

Plus le chef de ménage est âgé, moins son revenu est élevé. L'absence de la sécurité sociale pose énormément problème. Les personnes de troisième âge sont ainsi abandonnées à leur sort. Dans la plupart des cas, leurs revenus sont essentiellement constitués de transferts. Aussi, la taille de ménage élevée entraine une forte probabilité d'être pauvre. Les interventions devraient privilégier les familles nombreuses.

Les ménages se sentent plus exposés aux risques agricoles et naturels. La mise en place des structures coopératives et les mécanismes d'assurance et de crédit agricoles, tels que les coopératives agricoles, pourrait rendre les agriculteurs moins avers.

A la lecture de ces résultats, le développement intégral à Burhale doit prendre en compte la santé, la nutrition et l'éducation comme le soulignent d'ailleurs plusieurs auteurs comme Sen (1999).

5. Conclusion

Cette étude a porté sur les déterminants des inégalités de revenus à Burhale. La question était celle de savoir les sources de revenus, les déterminants de la distribution des revenus à Walungu ainsi que le lien entre le niveau de revenu et l'aversion au risque. L'étude s'est subdivisée en quatre chapitres.

Nous avons présenté les données, la méthodologie ainsi que les résultats de l'étude. Le seuil global de pauvreté est de 658 600 CDF par EA et par an (soit 1800 CDF par EA par jour). L'incidence de la pauvreté est de 82,6%, la profondeur est de 48% et la sévérité de 28%. Les ménages dont les chefs sont des femmes ont un taux de pauvreté plus élevé (88%) que ceux chapeautés par les hommes (81%). Le coefficient de Gini est de 41 % pour la distribution des revenus ; il est plus élevé que celui trouvé par le DSCRP (2006) pour le milieu rural (soit 36%) et celui trouvé par le PNUD (2009) pour le Sud-Kivu (33%). Le patrimoine est plus inégalitaire que le revenu (coefficient de Gini de 75%). La distribution des revenus et du patrimoine est moins inégalitaire entre les pauvres qu'entre les non pauvres.

En décomposant l'inégalité totale par source, la contribution la plus élevée provient du commerce et des activités minières soit 56%, en deuxième position les métiers contribuent à 15% à l'inégalité totale. La hausse des revenus issus du commerce et des activités minières augmente les inégalités tandis qu'une telle hausse du revenu agricole, du salariat, des métiers ou des transferts diminue les inégalités.

Le chef de ménage est âgé en moyenne de 44 ans. Il s'agit en majeure partie des hommes du niveau secondaire ; 70% d'entre eux sont monogames et 57% possèdent pour activité principale l'agriculture ; la taille du ménage est de 4 EA. Chaque ménage a en moyenne 7 actifs, et chaque EA possède 1546 mètres carrés des terres cultivables. Le chef de ménage affiche une faible tendance à l'aversion au risque avec un score moyen de -1,75.

Pour l'estimation du premier modèle, les variables significatives au seuil de 5% sont l'âge du chef de ménage, la taille du ménage, l'index des actifs et l'attitude face au risque. L'âge du chef et la taille du ménage affectent négativement le revenu alors que l'index des actifs et la risquophilie l'affectent positivement. Le deuxième modèle rapporte un lien positif entre inégalité et utilité. Ce résultat est contraire aux études antérieures. Pour le troisième modèle, relativement au cinquième quintile, la probabilité d'être très pauvre augmente avec le niveau bas d'éducation du chef de ménage, la taille du ménage élevée, le faible index d'actifs et la forte aversion au risque. Cette probabilité diminue avec la présence des membres ayant le niveau secondaire, l'index des actifs et la faible aversion au risque.

L'étude plaide pour les interventions en faveur de l'éducation et de l'agriculture pour la lutte contre la pauvreté ; cependant, la lutte contre les inégalités n'est pas primordiale. La première hypothèse n'a pas pu être validée car la variable « terre » n'est pas significative et possède un signe non attendu, par contre la seconde hypothèse est validée, l'amour du risque influe positivement sur le revenu.

Une limite non négligeable de ce travail est l'utilisation des données en coupe instantanée, plusieurs variables d'intérêt seraient plus pertinentes avec les données de panel. Il serait alors possible d'étudier la dynamique des inégalités et du risque dans la région. Une deuxième limite est d'avoir négligé les inégalités au sein du ménage. En effet, Sen (1984), cité par Peluso et Tranoy (2005), souligne que les discriminations (par exemple en défaveur des femmes) pourraient conduire aux inégalités intra-ménages. Notre étude n'a pas circonscrit cet aspect. Une troisième limite est le baromètre de mesure de l'attitude face au risque. En effet, la méthode la plus à même de révéler les caractéristiques de l'individu à l'égard du risque est celle des loteries avec des distributions de revenus aléatoires telles qu'utilisées par Binswanger (1980). Une autre étude pourrait utiliser cette méthode et comparer les résultats avec ceux de la présente recherche. Il s'agit d'autant de pistes que peuvent emprunter les recherches futures.

Bibliographie

Alesina, A., Tella, R. et R. MacCulloch (2004), "Inequality and happiness: Are Europeans and Americans different? ", *Journal of Public Economics*, Vol 88, p. 2009-2042.

Arrondel, L., Masson, A. et D. Verger (2004), « Mesurer les préférences individuelles à l'égard du risque », *Economie et statistique*, vol. 374, n° 1, p. 53-85.

Atkinson, A.B. (1970), "On the measurement of inequality", *Journal of Economic Theory* 2, 244-263.

Atkinson, A.B. et A. Brandolini (2004), *Global World Inequality: Absolute, Relative or Intermediate?* Paper prepared for the 28th General conference of The International, Association for Research in Income and Wealth, Cork, Ireland, August 22-28.

Babatunde R.O. (2008), "Income inequality in rural Nigeria: Evidence from farming households survey data", *Austrlian Journal of Basic and Applied Science* 2(1): 134-140.

BAD (2012), Notes d'information pour la stratégie à long terme de la banque, Note d'information n°5 : Inégalités des revenus en Afrique, préparée par Maurice Mubila *et al*, Mars.

Banque Mondiale (2012), *World Development Indicators.*

Bhalla, S. (2002), *Imagine There's No Country: Poverty, Inequality and Growth in the Era of Globalization*, Washington, D.C., Institute for International Economics.

Binswanger, H. (1980), "Attitudes toward risk : Experimental measurement in rural India", *American Journal of Agricultural Economics*, Vol. 62, N° 3, p. 395-407, Oxford Univesity Press .

Bourguignon, F. (2004), « Le triangle pauvreté-croissance-inégalités », *Afrique contemporaine*, 2004/3 n° 211, p. 29-56.

Bugandwa, D., (2009-2010), *Cours de théorie et pratique de sondages*, inédit, UCB.

Bucekuderhwa, B.C., Bidubula, J.G. et K.E. Balemba (2013), « Vulnérabilité et stratégies de gestion des risques dans les zones d'exploitation minière artisanale. Le cas des ressources d'or de Mukungwe, Burhinyi et Lwindja », *in* MARYSSE, S., OMASOMBO, J. (dirs.), *Conjonctures congolaises 2012 : Politique, secteur minier et gestion des ressources naturelles en RD Congo*, Tervuren/v Paris, MRAC/L'Harmattan, coll. Cahiers Africains, n° 82, 2013.

Cayotte J-L., (2009), *Microéconomie de l'incertitude*, Ouverture économique, 2ème édition, LMD, De Boeck, Bruxelles.

Chang, H.H. (2012), Consumption inequality between farm and nonfarm households in Taiwan: a decomposition analysis of differences in distribution, *Agricultural Economics*, 43, 487– 498.

Cogneau, D., Bossuroy, T., De Vreyer, P., Guénard, C., Hiller, V., Leite, P., Meslé-Somps

S., Pasquier-Doumer L., et T. Constance (2006), *Inégalités et équité en Afrique* , Agence Francaise de Dévelopement.

Cowell, F. (2009), *Measuring inequality.*

Diamond, A., Simon, J. et T. Warner., (1990), "A multinomial probability model of size income distribution", *Journal of Econometrics*, 43, 43-61, North Holland.

Dollar, D. et A. Kraay (2002), « Growth is good for the poor », *Journal of Economic Growth*, Vol. 7 n° 3, p. 195-225, Septembre.

Ferrer-i-Carbonell, A.et X. Ramos (2010), "Inequality Aversion and Risk Attitudes", *IZA Discussion Paper* No. 4703.

Flückiger Y. et R. Naga (2005), *Evaluation de différentes mesures de l'inégalité,* Observatoire Universitaire, laboratoire d'économie appliquée, Suisse.

Friedman, M. (1953), "Choice, chance and the personal distribution of income", Journal of Political *Economy,* 61(4), 277-90.

Gajdos, T. et J. Weymark (2012), "Inequality and risk", *Journal of Economic theory,147,* p.1313-1330.

Guénard, C. et J-L. Dubois (2001), « Inégalités, croissance et pauvreté en Afrique subsaharienne », in Winter Gérard (coord.), *Inégalités et politiques publiques en Afrique : pluralité des normes et jeux d'acteurs,* Paris : IRD, Karthala, p. 41-56.

Harley *et al,* (2003), *Etude Pilote de Risques et de la Vulnérabilité en République Démocratique du Congo,* Rapport Préliminaire (2e version).

Harsanyi, J.C. (1953), "Cardinal utility in welfare economics and in the theory of risk-taking", *Journal of Political Economy, vol* 61, p. 434-435.

Hoogeveen, J., Tesliuc E., Vakis, R.et S. Dercon (2005), "Guide to the Analysis of Risk, Vulnerability and Vulnerable Groups", Mimeo, Social Protection Unit, The World Bank, Washington D.C.

House, J. (1991), "The nature and determinants of socioeconomic inequality among peasant households in Southern Sudan", *World development,* Vol 19, N°7, juillet, p. 867-884.

Kodila, O. T. (2010), « Pauvreté en République Démocratique du Congo : Un rapide état de lieux », *Congo EconomicReview,* Université de Kinshasa, WP01/10-Mai 2010.

Kuznets, S. (1955), « Economic Growth and Income Inequality », *American Economic Review,* n° 43, p. 1-28.

Lachaud, J.-P. (2003), « Les déterminants de l'inégalité du bien-être au Burkina Faso : une décomposition de régression », Université Montesquieu-Bordeaux IV, France.

Lachaud, J.-P. (2000b), « Modélisation des déterminants de la pauvreté et marché du travail en Afrique : le cas du Burkina Faso », *Louvain EconomicReview,* Vol. 66, N°3, p. 309-361.

Lachaud, J.-P. (2000a), *Les déterminants de la réduction de l'inégalité et de la pauvreté en Mauritanie : Une approche micro-économique,* Université Montesquieu-Bordeaux IV, France.

Lawson, B., Baninganti K., Homevoh E. et E. Lamadokou (2006), « Analyse comparative de la pauvreté et d'inégalité au Togo : une approche multidimensionnelle basée sur l'indice de richesse », Rapport final, PMMA Network Session Paper, PEP, IDRC, CRDI.

Lerman, R. et S. Yitzhaki, (1985), « Income Inequalities Effects by Income Source: A New Approach and Applications to United States », *Review of Economicsand Statistics*, vol 67, p.151-156.

Lopez-Feldman, A. (2006), Decomposing inequality and obtaining marginal effects, *The Stata Journal*, 6, N° 1, p.106-111.

Mestre, C., Duray-Soundron, C., Huyghebaert, P.et O. Turot (2009), *Réduire les inégalités par des politiques publiques locales, Orientations méthodologiques*, Réseau IMPACT-CIEDEL, Mars.

Ministère du Plan (2011), *Document de la Stratégie de croissance et de réduction de la pauvreté de seconde génération, (D S C R P 2)*, Vol 1, RDC .

Montaud, J. M. (2002), *Ajustement structurel et inégalités des revenus en Afrique : Une analyse de décomposition appliquée au Burkina-Faso*, Université Montesquieu-Bordeaux IV.

Moummi, A. (2010), « Analyse de la pauvreté en République démocratique du Congo », *Workingpaper Series*, N° 112, August, BAD.

Mourji, F., Decaluwé P., et P. Plane (2006), « Développement économique, croissance et réduction de la pauvreté : arbitrage ou synergies ? », *Développement face à la pauvreté*, Réseau analyse économique et développement, Economica, l'Agence universitaire de la Francophonie, Centre de Recherches pour le Développement International, Paris.

Moyes, P. (2009), *Mesurer les inégalités économiques*, Université de Bordeaux, GREThA UMR CNRS 5113, n° 2009-06, France.

Mussard, S. et M. Terreza (2009), Décomposition des mesures d'inégalités : le cas des coefficients de Gini et d'entropie, *Louvain EconomicReview* 75 (2).

Nashold, F. (2009), "Microeconomic Determinants of Income Inequality in Rural Pakistan", *The Journal ofDevelopment Studies*, Vol 45, N° 5, p. 746-768.

Ortiz, I. et M. Cummins (2012), *L'inégalité mondiale. La répartition des Revenus dans 141 pays*, UNICEF, New York.

Peluso, E. et A. Trannoy (2005), "Does less inequality among households mean less inequality among individuals?", *Journal of Economic Theory*, 133, p. 568-578.

Petemoya, J-C. (2005), « La pauvreté au Sud-Kivu : concept et mesure », *Discussion Paper*, N° 2005-01, LEAD, UCB.

Petemoya, J.C. (2006), « Mesure et analyse de la pauvreté au Sud Kivu », *Discussion Paper*, N°15, Avril, LEAD UCB.

Picketty, T. (2002), *Economie des inégalités*, La Découverte, quatrième édition, Paris.

PNUD (2006), *Profil de pauvreté en milieu rural, Enquête sur les*

Conditions de Vie en milieu rural – ECVR – 2003, région de l'Equateur, République Centre Africaine.

PNUD (2009), *Province du Sud Kivu. Profil résumé, pauvreté et conditions de vie des ménages*, mars, PNUD/RDC.

PNUD (2011), *Rapport sur le développement humain 2011. Durabilité et équité : Un meilleur avenir pour tous*, New York, USA.

Ravallion, M. (1996), *Comparaisons de la pauvreté, concepts et méthodes*, LSMS, document de travail n°122, Banque Mondiale, Washington DC.

Rawls, J. (1987), *Théorie de la justice*, Seuil, Paris.

Sala-i-Martin, X. (2002), «The World Distribution of Income (Estimated from Individual Country Distributions) », *Working Paper*, 8933, Washington, D.C., NBER.

Sen, A. (1999), *Development as Freedom*, Oxford University Press, New Delhi.

Shorrocks, A.F., (1982), «Inequality Decomposition by Factor Component », *Econometrica*,vol 50, p.193-211.

Stewart, F., Brown, G., et L. Mancini (2005), "Why Horizontal Inequalities Matter: Some Implications for Measurement", Centre for Research on Inequality, Human Security and Ethnicity , CRISE WORKING PAPER N° 19, Juin; UK.

Von Neumann J., et O. Morgenstern, (1944), *Theory of Games and Economic Behavior*, Princeton: Princeton University Press.

Zhu, N. (2002), « Déterminants de la participation aux activités non agricoles et du revenu des ménages ruraux : le cas de la Chine », CERDI, Etudes et Documents, Ec 2002, p.23.

Capital humain et croissance du bien-être à Kagera, en Tanzanie

Christian Kamala Kaghoma

RÉSUMÉ/ABSTRACT

Objectif : Questionner l'effet du capital humain perçu comme stock de santé et d'éducation d'un ménage sur l'évolution du bien-être dans le temps dans la région de Kagera, en Tanzanie.

Méthodologie : Le papier prend appui sur le modèle de Ramsey de planification de la consommation étendu au cas d'un ménage qui, dans son processus de génération de revenu, bénéficie d'externalités liées à sa dotation en capital humain. Les données utilisées sont issues d'une enquête longitudinale collectée, entre 1991 et 2004, dans la région de Kagera en Tanzanie et connue comme la Kagera Health and Development Survey (KHDS). Les régressions en quantile y sont appliquées pour obtenir les résultats.

Résultats : En plus de l'existence d'une convergence de la croissance du bien-être des ménages entre les différents clusters et au sein d'eux, l'ensemble des résultats révèle un effet non-linéaire de l'éducation sur la croissance du bien-être du ménage. Ils permettent ainsi de généraliser, aux aspects autres que pécuniaires, la non-linéarité du retour sur investissement éducatif, déjà bien documenté dans le cas du salaire. Quant à la santé, elle a un effet positif et linéaire sur l'évolution du bien-être dans le temps. Un tel résultat contraste avec ceux des travaux portant sur les pays développés qui ont plutôt démontré une relation en "U renversé" entre la santé (surpoids ou obésité) et le salaire, la capacité de travailler et la pauvreté.

Mots-clés : Education, Santé, Bien-être, Régression en quantile.

JEL classification : I10, I21, I31, C29.

Introduction

Les travaux sur la croissance à partir des données microéconomiques, dans les pays en développement en général et en Afrique en particulier, ne sont pas nombreux, probablement faute d'existence des données appropriées. Cependant, en dépit de cette rareté, quelques travaux ont pris cette perspective, soit pour analyser les déterminants de la croissance microéconomique (Gunning *et al*, 2000 ; Deininger et Okidi, 2003), soit pour analyser les sources des divergences et convergences dans la croissance des ménages (Ravallion et Jalan, 1996) ou pour analyser les effets des risques aussi bien agricoles (Thomas, 2009 ; Elbers *et al*, 2007) que sanitaires (Dercon, 2004). Dans les cas respectifs de la Chine rurale et du Pérou, Jalan et Ravallion (2002) et Herrera *et al* (2005) se fondent sur le même cadre théorique pour, cette fois, analyser l'effet de la localisation géographique, les dotations publiques en ressources ainsi que l'offre des services publics qui leur sont associés sur la croissance du bien-être du ménage et la possibilité d'existence de trappes de pauvreté.

Si ces travaux ont le mérite d'avoir mis en évidence les facteurs à même d'influencer la dynamique du bien-être des ménages dans le temps, force est de constater qu'à l'exception de Dercon (2004), ces travaux n'insistent pas sur le rôle du capital humain, éducation et/ou santé, dans ce processus. Pourtant, depuis le travail séminal de Schultz (1961), il semble se dégager un consensus entre économistes et décideurs de politique économique non seulement sur le rôle de ce capital dans le développement mais surtout sur la nécessité d'orienter davantage de ressources vers l'investissement en capital humain, particulièrement dans les pays en développement[1].

L'idée sous-jacente à cette prescription est qu'étant le seul actif le plus à la disposition des populations pauvres, ne serait-ce qu'en termes de force de travail, l'investissement en capital humain, est de nature à doter les individus, des capacités leur permettant non seulement de participer activement au processus de croissance économique mais surtout d'accroître leurs capacités de génération de revenu et d'amélioration de leur propre bien-être (Schultz, 1975 ; Berthélemy, 2008; Unterhalter, 2009 ; Unterhalter 2012). D'autre part, et cela dans le cas particulier de ceux qui se focalisent sur la dynamique de la pauvreté, tout en analysant les flux d'entrée et de sortie de pauvreté à travers le temps, ils ne donnent qu'une information partielle aux décideurs de politique économique dont le souci est de connaître l'ampleur d'actions à entreprendre afin d'améliorer la situation globale de la société.

En effet, un ménage peut voir son bien-être varier, et parfois même sensiblement, d'une période à l'autre

1. Cette idée est relayée par le poids important accordé à ces investissements dans les Objectifs du Millénaire pour le Développement (OMD).

sans que cela ne le conduise à changer son statut de pauvreté. La prise en compte de cet aspect et l'approfondissement de la compréhension de la variation du bien-être, du fait du capital humain détenu par le ménage ou de ses investissements dans cette dernière forme de capital, requiert par conséquent d'appréhender aussi ces phénomènes de croissance du bien-être et d'identifier les déterminants socioéconomiques qui leur sont associés.

Ainsi, ce papier questionne l'effet du capital humain perçu comme stock de santé et d'éducation d'un ménage sur l'évolution du bien-être de ce dernier en prenant appui sur le cas de la région de Kagera en Tanzanie. En plus de la disponibilité des données de panel des ménages et des individus qui y vivent, le type des données appropriées pour une analyse dynamique du bien-être, la région de Kagera, dans le Nord-Ouest de la Tanzanie, présente les caractéristiques de bon nombre d'autres régions non seulement de la Tanzanie mais aussi celles du continent africain. En effet, pendant que la Tanzanie a connu une croissance économique de 4% l'an en moyenne entre 1994 et 2004 et que la pauvreté a sensiblement baissé à Dar-es-Salam, la capitale économique (passant d'une incidence de 28 à 18 %) et dans certains centres urbains, dans la partie continentale, en particulier, elle n'a été que très modeste.

A Kagera plus spécifiquement, elle n'a baissé que de 36.8 à 35.7% entre 1991 et 2000/2001 (United Republic of Tanzania, 2007 ; Demombynes and Hoogeveen, 2007 ; Woods, 2008 ; Wedgwood, 2010), traduisant le véritable défi de lutte contre la pauvreté pour le pays pris globalement. Bien plus, une telle image reflète les réalités de la majorité des pays d'Afrique Sub-saharienne qui, durant la dernière décennie, ont réalisé des taux de croissance très élevés sans que ces performances macroéconomiques n'aillent de pair avec l'amélioration des conditions de vie de leurs populations (UNECA, 2008).

Le reste de ce papier est structuré comme suit : la deuxième section discute le cadre théorique d'analyse, celui de la croissance du bien-être dans le temps sans que cette dernière ne soit associée à un quelconque état de pauvreté. La troisième section en présente la spécification économétrique adoptée, ainsi qu'une brève discussion des données utilisées. Avant la conclusion, la quatrième section présente les résultats empiriques et leur interprétation.

2. Cadre théorique d'analyse et spécification économétrique

2.1. Cadre théorique : le modèle de croissance microéconomique

Comme dans Jalan et Ravallion (2002) et Herrera *et al* (2005), le cadre d'analyse choisi ici est le modèle de Ramsey de planification de consommation étendu au cas d'un ménage qui fait face aux externalités liées à sa dotation en capital humain – dans le processus de génération de revenu. Le ménage finance sa consommation entièrement à partir de son revenu actuel, lequel est produit selon une fonction de production qui admet comme argument le capital et un vecteur de variables caractéristiques de la communauté et qui peuvent avoir un effet positif ou négatif sur le rendement du capital :

$$y_{ht}=F(K_{ht},GR_{ht}) \quad (1)$$

A la différence de Jalan et Ravallion et dans la lignée de Dercon (2004), le capital est considéré dans son sens le plus large possible en cela qu'il englobe à la fois le capital physique et le capital humain. Ainsi, y_{ht} est le revenu total à la Becker ou le revenu potentiel, c'est-à-dire le revenu que le ménage pourrait réaliser s'il utilisait entièrement son capital physique et humain pour le produire. Dans le modèle de départ, les ménages sont considérés comme n'ayant pas accès au marché du crédit et cela parait réaliste dans le cas de Kagera. Ainsi, le revenu potentiel peut être utilisé par le ménage soit pour accroître son stock de capital (en accumulant des actifs physiques ou en investissant dans le capital humain de ses membres) soit pour la consommation :

$$F(K_{ht},GR_{ht})=K_{h,t+1} - (1-\delta)K_{ht} + c_{ht} \quad (2)$$

avec δ le taux de dépréciation du capital, humain comme physique. En supposant que le ménage a une forte préférence pour le futur et qu'il maximise la valeur actuelle de son flux d'utilité (u_{ht}) au temps 0 sous la contrainte budgétaire (2), on peut écrire ce problème de manière suivante :

$$\underbrace{max}_{\{c_{ht}\}t=0...,+\infty} \quad \sum_{t=0}^{+\infty} \beta^t u_{ht}$$

$$s.c\ K_{h,t+1} = (1-\delta)K_{ht} + F(K_{ht}, GR_{ht}) - c_{ht}\ \forall t \geq 0 \quad (3)$$

Ce programme (3) conduit à l'ensemble des conditions de premier ordre traduites comme :

$$[F'_K(K_{ht}, G_{ht}) + 1 - \delta]u'_{ht}(c_{ht}) = u'_{h,t-1}(c_{h,t-1})\forall t \geq 1 \quad (4)$$

L'expression (4) indique qu'une augmentation dans la productivité marginale du capital induit une augmentation de la consommation si l'utilité marginale de la consommation est décroissante. La particularité de ce modèle est que les différentes externalités tant géographiques que celles liées au capital physique et humain peuvent influencer le taux de croissance de la consommation à travers les différents effets sur la productivité marginale du capital. Pour obtenir la forme estimable de cette équation, Jalan et Ravallion (2002) suggèrent que soit considérée une fonction d'utilité iso-élastique et de la forme suivante :

$$u_{ht}(c_{ht}) = \frac{(c_{ht})^{1-\delta}}{1-\delta} \quad (5)$$

avec $\delta \in$ 0,1. Jalan et Ravallion (2002) indiquent qu'après avoir remplacé des utilités marginales correspondantes dans les conditions de premier ordre et en linéarisant, la résolution de (3) conduit à la forme réduite suivante[1] :

$$lnc_{it} - lnc_{it-1} = \alpha + \beta lnc_{it-1} + \delta X_{it} + u_{it} \quad (6)$$

Avec c_{it} la consommation per capita du ménage, α une source de croissance commune pour tous les ménages, X_{it} l'ensemble des variables explicatives, y compris celles relatives aussi bien à la santé qu'à l'éducation au niveau du ménage ainsi que celles de contrôle.

2.2. *Spécification économétrique*

Une question standard dans l'analyse empirique de la croissance est celle de savoir s'il existe une convergence entre les niveaux de vie des populations des divers pays. Au niveau du ménage, la même question consiste à savoir si le bien-être des pauvres croît au même rythme que celui des non pauvres, après avoir contrôlé les autres variables qui déterminent l'état stationnaire. Une valeur négative pour β suggérerait donc une convergence[2]. Pour bien approfondir l'analyse, la consommation de l'année de base (1991) est désagrégée entre clusters[3] représentés par v et la différence entre cette moyenne et le niveau de consommation même est donnée par :

$$lnc_{it} - lnc_{it-1} = \alpha + \beta_1(lnc_{it-1} - lnc_{vt-1}) + \beta_2 lnc_{vt-1} + \delta X_{it} + u_{it} \quad (7)$$

Si β_1 n'est pas égal à β_2, on peut déduire des résultats que la convergence entre villages et entre ménages se fait à des vitesses différentes.

Les travaux existants dans la littérature (Herrera *et al*, 2003 ; Dercon, 2004 ; Thomas, 2009) estiment les coefficients de l'équation (7) par les moindres carrés ordinaires (MCO). Mais, dans le cadre de ce papier, on recourt aux régressions en quantile. En effet, dans le cadre théorique développé plus haut, les rendements des différentes variables explicatives sont supposés être identiques tout au long de la distribution de la variable dépendante. De plus en plus, les travaux empiriques sur le capital humain confirment l'hétérogénéité des rendements de l'investissement en capital humain entre individus, groupes sociaux et à travers le temps (Girma et Kedir, 2005 ; Söderbom *et al*, 2006 ; Kahyarara et Teal, 2008). Il est donc important d'adopter une modélisation empirique compatible avec les modèles de croissance et permettant, à la fois, de prendre en compte cette hétérogénéité à ces

1. Dans les travaux antérieurs comme ceux de Dercon (2004) ou Justino *et al* (2008), l'analyse part de cette forme réduite.

2. D'une part, quand, la variation de l'indicateur du bien-être croît avec l'indicateur lui-même, les riches de la période initiale vont plus de l'avant. Ceci est connu comme "divergence inconditionnelle". D'autre part, quand ce sont les pauvres de l'année de base qui avancent le plus, diminuera à mesure que augmente, et dans ce cas on est en présence d'une "convergence inconditionnelle" (Fields *et al*, 2003c).

3. Dans le cadre de l'enquête KHDS, chaque cluster contient 16 ménages.

trois différents niveaux d'analyse. La régression en quantile remplit bien une telle tâche.

Une régression en quantile est une régression économétrique dans laquelle un *quantile* (ou percentile) spécifique de la variable à expliquer est exprimé comme une fonction linéaire des caractéristiques du sujet étudié. Elle contraste avec une régression MCO, où c'est la moyenne d'une variable (de réponse) continue qui est exprimée comme une fonction linéaire d'un ensemble de variables indépendantes et explicatives. Le $p^{ième}$ quantile de la distribution d'une variable aléatoire y est un nombre q tel que P (y ≤ q) pour un modèle noté de la manière suivante :

$$y_i = \beta_0 + \beta_1 x_{1i} + \beta_2 x_{2i} + \cdots + \beta_k x_{ki} + \varepsilon_i \quad (8)$$

Dans une régression par la méthode des Moindres Carrés, les coefficients sont déterminés de façon à minimiser la somme des carrés des écarts de la droite de régression. Cependant, dans les régressions en quantile, si on veut modéliser le $p^{ième}$ quantile (o < p < 1) de la distribution conditionnelle comme une fonction linéaire des caractéristiques du sujet étudié, on définit la fonction suivante :

$$h_i = \begin{cases} p \; si \; e_i > 0 \\ (1-p) sinon \end{cases} \quad (9)$$

Les coefficients de la régression (b_0, b_1, b_2..., b_k) sont ainsi choisis de manière à minimiser la fonction suivante[1] :

$$\sum_{i=1}^{n} |e_i|_i \, h_i \quad (10)$$

où

$$e_i = y_i - (b_0 + b_1 x_{1i} + b_2 x_{2i} + \cdots + b_k x_{ki}) \quad (11)$$

Ainsi, le quantile voulu de la distribution de la variable de réponse, conditionnel aux valeurs des variables explicatives, peut être donné par :

$$Q_{y_i}[\tau \vee x_{1i}, x_{1i}, \ldots, x_{ki}] = \beta_0(\tau) + \beta_1(\tau) x_{1i} + \beta_2(\tau) x_{2i} + \cdots + \beta_k(\tau) x_{ki} \quad (12)$$

où Q représente le τ-quantile de la distribution conditionnelle y_i. Ainsi, les paramètres de la régression $\beta_k(\tau)$ représentent le changement dans le quantile spécifié, du fait d'un changement unitaire dans x_k.

Il est possible d'estimer l'équation (8) en utilisant les techniques proposées par Koenker et Bassett (1978) et développées par Rodgers (1992). Cependant, ces dernières sous-estiment l'écart-type des coefficients quand la distribution du terme aléatoire est hétéroscédastistique. Mais, le recours aux techniques d'estimation reposant sur le bootstraping permet d'y remédier.

1. Ainsi par exemple, pour un modèle de régression à la médiane (50ième percentile), sera égal à 0.5 pour toutes les observations. Les coefficients seraient alors choisis de telle sorte que soit minimisée la moitié de la somme de l'écart absolu de la ligne de la régression. C'est pour cette raison que la régression médiane est aussi connue comme la régression à moindres écarts absolus.

C'est ce qui est fait ici étant donné que l'analyse n'est pas menée séparément selon que les ménages vivent dans le milieu urbain ou rural et qu'une telle agrégation peut facilement exposer les estimations obtenues à une forte hétéroscédasticité.

Comparée à une régression MCO, la régression en quantile présente plusieurs avantages :

- (a) plutôt que d'évaluer comment le centre d'une distribution conditionnelle change avec le changement des caractéristiques du sujet analysé, elle permet d'évaluer comment chaque percentile de la distribution conditionnelle est affectée par des modifications dans les caractéristiques du sujet étudié. En examinant multiples percentiles de la distribution conditionnelle, on peut savoir si la distribution entière, plutôt que sa seule moyenne, change avec les caractéristiques du sujet étudié. En effet, il est possible que certains percentiles soient plus affectés que d'autres par certaines de ces caractéristiques ;
- (b) les modèles de régression en quantile sont additifs. Ainsi, les coefficients peuvent être interprétés comme un changement dans un percentile donné de la distribution associé avec un changement unitaire d'une caractéristique ;
- (c) il existe des versions censurées des régressions en quantile de sorte que si les valeurs de la variable à expliquer varient dans une certaine marge qu'elles ne peuvent dépasser, il est toujours possible d'appliquer cette méthode d'estimation ;
- (d) pour toute fonction monotone h, on a $Q_{h(y)}(\tau lx) = h(Q_y\ (\tau lx))$, un résultat en contraste avec le problème de transformation qui se pose généralement dans le cas des MCO pour lesquels $E(h(ylx))\neq h(E(yVx))$.

3. Données et variables utilisées

3.1. Les données

Les données utilisées dans le cadre de ce papier sont issues d'une enquête longitudinale collectée dans la région de la Kagera, dans le Nord-ouest de la Tanzanie, et connue comme la *Kagera Health and Development Survey* (KHDS)[1]. Initialement menée par la Banque Mondiale et *Muhimbili University College of Health Sciences* (MUCHS), la base KHDS contient à ce jour 6 vagues d'enquêtes et couvre la période allant de 1991 à 2010. Les quatre premières vagues ont été collectées entre septembre 1991 et janvier 1994, à 6 ou 7 mois d'intervalle ; la cinquième vague en 2004, soit 13 ans après la première vague et la sixième au cours du dernier trimestre de l'année 2010[2]. La fusion des quatre premières vagues a permis de constituer la base à partir de laquelle ont été retracées les unités statistiques reprises dans les enquêtes de 2004 et 2010. Des 912

1. Voir Beegle et al (2006) pour tous les détails techniques sur la base KHDS ou le site web de Economic Development Initiatives (EDI-Kagera): http://www.edi-africa.com/research/KHDS.htm.
2. Les données de cette dernière vague n'étaient pas encore accessibles pendant la rédaction de ce papier.

ménages initialement interviewés en 1991, 832 ont été recontactés en 2004. Avec la possibilité d'éclatement des ménages, la vague d'enquête de 2004 a couvert un total de 2774 ménages ; ce qui traduit un taux d'attrition très faible comparativement à ceux observés dans les panels existants sur les pays en développement[1].

Couvrant une si longue période, cette base reste l'une des rares à même de permettre une analyse des effets du bien-être dans une perspective de long terme dans un pays en développement. En effet, en plus de la prise en compte du volet santé qui en est le principal objectif, elle couvre plusieurs dimensions relatives au bien-être des individus observés et de leurs ménages respectifs. Le comportement de survie des ménages est conditionné par les prix locaux, les services et les programmes disponibles. Pour en tenir compte, KHDS a aussi collecté des données sur les communautés à partir desquelles les ménages ont été tirés, les marchés locaux, les structures de soins médicaux les plus proches et toutes les écoles primaires existant dans la communauté. Pour permettre l'analyse du bien-être au sein des ménages, un module extensif sur la consommation a été administré en 1991 et en 2004. Ce module a été explicitement construit par l'équipe de *Economic Development Initiatives-Kagera* (EDI) pour permettre la comparaison de la consommation entre 1991 et 2004. La base KHDS ayant collecté aussi les prix des divers produits consommés par les ménages, dans la construction des dépenses de consommation, toutes les valeurs reportées en 2004 ont été déflatées à partir des niveaux des prix observés en 1991 pour chaque produit retenu dans la base (Beegle *et al*, 2006, p30[2]).

De ces 2774 repris dans la base KHDS en 2004, seuls 2236 sont retenus pour l'analyse dans ce papier du fait du traitement des données et de la conciliation des variables entre les vagues de 1991 et celle de 2004. En effet, ces 2236 ménages sont ceux qui ont fait l'objet de toutes les cinq vagues d'enquête réalisées entre 1991 et 2004. Pour une si longue période, il y a eu certes une variation de niveau de bien-être entre 1991 et 2004 sans que celle-ci ne soit nécessairement

1. Alderman et al (2001) font une revue des panels dans les pays en développement et trouvent un taux d'attrition, c'est-à-dire une perte d'individus observés à travers le temps, allant de 15.5 à 1.5 % par an, pour des bases couvrant une période généralement plus courte (2 à 5 ans) que la KHDS. Par exemple, les Living Standards Measurement Study (LSMS) de la Banque Mondiale qui sont une autre source de données de panels largement utilisée et citée dans le cas des pays en développement, retiennent la moitié des observations et remplacent l'autre moitié des ménages enquêtés entre les années. Ceci rend impossible le suivi des individus ou des ménages pour plus de deux ans et réduit, de ce fait, toute possibilité d'évaluer l'importance de la variation du bien-être pendant un temps relativement long.

2. Un module spécial sur la consommation et sa comparabilité entre 1991 et 2004, est disponible sur le site de EDI - Kagera : http://www.edi-africa.com/research/khds/introduction.htm.

associée à un mouvement d'entrée ou de sortie de la pauvreté.

3.2. *Présentation des variables.*

3.2.1. *La variable dépendante*

Le logarithme naturel du total mensuel des dépenses de consommation par tête en équivalent adulte[1] est retenu comme variable dépendante. Cette transformation logarithmique de l'indicateur du bien-être est dictée par le fait que, dans l'estimation économétrique, elle permet de mieux approximer une distribution normale que l'indicateur lui-même.

3.2.2. *Les variables explicatives*

Le choix des variables explicatives du bien-être est essentiellement fait de manière à ne retenir que des variables dont l'exogénéité par rapport à la consommation peut être établie soit directement soit indirectement. Un nombre varié d'éléments représentant les dotations du ménage déterminent, selon certaines conditions de l'environnement physique, sociopolitique et économique dans lequel ledit ménage évolue, son niveau de bien-être. De ces éléments, le capital humain et le capital physique restent certes les deux principales dotations mais globalement, ils peuvent être regroupés en deux grands ensembles : ceux relatifs au ménage lui-même et aux individus qui le composent d'une part et, ceux relatifs à la communauté dans laquelle ils évoluent, d'autre part.

L'attention étant ici focalisée sur le capital humain, les variables y relatives sont regroupées en deux grands ensembles, dont l'un englobe les variables relatives à l'éducation et l'autre celles relatives à la santé. Comme déjà indiqué plus haut, le capital humain est incarné dans les différents membres qui constituent le ménage ; et la capacité de ceux-ci à l'utiliser ou à le faire valoir efficacement sur le marché du travail dépend fortement de l'âge et du sexe des membres du ménage. Ainsi, en association avec les éléments démographiques comme suggéré par quelques études antérieures (Grootaert, 1997 ; Rolleston, 2011), le premier ensemble des variables saisissant le capital humain comprend la proportion d'enfants (de 0 à 14)[2] et la proportion des vieux (65 ans et plus) qu'il y a dans le ménage. Ces deux variables du capital humain permettent aussi de saisir l'effet du taux de dépendance.

L'éducation du ménage est perçue à travers celle des tous ses membres en âge de scolarisation et qui ne

1. Ne pas tenir compte de cet ajustement implique (i) que tous les membres du ménage reçoivent une allocation égale des biens consommés compte non tenu de l'âge et du sexe, (ii) tout membre du ménage a les mêmes besoins compte non tenu de l'âge et du genre et (iii) le coût par individu, pour deux, trois ou plusieurs personnes vivant ensemble est le même que s'ils vivaient séparément (Mukherjee et Benson, 2003 ; Lanjouw, 1999).

2. Une telle perception repose essentiellement sur l'acception consacrée par le Bureau International du Travail (BIT) pour lequel, toute personne de moins de 14/15 ans qui travaille, est un enfant travailleur.

vont plus à l'école : chef de ménage et tous les autres adultes qui s'y trouvent. Il s'agit d'une variable continue représentée par le nombre d'années de scolarité achevées. Mais pour tenir compte de la particularité de la Tanzanie, on considère aussi l'alphabétisation des adultes et la formation de l'école coranique[1] qui sont considérées comme correspondant à une année d'éducation achevée. Ainsi, la variable niveau d'instruction (éducation) prend la valeur 1 pour toute personne qui a bénéficié d'un programme d'alphabétisation ou, alternativement, a fait l'école coranique alors que dans le cas d'absence totale d'instruction d'une quelconque forme, elle prend la valeur « zéro ». De ce fait, pour le reste des niveaux d'instruction, la valeur retenue correspond à la classe achevée la plus élevée plus l'unité. Ainsi, l'éducation est subdivisée en plusieurs catégories selon le niveau d'instruction le plus élevé atteint par chacun des membres du ménage : sans instruction, primaire, secondaire premier-cycle, secondaire second-cycle et postsecondaire.

L'éducation du chef du ménage et son expérience professionnelle pouvant profondément influencer la manière dont le ménage est relié au marché de l'emploi (type d'emploi recherché ou même exercé déjà ou en cours d'exercice, installation d'une entreprise familiale, etc.), l'accent est mis sur le niveau d'instruction du chef de ménage. Ainsi, le fait d'avoir un certain niveau d'instruction pour le chef de ménage et l'appartenance de ce dernier à une catégorie donnée de détention du capital-éducation que cela implique, peuvent être un atout important pour permettre au ménage d'éviter la pauvreté, du fait qu'ils pourraient induire un accès à des emplois hautement rémunérés dans le secteur formel. Enfin, l'âge du chef de ménage, en niveau et élevé au carré, capte l'expérience professionnelle et la phase atteinte dans le cycle de la vie du ménage.

La santé est une notion très complexe du fait qu'elle sous-entend plusieurs dimensions et, pour cette même raison, sa mesure reste encore un sujet à controverse (Mwabu, 2001 ; Audibert *et al*, 2003, Audibert, 2009). Plus que la seule absence de maladie ou d'infirmité, l'Organisation Mondiale de la Santé (OMS) définit la santé en des termes qui renvoient non seulement à la promotion du bien-être mais aussi impliquent un accès au traitement et une réhabilitation des personnes affectées tant par des désordres physiques et mentaux que sociaux. Cette définition renvoie beaucoup plus à la détermination d'indicateurs à même de mesurer ces diverses dimensions de la santé. On comprend dès lors la complexité desdites mesures et, en conséquence, la multiplicité d'indicateurs y associés étant donné que

1. L'inclusion de cette catégorie est motivée par le besoin de faire ressortir l'effet qu'une telle formation pourrait avoir sur le niveau de vie de celui qui en dispose et qui le différencierait de celui qui n'a tout simplement pas appris.

différentes dimensions de la santé sont enclines à avoir différents effets sur les possibles issues de la participation au marché du travail. Ainsi, on retrouve dans la littérature empirique une série d'indicateurs dont les principaux sont notamment la morbidité, les mesures anthropométriques et la consommation des nutriments (kilocalories, grammes de protéines, micronutriments).

Les données sur la morbidité sont généralement basées sur l'autoévaluation qui est une mesure subjective et, très souvent, porteuse d'importantes erreurs de mesure. Ces dernières peuvent être dues à l'information, au niveau d'instruction et donc au revenu[1]. Les mesures objectives comprennent la consommation des nutriments et tous les aspects anthropométriques utilisés pour capter la santé. Les mesures anthropométriques les plus couramment utilisées sont la taille et l'Indice de Masse Corporelle[2] (IMC, égal au rapport du poids en Kg sur la taille en mètres au carré). Bien qu'objectives, ces mesures anthropométriques impliquent aussi plusieurs dimensions de la santé. Etant une combinaison de la taille et du poids d'un individu, l'IMC est considéré comme l'indicateur adéquat du statut sanitaire individuel particulièrement quand les adultes constituent l'unité de référence dans l'analyse (Cawley, 2004 ; Wagstaff, 2007 ; Molini *et al*, 2010) et que celle-ci porte sur un milieu où il y a une relative diversité ethnique (Khongsdier, 2001).

En effet, pendant que le poids est considéré comme un très bon indicateur du statut nutritionnel actuel, la taille capte les absorptions nutritionnelles cumulées depuis l'enfance, de sorte que la combinaison des deux induit une bonne synthèse du stock (long terme) et du flux (court terme) du statut sanitaire. La première contribue aux variations de l'IMC et un faible niveau ainsi qu'un niveau très élevé de ce dernier accroissent la vulnérabilité face à des épisodes de maladie. En tant que tel, il est à la fois fonction des investissements tant présents que passés dans la santé (Ainsworth et Dayton, 2003 ; Strauss et Thomas, 2008). Bien plus, il existe une relation bidirectionnelle entre la morbidité et l'IMC d'une part, et d'autre part, entre l'IMC et la mortalité[3]. De ce fait, il semble bien convenir pour l'analyse menée dans ce travail étant donné que l'indicateur choisi pour la mesure du bien-être est la consommation qui, elle-même, a un pendant plus "permanent" que ponctuel.

Ainsi, la santé du ménage est captée par une mesure

1. En effet, si les individus à revenu élevé sont plus enclins à se considérer comme malades alors, caeteris paribus, il sera difficile de séparer l'effet de l'incidence de la maladie sur le salaire de celui lié à l'erreur dans le report.

2. En effet l'OMS admet la classification suivante d'états nutritionnels :

– Sous poids si	IMC < 18.5 ;
– Marge normale si	IMC [18.5 – 24.9] ;
– Surpoids si	IMC ≥ 25 ;
– Pré-obésité si	IMC [25 – 29.9] ;
– Obésité si	IMC ≥ 30.

3. Voir Ainsworth et Dayton (2003) pour un petit survol des travaux cliniques sur ce lien.

anthropométrique, la moyenne de l'Indice de Masse Corporelle (IMC) des adultes du ménage. Comme le montrent certains travaux empiriques (Strauss, 1986 ; Thomas et Strauss, 1997), en tant qu'indicateur de santé, l'IMC est corrélé avec la productivité et le niveau de salaire auquel hommes comme femmes peuvent prétendre sur le marché du travail, particulièrement dans les catégories les moins instruites de la population[1]. En conséquence, il peut, comme toute variable de santé, avoir un effet sur le niveau du bien-être d'un ménage, à travers son effet sur la capacité de ses membres à générer un revenu (Kedir, 2009 ; Classen, 2010 ; Abegunde et Stanciole, 2008)[2].

Le capital physique constitue la deuxième composante importante de la dotation des ménages en actifs. Ainsi, des informations sur deux ensembles d'actifs productifs sont incluses dans la régression : la quantité de terre agricole détenue par le ménage quel que puisse en être le mode d'acquisition et la valeur des équipements agricoles (la part des actifs agricoles dans le total des actifs du ménage). Ces deux éléments sont les indicateurs les plus importants du potentiel du ménage à créer un revenu à travers sa propre activité. A ceux-ci s'ajoute la valeur d'actifs détenus par le ménage. Il est vrai que ces derniers ne contribuent pas directement au processus de création de revenu par le ménage. Leur contribution est indirecte en cela qu'ils peuvent servir de garantie contre d'éventuels chocs sur le revenu du ménage ou dans le cas de la sollicitation d'un prêt par exemple. Ils servent ainsi au lissage du revenu dans le temps (Holmes, 2003).

La composante productive du capital physique lie le ménage au marché du travail à travers deux canaux. Le premier est relatif au volume de travail que le ménage sera prêt à offrir pour générer le revenu ; c'est dans ce cadre qu'il conviendrait de placer l'auto-emploi. Ainsi, bien que le rendement de chaque type d'actifs soit différent et dépendant de l'importance du capital-éducation et du degré d'entrepreneuriat des membres du ménage, plus un ménage détient un tel capital, moins il est exposé au risque d'être pauvre. Ensuite, la présence ou mieux le niveau du capital physique détenu par un ménage peut influencer son choix en termes de segment de l'emploi salarié du marché du travail. Ce lien peut tout aussi bien être positif que négatif. L'existence d'une entreprise ou une activité du ménage peut dissuader ou pousser ses membres à rechercher un type d'éducation conduisant aux travaux rémunérés par de hauts salaires. Alternativement,

1. En effet, il est relié à l'absorption d'énergie ainsi qu'à la capture du maximum d'oxygène (VO2 maximum) pendant le travail physique qui est, lui-même, associé à la capacité aérobie et à l'endurance indépendamment de l'énergie absorbée (Strauss et Thomas, 1998).

2. Classen (2010) fait une large revue des travaux qui ressortent l'effet de la santé, particulièrement celui d'un excès de poids, sur l'accès à l'emploi d'une part et de l'autre sur la productivité au travail.

l'absence de capital physique dans le ménage - et l'incapacité d'emprunter qui s'ensuit - peut forcer les membres de ce dernier à accepter des travaux offrant de bas salaires, quand bien même ils peuvent être en mesure de générer des rendements élevés à partir de la capacité de travail qu'ils détiennent.

Les régressions saisissant le lien entre actifs productifs et bien-être procèdent de deux manières alternatives. La première qui est déjà décrite plus haut procède par l'inclusion, dans la régression, de la valeur des actifs comme une mesure des gains (revenus) potentiels. La voie alternative consiste à analyser les revenus courants réalisés par le ménage ; ce qui peut être fait à travers l'inclusion dans le modèle de la part des revenus provenant des diverses sources : salaire, revenu agricole, revenu non agricole. Pour ce qui est des variables de segmentation, elles peuvent être nombreuses mais pour les besoins de l'analyse menée ici, seules les plus importantes d'entre elles sont considérées. Au premier rang de celles-ci, figure le statut matrimonial du chef de ménage. A la suite des auteurs comme Bartlett et Callahan (1984) qui relèvent l'effet du statut matrimonial sur le gain d'un individu dans les pays industrialisés, Schoeni (1995) le démontre dans le cas des pays en développement[1]. Enfin, le secteur d'activité des adultes du ménage est inclus comme un ensemble de variables catégorielles.

4. Présentation et discussion des résultats

Dans l'estimation du modèle de croissance de la consommation, les travaux antérieurs (Jalan et Ravallion, 2002 ; Herrera *et al*, 2003 ; Dercon, 2004 ; Thomas, 2009) soulignent l'éventuelle endogénéité de la consommation décalée, celle de l'année initiale dans le cas de ce chapitre. Ne pas tenir compte de ce problème, quand il existe, résulte tout simplement en une surestimation de l'effet de cette consommation décalée dans l'explication de la variation de la consommation. Cela revient alors à renforcer fallacieusement l'existence de la convergence entre ménages pendant la période sous étude. Ainsi, pour se fixer d'abord sur la plausibilité de l'endogénéité et déterminer la technique à adopter dans l'estimation, un test d'endogénéité

1. En effet, après avoir contrôlé l'effet de plusieurs variables comme l'éducation, la race, la localisation et le nombre d'heures prestées, il trouve que le fait d'être marié justifie la différence dans la marge de 0 à 30 % pour les travailleurs de sexe masculin. La littérature empirique sur le fonctionnement du marché du travail dans les pays en développement relève que celui-ci fonctionne de manière imparfaite (Vijverberg, 1993 ; Tansel, 1997). La Tanzanie en général et la région de Kagera tout particulièrement ne dérogent pas à cette observation. Les travaux comme ceux de Knight et Sabot (1982) ou Sandefur et al (2006) indiquent que le genre est une potentielle source de segmentation du marché et de discrimination. Pour en tenir compte, le sexe du chef de ménage est considéré comme variable explicative dans les diverses régressions.

à la Durbin-Wu-Hausman est préalablement appliqué sur la consommation décalée.

Ce test procède en deux étapes dont la première consiste à régresser, sur la variable X supposée endogène, l'ensemble de tous ses corrélats. Ceux-ci sont constitués des variables considérées comme exogènes et entrant dans l'explication de la variable X. Dans la deuxième étape, on extrait les résidus que l'on joint à la variable X dans la régression du modèle initial, celui à partir duquel il y a eu soupçon d'endogénéité de X. Si les résidus de X sont significativement différents de zéro dans ce dernier modèle, alors on conclut à l'endogénéité de X et dans ce cas l'OLS n'est plus approprié pour l'estimation[1].

Le tableau 1 présente les résultats de la régression de la croissance de la consommation entre 1991 et 2004, après contrôle des variations de certaines caractéristiques du ménage comme spécifié dans l'équation (7). Le tableau 2 présente les mêmes résultats mais pour les régressions en quantile. En plus des variables relatives à la santé et à l'éducation dans le ménage, le choix des variables de contrôle est justifié par la possible influence que ces dernières pourraient avoir sur les préférences du ménage. Les autres variables qui interviennent dans l'analyse de la dynamique de la pauvreté menée au point précédent mais qui n'apparaissent pas directement ici ont été utilisées dans l'instrumentation de la consommation au cours de la période initiale.

Dans le tableau 1, la colonne (1) donne les résultats de l'équation permettant de tester à la fois la convergence au sein et entre les clusters. Le test de Wald d'égalité de coefficients et dont le résultat est donné dans la dernière ligne du tableau suggère une absence d'égalité entre les deux coefficients. Pour une première évaluation de la robustesse des résultats, les colonnes (3) et (4) reprennent les résultats de la régression en Double Moindre Carré (DMC) mais désagrégé respectivement pour, d'une part, les ménages qui ont connu une augmentation de leur consommation entre 1991 et 2004 et de l'autre, ceux pour qui elle a plutôt baissé[2].

Le coefficient correspondant à la valeur de la consommation de l'année initiale est négatif (-0.865[3])

1. Les résultats de l'application du test de Durbin-Wu-Hausman sont contenus dans le tableau A.1 en annexe. Le fait que le résidu soit largement significatif permet de conclure à l'endogénéité de la consommation de la période initiale, 1991 et par conséquent à la nécessité de son instrumentation. Ainsi, pour en tenir compte, on procède plutôt à l'estimation des moindres carrés en deux étapes.

2. Cette subdivision binaire est essentiellement dictée par le fait que tout au long de la distribution de la variation du logarithme de la consommation entre 1991 et 2004, les observations correspondant à une valeur égale à zéro sont très peu nombreuses. Ainsi, il n'y a aucun ménage qui ait maintenu exactement le même niveau de consommation entre les deux périodes.

3. Une telle valeur est certes légèrement supérieure à celle obtenue par les travaux précédents qui ont utilisé le même type de modèle (Dercon, 2004 ; Herrera et al, 2003 ; Thomas, 2009) et qui ont plutôt trouvé un coefficient oscillant autour de 0.3. Mais étant largement significatif (à 1%), il n'y a aucune raison de le rejeter.

TABLEAU 1 DÉTERMINANTS DE LA CROISSANCE DU BIEN-ÊTRE, 1991 – 2004				
	(1)	(2)	(3)	(4)
Log. Cons.:Différence vav Moyenne du Cluster	-0.865***			
	(33.81)			
Log. Cons.:Moyenne du Cluster	-0.298***			
	(7.34)			
Age du Chef de Ménage	0.002	-0.013***	-0.007*	-0.007
	(0.37)	(2.79)	(1.80)	(1.30)
Age du Chef de Ménage au Carré	-0.000	0.000**	0.000	0.000
	(0.78)	(2.14)	(0.96)	(1.43)
Taille du Ménage	-0.010	0.014	-0.013	0.034**
	(0.55)	(0.64)	(0.85)	(2.04)
Taille du Ménage au Carré	-0.005***	-0.006***	-0.003***	-0.003***
	(3.67)	(3.89)	(2.86)	(3.89)
IMC Moyen Mén.: Catég. Sous poids	-0.066**	-0.070**	-0.056*	-0.083**
	(2.27)	(2.07)	(1.75)	(2.26)
IMC Moyen Mén.:Catég. Surpoids ou Obèse	0.160**	0.044	0.056	-0.059
	(2.30)	(0.60)	(0.95)	(0.84)
Superficie Terre Mén. en Acre	0.008	-0.006	-0.010	-0.005
	(1.32)	(0.82)	(1.48)	(0.55)
Part Animal ds Actifs Physique	-0.087	-0.361***	-0.390***	-0.105
	(1.21)	(4.27)	(4.68)	(1.05)
Part Agricole ds Actifs Physique	-1.071	-5.405***	-7.123***	-1.680**
	(1.58)	(4.97)	(3.93)	(2.26)
Part Non-Agr. ds le Revenu HH	0.030	-0.319***	0.286**	-0.082
	(0.31)	(2.79)	(2.16)	(0.76)
CM a Format. Primaire	0.068**	0.008	-0.072**	0.055
	(2.39)	(0.25)	(2.30)	(1.56)
CM a Format. Sec. O-A ou Univ.	0.274***	0.024	-0.069	0.133*
	(4.58)	(0.36)	(1.15)	(1.89)
Variation Taille Ménage	-0.113***	-0.128***	-0.087***	-0.019**
	(14.40)	(15.13)	(10.69)	(2.07)
Variation Tx Dépendance	-0.005***	-0.006***	0.000	-0.002*
	(4.86)	(5.30)	(0.02)	(1.84)
Variation Nbre Enfants"15ans	0.066***	0.083***	0.042***	0.015
	(5.65)	(6.65)	(3.43)	(1.13)
Variation %âge d'adultes Men.	-0.235**	-0.331***	0.038	-0.105
	(2.13)	(2.77)	(0.11)	(0.98)
Variation Moyenne d'Educ. Men.	0.003	-0.002	0.002	-0.004

	(0.77)	(0.54)	(0.45)	(0.85)
Variation %âge Ad. Trav. off-farm	0.406***	0.450***	0.291***	0.093**
	(10.25)	(10.67)	(6.84)	(2.12)
Variation de la Moyenne d'IMC du Mén.	0.009***	0.006***	0.003***	0.006**
	(5.34)	(2.79)	(2.83)	(2.12)
Log Cons. Men. en Equivalent Adulte		-0.264***	-0.078	-0.204***
		(4.26)	(1.50)	(2.81)
Constant	3.864***	3.830***	1.892***	2.194**
	(7.51)	(5.19)	(3.01)	(2.50)
F statistic	97.97	.	.	.
Adjusted R-squared	0.49	0.36	0.22	0.17
Observations	2,236	2,211	1,281	930
Test de Wald (Prob " Chi2)	0.0000			

Variable dépendante : Variation de la consommation du ménage en équivalent adulte entre 1991 et 2004.
Valeurs absolues des t de Student entre parenthèses ; * significatif à 10%; ** significatif à 5%; *** significatif à 1%.

Source : Résultats obtenus sur base des données de KHDS.

et significatif à 1%, suggérant une forte tendance de convergence vers la moyenne de la consommation du cluster. Ainsi, plus la consommation du ménage en équivalent adulte en 1991 est éloignée de la moyenne du cluster dans lequel le ménage se retrouve, plus ledit ménage est enclin à subir une baisse de sa consommation (bien-être) au cours des 13 ans qui séparent les deux vagues sous analyse. Ce processus de convergence au sein des clusters est confirmé avec la désagrégation de l'analyse au niveau des quantiles de consommation comme avec la séparation des ménages qui ont connu une baisse de la consommation de ceux qui ont plutôt connu son augmentation ou soit sont restés au même niveau. Les ménages qui ont un niveau de consommation inférieur à la moyenne de leur quantile ont des taux de croissance plus élevés alors que ceux qui ont un niveau de consommation supérieur croissent à un taux plus faible. La même convergence est aussi observée entre les clusters : la moyenne de consommation par cluster est non seulement significativement liée à la variation de la consommation dans le temps mais surtout, elle est munie d'un signe négatif. Le test de Wald d'égalité de coefficient rejette l'égalité de ceux associés respectivement à la moyenne de consommation par cluster et la différence entre celle-ci et la consommation

Tableau 2
Déterminants de la croissance du bien-être, 1991 – 2004 : régression en quantile

Modèle Elargi	1er quartile	2ème quartile	3ème quartile	4ème quartile
Log Cons. Mén. en Equivalent Adulte	-0.726***	-0.675***	-0.668***	-0.805***
	(27.65)	(25.47)	(19.15)	(10.38)
Age du Chef de Ménage	-0.007*	-0.002	-0.002	-0.003
	(1.66)	(0.56)	(0.38)	(0.21)
Age du Chef de Ménage au Carré	0.000*	0.000	0.000	-0.000
	(1.77)	(0.45)	(0.13)	(0.19)
Taille du Ménage	0.032	-0.001	-0.040	-0.020
	(1.29)	(0.04)	(0.97)	(0.50)
Taille du Ménage au Carre	-0.007***	-0.006***	-0.003	-0.003
	(6.06)	(3.64)	(0.82)	(1.28)
IMC Moyen Mén.: Catég. Sous poids	-0.142***	-0.176***	-0.067*	-0.066
	(3.11)	(4.81)	(1.89)	(0.67)
IMC Moyen Mén.: Catég. Surpoids ou Obèse	0.062	0.146***	0.098	0.339***
	(0.52)	(3.00)	(0.58)	(2.80)
Superficie Terre Mén. en Acre	0.021**	0.006	-0.001	0.021
	(2.21)	(0.76)	(0.13)	(1.58)
Part Animal ds Actifs Physique	-0.218	-0.223***	-0.518***	-0.384
	(1.36)	(4.19)	(5.50)	(1.24)
Part Agricole ds Actifs Physique	-1.758***	-3.433***	-3.638***	-3.140
	(3.12)	(4.04)	(2.58)	(0.89)
Part Non-Agr. ds le Revenu HH	0.089	-0.037	0.054	0.296
	(0.61)	(0.31)	(0.35)	(0.99)
CM a Format. Primaire	0.080*	0.090**	0.036	-0.234***
	(1.70)	(2.38)	(0.72)	(2.68)
CM a Format. Sec. O-A ou Univ.	0.249***	0.244***	0.193**	0.128
	(2.67)	(3.93)	(2.25)	(0.82)
Variation Taille Ménage	-0.112***	-0.130***	-0.128***	-0.143***
	(10.78)	(15.07)	(9.70)	(7.23)
Variation Tx Dépendance	-0.004*	-0.005***	-0.006**	-0.007*
	(1.89)	(4.69)	(2.00)	(1.73)
Variation Nbre Enfants"15ans	0.092***	0.089***	0.059**	0.073**
	(5.09)	(5.15)	(2.44)	(2.02)
Variation %âge d'adultes Men.	-0.009	-0.191	-0.341	-0.670*
	(0.04)	(1.47)	(1.04)	(1.69)
Variation Moyenne d'Educ. Mén.	0.002	-0.000	0.003	0.018**

	(0.25)	(0.01)	(0.60)	(1.96)
Variation %âge Ad. Trav. off-farm	0.268***	0.460***	0.469***	0.345***
	(3.41)	(8.67)	(7.84)	(3.49)
Variation de la Moyenne d'IMC du Mén.	0.011	0.004	0.006	0.011***
	(1.61)	(1.25)	(1.58)	(5.33)
Constant	8.968***	8.675***	9.036***	11.483***
	(23.99)	(24.44)	(20.13)	(9.77)
Observations	2,236			
Variable dépendante : Variation de la consommation du ménage en équivalent adulte entre 1991 et 2004. Valeurs absolues des t de Student entre parenthèses ; * significatif à 10%; ** significatif à 5%; *** significatif à 1%.				
Source : Résultats obtenus sur base des données de KHDS.				

du ménage. La convergence est beaucoup plus rapide entre clusters qu'au sein d'eux.

Parmi les variables de contrôle sociodémographiques, la taille du ménage pris en niveau n'est pas significative alors que son carré l'est, aussi bien dans le cas de l'échantillon pris dans son ensemble que dans ceux des deux premiers quartiles de la distribution de la variation de la consommation. La taille du ménage dans la période initiale et son carré ne sont conjointement significatifs que pour la portion des ménages qui ont connu une baisse de leur consommation entre 1991 et 2004 (colonne 4 du tableau 1). Munie d'un coefficient positif, elle affecte donc positivement la baisse de la consommation. Concrètement, elle indique le fait que cet effet régressif de la taille du ménage sur la variation consommation du ménage entre 1991 et 2004 ne joue que jusqu'à une certaine taille étant donné que la même variable élevée au carré est significative et associée à un coefficient négatif.

Ainsi, cette relation quadratique permet de situer la taille maximum à 5.7 ou approximativement à 6 personnes. C'est donc seulement au-delà d'une taille dépassant 6 personnes que l'augmentation d'une personne supplémentaire pour un ménage n'altère pas l'évolution de son bien-être dans le temps. Ce résultat est renforcé par celui de l'effet de la variation de la taille du ménage qui exerce un effet négatif sur la variation de la consommation pour l'ensemble des ménages de l'échantillon.

Alors que la part d'actifs agricoles dans le total d'actifs du ménage n'est pas significative dans le cas de l'échantillon pris dans son ensemble, elle l'est dans les deux sous-groupes de ménages pris séparément. Cependant, du fait que le signe de l'effet soit le même pour deux mouvements opposés dans la variation de la consommation, il est difficile de trancher, à ce niveau, sur l'effet de cette variable. La désagrégation de l'effet pour divers quantiles de consommation indique que la part d'actifs agricoles dans le total d'actifs du ménage affecte négativement la variation de la consommation du ménage mais seulement dans les cas respectifs des deuxième et troisième quartiles. Il en est de même de la part non agricole du revenu du ménage qui n'est significative que dans le cas des ménages qui ont connu une augmentation de la consommation entre 1991 et 2004. Ainsi, il apparaît clairement que ces deux variables affectent ou n'affectent pas la variation du bien-être d'un ménage selon sa localisation dans la distribution de la consommation et selon le sens de la variation qu'il a connu dans la variation de sa consommation. Ce résultat conforte et complète celui de De Weerdt (2010) qui, à partir des mêmes données que celles utilisées ici, complétées par d'autres tirées du *Core Welfare Indicator Questionnaire* (CWIQ), a trouvé un effet différencié de cette variable selon la transition du statut de pauvreté du ménage, mais dans les seuls cas des effets de la maladie et des chocs agricoles.

Les variables qui captent le capital humain comprennent d'une part celles relatives à l'éducation et d'autre part celles relatives à la santé. Pour ce qui est de l'éducation, les deux variables retenues sont l'éducation du chef de ménage et la variation de la moyenne de l'éducation des membres du ménage entre 1991 et 2004. L'éducation du chef de ménage mesurée en termes de nombre d'années de scolarité est subdivisée en trois autres catégories : sans instruction, éducation primaire et éducation secondaire et/ou postsecondaire. La première modalité est considérée comme modalité de référence. Dans le cas de la santé, deux variables sont également utilisées : l'IMC moyen des adultes du ménage et la variation de ce même indicateur de la santé au cours de la période étudiée[1].

L'effet moyen du niveau d'instruction du chef de ménage, primaire comme secondaire, sur la croissance de la consommation est significatif et positif. La désagrégation des ménages de l'échantillon en quartiles indique que l'éducation primaire et secondaire du chef de ménage sont toutes deux significatives et affecte la croissance de la consommation dans les deux premiers quartiles, c'est-à-dire celui des ménages qui ont connu les deux plus faibles variations de la consommation. Dans le troisième quartile, seule l'éducation secondaire ou

1. En effet, Wagstaff (2007) suggère que la variation de l'IMC du chef de ménage serait un bon indicateur du choc de santé pour une analyse longitudinale comme c'est le cas ici. Cependant, le choix de la variation de la moyenne d'IMC des adultes du ménage plutôt que celle de l'IMC du chef de ménage est en conformité avec la variable utilisée pour mesurer la santé, à partir du chapitre 2 précédent. Il peut également se justifier par la nature longitudinale des données utilisées ici. En effet, les ménages de 2004 comprennent ceux qui ont été directement observés en 1991 et ceux qui en dérivent 13 ans plus tard. Il va donc de soi que la notion de chef de ménage ne renvoie pas nécessairement à la même personne selon que le ménage est dérivé ou observé depuis 1991. De ce fait, la variation de l'IMC du chef de ménage n'aurait aucune pertinence pour les ménages dérivés.

postsecondaire exerce cet effet positif sur la croissance de la consommation. Par ailleurs, dans le dernier quartile, celui des ménages qui dont la variation de la consommation a la plus grande amplitude, l'éducation secondaire du chef de ménage est non-significative. En revanche, l'éducation primaire pour cette même catégorie des ménages affecte négativement la variation de la consommation. En considérant l'effet de l'éducation sur la croissance de la consommation parallèlement à celui qu'elle exerce sur la dynamique de la pauvreté, il apparaît donc qu'en dépit du fait qu'elle pourrait ne pas induire nécessairement un changement dans le statut de pauvreté, l'éducation affecte significativement la croissance de la consommation du ménage du ménage dans le temps.

L'ensemble de ces résultats confirment la non-linéarité de l'effet de l'éducation du chef de ménage sur le bien-être (mesurée ici par la consommation) du ménage. Ils complètent, de ce fait, ceux des études antérieures ne portant que sur les rendements financiers de l'éducation sur le marché du travail tanzanien (Kahyarara et Teal, 2008). Ainsi, la non-linéarité des rendements de l'éducation paraît généralisable, même aux rendements non-pécuniaires. Bien que servant de catalyseur d'effets d'autres actions de réduction de la pauvreté (Hanjra *et al*, 2009 ; Rolleston, 2011), l'éducation se révèle être un actif dont la qualité et le volume détenu par un ménage déterminent sa capacité d'accroître son bien-être dans le temps.

En ce qui concerne la santé, l'IMC moyen des adultes du ménage est significativement et négativement relié à la variation de la consommation quand il correspond à la catégorie de sous-poids. La désagrégation de l'analyse selon la trajectoire de leur bien-être dans le temps, indique qu'un IMC faible pour l'ensemble d'adultes du ménage affecte négativement l'augmentation de son bien-être dans le temps. Il se révèle ainsi être un frein à la variation de la consommation. Cela est le cas aussi bien pour les ménages qui ont connu une augmentation de leur consommation que pour ceux dont cet indicateur du bien-être a baissé dans le temps. En effet, dans cette dernière catégorie des ménages, un IMC moyen des adultes du ménage relevant de la catégorie des sous-poids est muni d'un signe négatif dans le résultat de la régression. Cet effet négatif de l'IMC sur la baisse du bien-être implique une liaison positive entre ces deux variables. Ces résultats sont en phase avec ceux des travaux antérieurs aussi bien à Kagera, en Tanzanie (Beegle *et al*, 2008) que dans d'autres pays en développement[1]. En effet, la région est essentiellement agricole et les travaux ci-haut évoqués indiquent que dans un tel contexte où la force

1. Cfr. Strauss (1986) dans le cas de la Guinée ; Schultz et Tansel (1997) dans le cas de la Côte d'Ivoire et du Ghana ; Asfaw (2004) dans le cas de l'Ethiopie et Godlonton et Keswell (2005) dans le cas de l'Afrique du Sud.

physique intervient pour beaucoup dans le processus de production, l'IMC est un vecteur important de la capacité de production des individus. La persistance d'un tel lien dans le temps présente le risque d'existence, à Kagera, d'un piège de pauvreté lié à la santé ou à la nutrition (Gupta, 1997).

Par ailleurs, quand il correspond à la catégorie de surpoids ou d'obésité, l'IMC moyen des adultes du ménage n'est pas significatif dans l'explication de la variation de la consommation des ménages quand l'ensemble de ceux-ci est considéré. En revanche, la désagrégation de l'analyse au niveau des quartiles révèle qu'un IMC moyen correspondant à cette catégorie de santé affecte positivement la consommation mais seulement dans les cas respectifs du deuxième et du quatrième quartile de la variation de la consommation. Un tel effet suggère que l'effet de la santé, mesurée par l'IMC, sur la variation du bien-être dans le temps est linéaire étant donné l'alternance des signes lui associés selon les catégories d'IMC. Un tel effet contraste avec les résultats des travaux portant sur les pays développés qui ont plutôt trouvé une relation en "U renversé" entre le surpoids ou l'obésité et le salaire, la capacité de travailler et la pauvreté (Greve, 2008 ; Brunello et D'Hombres, 2007 ; Jolliffe, 2011).

Dans le cas de Kagera, un tel résultat peut s'expliquer par le contexte global de la Tanzanie, en plus de la particularité soulignée par les travaux d'Ainsworth et Dayton (2003) et celui de Khan *et al* (2006) qui sont évoqués dans le point précédent. En effet, comme le souligne l'OMS (OMS, 2006) dans son rapport sur les maladies chroniques, dans bien de pays en développement, l'obésité fait partie des troubles de santé que l'on retrouve le plus dans les classes moyenne et supérieure des populations des pays en développement (OMS, 2006). La Tanzanie fait, en plus du Nigeria, partie des deux pays africains qui ont fait l'objet d'analyse dans le cadre de cette étude de l'OMS. Si un tel phénomène s'observe au niveau national, il peut renseigner sur le fait que l'obésité ait un lien positif avec la croissance de la consommation.

Conclusion

Comment le capital humain, perçu comme étant la santé et l'éducation, détermine t-il l'évolution du bien-être d'un ménage dans le temps ? Telle est la question à laquelle ce papier a cherché à apporter une réponse. Pour y parvenir, il prend appui sur les données issues de la *Kagera Health and Development Survey* (KHDS), collectées dans la région de Kagera, dans le Nord-Ouest de la Tanzanie. La forte prévalence de la pauvreté malgré la croissance économique que la Tanzanie a connue les deux dernières décennies, le faible niveau d'investissement éducatif et le grand héritage de la pandémie du VIH/SIDA que cette région a connu font d'elle une bonne maquette des économies africaines qui, globalement, traduisent les mêmes caractéristiques. Se distinguant du lot des papiers qui, à partir des données longitudinales sur les ménages ou les individus, se focalisent sur le statut de pauvreté ou la variation de celui-ci dans le temps, ce papier se concentre sur l'évolution du bien-être des ménages entre 1991 et 2004. Il utilise la régression en quantiles pour faire ressortir l'effet du capital-santé et du capital-éducation sur diverses portions de la distribution de la croissance du bien-être dans le temps. Les résultats obtenus révèlent l'existence d'une convergence conditionnelle du bien-être des ménages entre les différents clusters et au sein d'eux.

Dans le cas de l'éducation, l'ensemble de ces résultats confirme la non-linéarité de l'effet de l'éducation du chef de ménage sur le bien-être du ménage. Ils permettent ainsi de généraliser la non-linéarité du retour sur investissement éducatif même aux aspects autres que pécuniaires. L'éducation se révèle être un actif dont la qualité et le volume détenu par un ménage déterminent sa capacité d'accroître son bien-être dans le temps. Pour ce qui est de la santé, elle a un effet positif et linéaire sur l'évolution du bien-être dans le temps. Un tel effet contraste avec les résultats des travaux portant sur les pays développés qui ont plutôt trouvé une relation en "U renversé" entre le surpoids ou l'obésité et le salaire, la capacité de travailler et la pauvreté.

Bibliographie

Abegunde, D. O. et A. E. Stanciole (2008), "The economic impact of chronic diseases: How do households respond to shocks? Evidence from Russia", *Social Science & Medicine*, Vol.66, No. 11, p. 2296-2307.

Adams, P., M. D. Hurd, D. McFadden, A. Merrill et T. Ribeiro (2003), "Healthy, wealthy, and wise? Tests for direct causal paths between health and socioeconomic status", *Journal of Econometrics*, 112, p.3-56.

Ainsworth, M. et J. Dayton (2003), "The Impact of the AIDS Epidemic on the Health of Older Persons in Northwestern Tanzania", *World Development*, Vol. 31, No. 1, p. 131-148.

Alderman, H. , J.R. Behrman, H. Kohler, J. Maluccio et S. C. Watkins (2001), "Attrition in Longitudinal Household Survey Data: Some Tests for Three Developing-Country Samples", *Demographic Research*, Vol. 5, Art. 4, p. 79-124.

Alderman, H., H. Hoogeveen et M. Rossi (2009), "Preschool Nutrition and Subsequent Schooling Attainment: Longitudinal Evidence from Tanzania", *Economic Development and Cultural Change*, Vol. 57, No. 2, p. 239-260.

Al-Samarrai et T. Peasegood (1998), "Educational Attainments and Household Characteristics in Tanzania", *Economics of Education Review*, Vol. 17,N o. 4, p. 395-417.

Al-Samarrai, S. et B. Reilly (2000), "Urban and rural differences in primary school attendance: an empirical study for Tanzania", *Journal of African Economies*, Vol. 9, No. 4, p. 430-474.

Appleton, S. (2000), "Education and health at the household level in Sub-Saharan Africa", *CID Working paper*, n°33.

Appleton, S. (2001), "Education, incomes and poverty in Uganda in the 1990s", *CREDIT Research Paper*, No. 01/22.

Appleton, S., J. Hoddinot et J. MacKinnon (1996), "Education and Health in Sub-Saharan Africa", *Journal of International Development*, Vol. 8, No. 3, p. 307-339.

Appleton, S., J. Hoddinott et P. Krishnan (1999), "The Gender Wage Gap in Three African Countries", *Economic Development and Cultural Change*, Vol. 47, No. 2, p. 289-312.

Arcand, J-L. et K. Labart (2008), "Santé et salaires : une estimation en variables instrumentales sur un panel de travailleurs chinois", *Economie & prévision*, Vol.5, No. 186, p. 89-100.

Audibert, M. (2009), "Issues and Challenges of Measurement of Health: Implications for Economic Research", *Prepared for the African Economic Research Consortium "Health, Economic Growth and Poverty Reduction in Africa" Framework Papers Review Workshop.*

Bartlett R.L. et C. Callahan (1984), "Wage determination and marital status: Another look", *Industrial Relations*, 23, p. 90-96.

Beegle, K. (2005), "Labor Effects of Adult Mortality in Tanzanian Households", *Economic Development and Cultural Change*, Vol.53, No.3, p.655-683.

Beegle, K. , J. De Weerdt et S. Dercon (2010), "Orphanhood and Human Capital Destruction: Is There Persistence Into Adulthood?", *Demography*, Vol. 47, No. 1, p. 163-180.

Beegle, K., J. De Weerdt et S. Dercon (2008a), "Adult Mortality and Consumption Growth in the Age of HIV/AIDS", *Economic Development and Cultural Change*, Vol. 56, No. 2, p. 299-326.

Beegle, K., J. De Weerdt, et S. Dercon (2006), "Kagera Health and Development Survey 2004 Basic Information Document", mimeo. The World Bank.

Berthélemy, J.C. (2008), "Les relations entre santé, développement et réduction de la pauvreté", *Comptes Rendus Biologies*, Vol. 331, No.12, p.903-918.

Berthélemy, J.C. et J. Seban (2009), "Dépenses de santé et équité dans l'accès aux services de santé dans les pays en développement", *Revue d'Economie du Développement*, Vol. 1-2, No. 23, p. 33-71.

Berthélemy, J.C (2011),"Health, Education and Emergence from the Development Trap", *African Development Review*, Vol. 23, No. 3, 2011, p.300-312.

Brunello, B. et B. D'Hombres (2007), "Does body weight affect wages? Evidence from Europe", *Economics and Human Biology*, Vol. 5, No.1, p.1-19.

Cawley, J. (2004), "The Impact of Obesity on Wages", *Journal of Human Resources*, Vol. 39, No. 2, p. 451-474.

Classen, T.J. (2010), "Measures of the intergenerational transmission of body mass index between mothers and their children in the United States, 1981-2004", *Economics and Human Biology*, Vol.8, No.1, p.30-43.

De Weerdt, J. (2010), "Moving out of Poverty in Tanzania: Evidence from Kagera", *Journal of Development Studies*, Vol. 46, No.2, p. 331-349.

Deininger, K. and J. Okidi (2003), "Growth and Poverty Reduction in Uganda, 1999-2000: Panel Data Evidence", *Development Policy Review*, Vol. 21, No. 4, p. 481-509.

Deininger, K. (2003), "Does cost of schooling affect enrollment by the poor? Universal primary education in Uganda", *Economics of Education Review*, Vol. 22, No.3, p. 291-305.

Demombynes, G. et J.G. Hoogeveen (2007), "Growth, Inequality and Simulated Poverty Paths for Tanzania, 1992-2002", *Journal of African Economies*, Vol. 16, No. 4, p. 596-628.

Dercon, S. (2004), "Growth and shocks: evidence from rural Ethiopia", *Journal of Development Economics*, Vol.74, No.2, p.309-329.

Elbers, C., W. Gunning et B. Kinsey (2007), "Growth and Risk : Methodology and Micro Evidence", *The World Bank Economic Review*, Vol. 21, No.1, p. 1-20.

Fields, G. S., P. L. Cichello, S. Fieije, M. Menendez et D. Newhouse (2003), "Escaping from Poverty: Household Income Dynamics in Indonesia, South Africa, Spain, and Venezuela", in

Fields and Pfeffermann (eds), *Pathways Out of Poverty; Private Firms and Economic Mobility in Developing Countries,* Kluwer Academic Publishers Group, Dordrecht, The Netherlands.

Girma, S. et A. Kedir (2005), "Heterogeneity in returns to schooling: Econometric evidence from Ethiopia", *Journal of Development Studies*, Vol.41, No.8, p.1405-1416.

Glewwe, P., Jacoby, H. G., et E.M. King (2001), "Early childhood nutrition and academic achievement: A longitudinal analysis", *Journal of Public Economics*, Vol.81, No.3, p.345-368.

Glewwe, P; M. Gragnolati et H. Zaman (2002), "Who Gained from Vietnam's Boom in the 1990's", *Economic Development and Cultural Change*, Vol.50, No.4, p.773-792.

Godlonton, S. et M. Keswell (2005), "The impact of health on poverty: evidence from the south African Integrated Family Survey", *South African Journal of Economics*, Vol.73, No.1, p.133-148.

Gondard-Delcroix, C. (2009), "Spécificités des dynamiques de pauvretés dans deux régions rurales de Madagascar", *Economie rurale*, Vol.3, No.311, p.49-66.

Greve, J. (2008), "Obesity and labor market outcomes in Denmark", *Economics and Human Biology*, Vol.6, No.3, p.350-362.

Gunning, J., J. Hoddinott, J, B. Kinsey et T. Owens (2000), “Revisiting Forever Gained: Income Dynamics in the Resettlement Areas of Zimbabwe, 1983-96”, *The Journal of Development Studies*, Vol.36, p.131-154.

Gupta, I. et A. Mitra (2004), “Economic Growth, Health and Poverty: An Exploratory Study for India”, *Development Policy Review*, Vol.22, No.2, p.193-206.

Hanjra, M., T. Ferede et D. G. Gutta (2009), “Pathways to breaking the poverty trap in Ethiopia: Investments in agricultural water, education, and markets”, *Agricultural Water Management*, Vol.96, No.11, p.1596-1604.

Herrera, J. et F. Roubaud (2005), “Urban Poverty Dynamics in Peru and Madagascar, 1997-99: A Panel Data Analysis”, *International Planning Studies*, Vol. 10, No. 1, p.21-48.

Herrera, J., S. Mesple-Somps et P. De Vreyer (2003), “Consumption growth and spatial poverty traps: an analysis of the effects of social services and community infrastructures on living standards in rural Peru”, *DIAL Document de Travail*, DT/2002/17.

Jalan, J. et M. Ravallion (2002), “Geographic Poverty Traps? A Micro Model of Consumption Growth in Rural China”, *Journal of Applied Econometrics*, Vol.17, No.4, pp. 329-346.

Jolliffe, D. (2011), “Overweight and poor? On the relationship between income and the body mass index”, *Economics and Human Biology*, Vol.9, No.4, p. 342-355.

Kahyarara, G et F. Teal (2008), “The Returns to Vocational Training and Academic Education: Evidence from Tanzania”, *World Development*, Vol. 36, No.11, p. 2223-2242.

Kedir, A. M. (2009), “Health and Productivity: Panel Data Evidence from Ethiopia”, *African Development Review*, Vol.21, No.1, p.59-72.

Khan, M.M., D. R. Hotchkiss, A. Berruti et P. L. Hutchinson (2006), “Geographic aspects of poverty and health in Tanzania: does living in a poor area matter?”, *Health Policy and Planning*, Vol.21, No.2, p.110-122.

Knight, J.B. et R.H. Sabot (1982), “Labour Market Discrimination in a Poor Urban Country,” *Journal of Development Studies*, Vol.19, No.1, p. 67-87.

Khongsdier, R. (2001), “Body mass index of adult males in 12 populations of Northeast India”, *Annals of Human Biology*, Vol.28, No.4, p.374-383.

Koenker, R. et G. Bassett (1978), “Regression quantiles”, *Econometrica*, Vol.46, No.1, p. 33-50.

Minot, N. (2007), “Are Poor, Remote Areas Left behind in Agricultural Development: The Case of Tanzania”, *Journal of African Economies*, Vol. 17, No. 2, p. 239-276.

Molini, V., M. Nubé et B. Van den Boom (2010), “Adult BMI as a Health and Nutritional Inequality Measure: Applications at Macro and Micro Levels”, *World Development*, Vol. 38, No. 7, p. 1012-1023.

Mukherjee, S. et T. Benson (2003), "The Determinants of Poverty in Malawi, 1998", *World Development*, Vol.31, No.2, p.339-358.

Mwabu, G. (2001), "Health Status in Africa: A Regional Profile", *The South African Journal of Economics*, Vol. 69, No. 2, p.319-335.

Ravallion, M. et J. Jalan (1996), "Growth divergence due to spatial externalities", *Economics Letters*, Vol.53, No.2, p.227-232.

Rodgers, J.R. et J.L. Rodgers (1993), "Chronic Poverty in the United States", *Journal of Human Resources*, Vol.28, No.3, p. 25-54.

Rolleston, C. (2011), "Educational access and poverty reduction: The case of Ghana 1991-2006", *International Journal of Educational Development*, Vol.31, No.4, p. 338 - 341.

Sandefur, J., P. Serneels et F. Teal (2006), "African poverty through the lens of labor economics: Earnings and mobility in three countries", *GPRG-Working papers series*-060.

Schoeni, R.F. (1995), "Marital status and earnings in developed countries", *Journal of Population Economics*, Vol.8, No.4, p.351-359.

Schultz, T. W. (1961), "Investment in human capital", *American Economic Review*, Vol.51, No.1, p. 1-17.

Schultz, T.W. (1975), "Human Capital and Disequilibrium", *Journal of Economic Literature*, Vol.13, No.3, p.827-846.

Schultz, T.P. et A. Tansel (1997), "Wage and labor supply effects of illness in Côte d'Ivoire and Ghana: instrumental variable estimates for days disabled", *Journal of Development Economics*, Vol.53, No.2, p.251-286.

Strauss, J. (1986), "Does Better Nutrition Raise Farm Productivity?", *The Journal of Political Economy*, Vol.94, No.2, p.297-320.

Thomas, A-C. (2009), "The impact of agricultural shocks on households growth performance in rural Madagascar", *Document de Travail DIAL*, DT/2009-05.

Thomas, D. et J. Strauss (1997), "Health and wages: Evidence on men and women in urban Brazil", *Journal of Econometrics*, Vol.77, No.1, p.159-185.

United Republic of Tanzania (2005), *National Strategy for Growth and Reduction of Poverty*, Vice - President's Office, p 109.

United Republic of Tanzania (2007), *Household Budget Survey*, Dar-es-Salaam: National Bureau of Statistics.

Unterhalter, E. (2009), "Education", Chapitre 9 dans S. Deneulin and L. Shahani (Eds) *An Introduction to the Human Development and Capability Approach Freedom and Agency*, Earthscan/IDRC,London, p.207-227.

Unterhalter, E. (2012), "Inequality, capabilities and poverty in four African countries: girls' voice, schooling, and strategies for institutional change", *Cambridge Journal of Education*, Vol.42, No.3, p.307-325.

Vijverberg, Wim P. M. (1993), "Educational Investments and

Returns for Women and Men in Côte d'Ivoire", *The Journal of Human Resources*, Vol. 28, No.4, p. 933-974.

Wagstaff, A. (2007), "The economic consequences of health shocks: Evidence from Vietnam", *Journal of Health Economics*, Vol.26, No.1, p.82-100.

Wedgwood, R. (2007), "Education and poverty reduction in Tanzania", *International Journal of Educational Development*, Vol. 27, No.4, p. 383-396.

Wedgwood, R. (2010), "Tanzania", dans *Peterson, P., E. Baker and B. McGaw (Eds.), International Encyclopedia of Education*, 3rd Edition, p. 841-846.

Woods, E. (2008), "Progress towards EFA in Tanzania", *Prospects*, Vol.38, No.3, p.425-430.

Tableau A.1
Résultat du test d'endogénéité (D-H-W) de la consommation de 1991

Variables	Coefficient
Log Consommation du Ménage en Equivalent Adulte	-0.429***
	(0.052)
Le Résidu de l'Estimé de la Consommation en Equiv. Adulte	-0.377***
	(0.058)
Superficie Terre dont dispose le ménage, en Acre	-0.027***
	(0.007)
Part d'actifs Animaux dans le total d'Actifs Physiques	-0.450***
	(0.078)
Part Agricole dans le total d'Actifs Physiques	-4.296***
	(0.767)
Part Non-Agr. dans le Revenu du ménage	-0.276***
	(0.083)
Niveau d'Instruction du Chef ménage	0.011***
	(0.004)
Prop. Adultes du ménage avec Education Primaire	0.089**
	(0.044)
Prop. Adultes du ménage avec une éducation secondaire	0.335***
	(0.101)
Variation de la Taille du ménage	-0.072***
	(0.006)
Variation du taux de Dépendance	-0.005***
	(0.001)

Variation Nbre. d'enfants"15ans	0.095***
	(0.012)
Variation %âge d'adultes de sexe féminin	-0.573***
	(0.077)
Variation %âge d'adultes mâles	-0.480***
	(0.083)
Variation Moyenne de l'Education du ménage	0.006
	(0.004)
Variation %âge Adultes qui Trav. off-farm	0.460***
	(0.039)
Variation de la Moyenne d'IMC du ménage	0.009***
	(0.002)
Constant	5.377***
	(0.632)
F statistic	111.14
Adjusted R-squared	0.45
Observations	2,236
Valeurs absolues des t de Student entre parenthèses; * significatif à 10%; ** significatif à 5%; *** significatif à 1%.	
Source: Résultats obtenus sur base des données de KHDS.	

Smuggling at the Congolese-Rwandan border: drivers, context and welfare impact

Morisho Mwana Biningo Nene & Martin Doevenspeck

Bukavu Journal of Economics and Social Sciences (BJESS) numéro 3, 2016

RÉSUMÉ/ABSTRACT

Objective: Make a new contribution to the smuggling debate by assessing the welfare impact of smuggling at the border between the city of Goma in the Democratic Republic of Congo and the city of Gisenyi in Rwanda.

Methodological approach: Given that the lack of reliable data does not allow measuring the nationwide net welfare impact of smuggling, this study focuses on welfare impact at the local level of consumers in the two border towns. Our approach was to first consider a sample of the most smuggled commodities between the two cities, to assess then the capacity of smuggling to reduce prices on the markets, and lastly to measure the welfare impact on consumers in terms of consumer surplus. We used both quantitative and qualitative data collected during several fieldwork periods between October 2008 and March 2013.

Major findings: The results of the current study indicate that, on average, prices at which households purchase smuggled commodities are 38.3 per cent (Gisenyi) and 19 per cent (Goma) lower than the tax-inclusive prices. The average decrease in the prices of imported commodities due to smuggling in the two cities, taken together, is about 29 per cent. The study also shows that the low level of smuggling prices is mainly explained by the capacity of smugglers to reduce risks and thus transaction costs, rendering their business environment more predictable. This makes it easier for them to smuggle large quantities of goods at low cost and sell them at cheaper prices in Goma and Gisenyi. The study also shows that due to smuggling, households in a suburb of Gisenyi called Mudugudu are able to save up $10 per month. This means that smuggling generates for them a consumer surplus of $10 per month, which represents 6.2 per cent of the households' total monthly expenditure. For inhabitants of Birere in Goma, smuggling generates a monthly consumer surplus of $7 for the households living in this suburb. This surplus represents 3 per cent of the monthly expenditure of these households.

Limit: The major limit of the current study is the lack of national data on smuggling. Their availability would allow using a more rigorous methodological approach, especially measuring the welfare impact by using the concept of national utility (satisfaction) developed by Pitt (1981), Sheikh (1974), and Kemp (1976).

Key words: Smuggling, welfare impact, cross border trade, Goma, Gisenyi.

Introduction

For more than five decades, the low level of intra-African trade has been persistent, as underlined in different reports by international organizations (IMF, WTO or UNICTAD). In 2009, for example, intra-African trade accounted for about 10 per cent of the continent's total trade, as against 22 per cent in Latin America and 50 per cent in Asia (Barka, 2012). This study takes the case of the Democratic Republic of Congo (DRC) and Rwanda, whose formal economic cooperation has been minimal over the last 30 years, despite their close geographical and historical links. Official statistics show that official trade between the two countries represents a very small part of their international trade. For example, trade with Rwanda represented less than 0.5 per cent of DRC's total exports and 1 per cent of its imports between 2007 and 2010. Similarly, Rwandan imports and exports to DRC represented 4 per cent and 5 per cent of its total imports and exports respectively during the same period.

However, Golub (2010) points out that official statistics relating to intra-African trade are problematic as they capture only recorded cross-border trade. He argues that activities involving unrecorded informal cross-border trade in food grains, animals and manufactured goods are not considered. Given the importance of such activities in African regional trade, this lack of data substantially reduces the official level of intra-African trade (ECA, 2010).

As acknowledged in the 2010 report of the Economic Commission for Africa, it is very rare in Africa to find adequate secondary data on smuggling, and in countries where such data are available they are often incomplete or related to case studies of selected commodities (ECA, 2010). However, after gathering existing studies of informal trade in Africa, the ECA estimated that 5.6 per cent to 11 per cent of intra-African trade is informal, and in some parts of the continent, like at the border between DRC and its neighbors (Rwanda for example), the level of smuggling exceeds that of formal trade. Therefore, research into the potential welfare impact of this business in the African context is primordial.

The debate on the welfare impact of smuggling started in 1973 with the pioneering work of Bhagwati and Hansen. For them, smuggling was not only a moral and legal problem, but also an economic phenomenon, which deserves to be analyzed. They pointed out the fact that smuggling, due to the wastage of resources, is often welfare decreasing. Authors such as Deardorff and Stolper (1990), Falvey (1978) and Connolly, Devereux and Cortes (1995) have shown that in many developing countries, especially in Africa, smuggling may have a positive welfare impact. Here, it is argued, smuggling reduces policy distortions, inefficiencies of the customs administration, and cumbersome regulations and controls, which make legal cross-border trade difficult and therefore less profitable.

Surprisingly there has been no significant contribution to smuggling welfare impacts since the end of the nineties. In Africa though, borders are still of utmost importance both for the everyday life of people and as a major source of revenue for many different actors. Informal cross border trade is a mass phenomenon from which hundreds of thousands of people earn their living (Azam, 2007; Deardorff and Stolper, 1990). To give an example, in 2005 the total value of Uganda's informal exports and imports to and from its neighboring countries were estimated at US$ 200 million and US$ 66 million respectively, representing about 25 per cent of its total exports, and 3 per cent of its total imports. According to Little (2007), 95 per cent of the livestock trade between countries in the Horn of Africa is informal, and a World Bank study (2011) shows that in 2009 the DRC's volume of informal trade in food staples was estimated at 16,078 tons while formal trade represented only 3,276 tons.

However, only a few studies have attempted to analyze this phenomenon on the continent and the aim of this paper is to make a new contribution to the debate by assessing the welfare impact of smuggling at the border between the city of Goma in the Democratic Republic of Congo and the city of Gisenyi in Rwanda. After an introduction to informal trade at the Goma-Gisenyi border, and a presentation of the methodological approach, the empirical chapters analyze different impacts of smuggling on local markets. The paper ends with a discussion of the empirical results and some reflections on the contribution made by this research.

Situating the problem: informal trade between Goma and Gisenyi

The Kivu region is an important transit region for long-distance trade connecting the east and the west of Central Africa. At the Goma-Gisenyi border, foodstuffs such as beans and bananas are taken to Rwanda, and minerals from the mines of North Kivu are exported overseas through Rwanda and East African ports. In return, construction materials

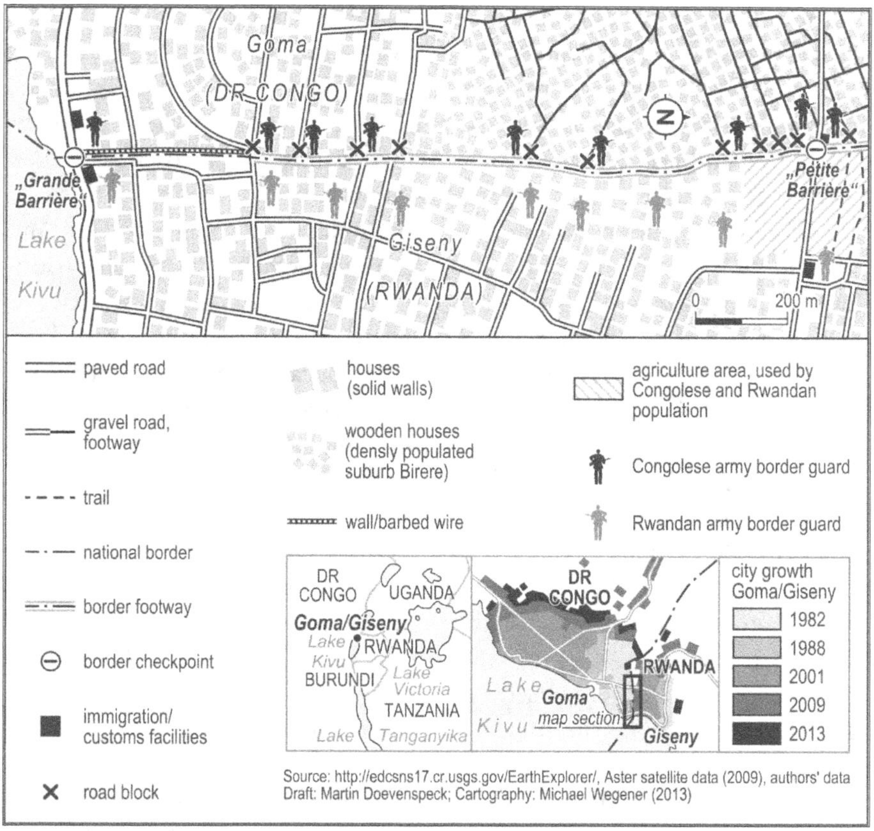

Figure 1
The Congo-Rwanda state border between Goma and Gisenyi

and petroleum products, as well as consumer goods, are imported (Tegera & Johnson, 2007).

Additionally, meat, milk products and vegetables from Rwanda are sold in local markets in Goma. From the beginning of the violent conflict in Eastern Congo in the early 1990s until today, Goma's population has shot up from 170,000 inhabitants to approximately one million. Refugees from war-torn rural areas and other migrants were attracted by the relative security provided by the UN peace forces, and by the job market created by the concentration of international humanitarian organizations (Büscher & Vlassenroot, 2010) and a construction boom, in which much money from the mineral trade is reinvested. The economy of Gisenyi, the neighboring town with about 100,000 residents, depends heavily on cross-border trade.

Goma has a key position in regional informal trade, which was reinforced by the political changes and their economic impacts in the 1990s. War and political instability in the DRC, the incapacity of its government to control its borders, and the new political regime in Rwanda boosted and reshaped informal cross-border transactions. For example, since the middle of the 1990s, agricultural products have become scarce on the markets of Goma due to the permanent instability in rural areas. Since then, traders in Gisenyi have become important providers of these commodities. While before the 1990s small exchanges between Goma and Gisenyi were exclusively based on agricultural products, the increase in customs tariffs for manufactured commodities in Rwanda has made them very attractive for small traders.

Economic growth in Rwanda has boosted inequalities, particularly in rural areas, leading to an increase in migration to cities such as Gisenyi (Ansoms, 2008; National Institute of Statistics of Rwanda, 2011) and many of these poorly skilled migrants engage in informal cross-border trade. Moreover, the Rwandan government tries to develop the manufacturing sector and encourages its citizens to consume locally produced commodities. The Rwanda Revenue Authority imposes high tariffs on imported commodities originating from Goma, thus creating scarcity on the markets of Gisenyi. This applies to products such as tomato paste, powdered milk, and the woven fabric known as "kitenge". Customs duties on these products have almost doubled in less than ten years. Combined with high unemployment rates in the city and marked poverty in the surrounding rural areas, this scarcity has led to an increase in smuggling, which became an important source of revenue of the local population. Smuggling is also a means whereby households in Gisenyi continue to have access to commodities that are no longer supplied through official channels due to the high import tariffs.

In the case of the DRC, and in particular in the North Kivu province, armed conflict and enduring political instability have had a devastating impact on the economy. Due to insecurity in the rural areas trade in agricultural commodities to Goma and other DRC cities, formerly a main source of revenue, has significantly declined and the informal sector has become the major source of income for a majority of people in Goma. As for many inhabitants of Gisenyi, the border is an opportunity for people in Goma not only to exercise a remunerated activity, but also to compensate the lack of agricultural products on the markets.

Between 20,000 and 30,000 people do cross the border every day (Kinamuka & Lange, 2010). However, due to due to harassment on the Congolese side of the border, and the rigidity of the Rwanda

Revenue Authority (RRA), smuggling is not easy. While it seems to be tolerated, or even encouraged by Congolese border officials, Rwandan authorities severely punish smugglers and those soldiers, police or customs agents who collaborate with them. Smugglers therefore navigate in two completely different contexts. As a result of the political instability in the region, the border is heavily militarized and the soldiers should normally negatively affect smuggling. However, this is not the case. Instead, the presence of soldiers at the border is an important facilitating factor as smugglers negotiate with them to cross the border uncontrolled.

The success of smugglers at this border can be explained by their capacity to minimize the transactions costs (bribe, remuneration of middlemen, transportation cost, and time spent at the border) and risks in the business. There are two major reasons why transaction costs and risk are low in smuggling: group membership (network of traders) and middlemen. Smugglers are organized in small groups of 10 or 20 traders from the same village or district, which allows them to reduce the cost for middlemen, who help them to get the goods across the border. Working in a group also allows smugglers rescuing their business, in particular when facing financial difficulties, through solidarity mechanism. Middlemen have a good knowledge of the border and established friendly relations with enforcement agents. Using middlemen reduces the bribe that has to be paid to border agents and minimizes the risk of being arrested and of the goods being seized.

Methodological approach

Analysis of the nationwide net welfare impact of smuggling is always difficult, and, as argued by Lovely (1994), generally indeterminate. Two approaches are often used. The first one, suggested by Bhagwati and Hansen (1973) and Deardorff and Stolper (1990) measures welfare impact by comparing the level of consumption in an economy with and without smuggling. Smuggling is welfare-increasing when the level of national consumption is higher with it than without. The second approach (Pitt 1981; Sheikh 1974; Kemp 1976) uses the concept of national utility (satisfaction). However, for both approaches, it is important to note that the lack of consistent data on intra-African trade does not allow for such an analysis at the national level. The official data are often useless, due to the porosity of borders and the carelessness of customs administrations in the collection and recording of data on international trade (ECA, 2010; Deardorff & Stolper, 1990). Therefore, data sources such as the customs authority, central bank and ministry of trade, are not reliable. The same applies to international sources (UN, UNECA, UNCTAD and WTO) that rely on national data sets. Hence, an alternative is to conduct field research, as done in this study.

Given that the lack of reliable data does not allow measuring the nationwide net welfare impact of smuggling, this study focuses on welfare impact at the local level of consumers in the two border towns. Our approach was to first consider a sample of the most smuggled commodities between the two cities, to assess then the capacity of smuggling to reduce prices on the markets, and lastly to measure the welfare impact on consumers in terms of consumer surplus.

Previous studies have suggested three different concepts for measuring the effect of price changes on households' well being: compensating variation, equivalent variation and consumer surplus (Janvry and Sadoulet 2009). Compensating variation measures how much (money) is needed to increase/decrease the consumer's income if we want her or his welfare to remain the same after a change in the prices of goods. In this case, the question is how much extra money has to be given to a consumer in order to completely offset the harm resulting from a price increase. The measure is called compensating variation because its focus is on the money to be given to the consumer to compensate him for the decrease of utility. In terms of economic policy, compensating variation enables measurement of the amount of money that the government would have to give to the consumer if it wanted to exactly compensate the consumer for the price variation. Equivalent variation measures the extent to which the consumer's income should be increased or decreased to induce the same welfare loss as a change in prices. The interest here lays on the amount of money that should be taken away from the consumer in order to harm him as much as the price increases. The measure is called "equivalent" because it is the same (equivalent) harm as with the price change. Both approaches focus exclusively on the income effects of a price change, and answer the question how much change in income is necessary to offset a change in price so that the consumer keeps the same level of satisfaction (Perloff, 2003).

The concept of consumer surplus can be defined either (Henderson 1941) as the excess of the price which the consumer would be prepared to pay over that he actually pays or in terms of the gain for a consumer which results from a fall in price. The second definition is closest to our purpose of measuring the gain that consumers in Goma and Gisenyi obtain from the decrease in prices of imported commodities due to smuggling. However, when the income effect of price modification is zero, as in the Goma-Gisenyi borderland, consumer surplus is the most appropriate measure of the effect of a price change on the consumer's well-being (Janvry & Sadoulet, 2009).

Households, smugglers, middlemen, soldiers, police officers, government officials and customs agents are all directly affected by smuggling. Thus, the aim of our smuggling impact analysis is to estimate the gain generated for these actors. We use both quantitative and qualitative data collected during several fieldwork periods between October 2008 and March 2013. Data on trade flows and types of goods involved in this business were collected through standardized questionnaires and open interviews conducted at the border and in the two cities. For the questionnaire, a sample of 136 smugglers and 25 formal traders was used. 71 interviews were conducted. Data on smuggling impacts on households' welfare were collected from a sample of 200 households in the districts of Birere in Goma and Mudugudu in Gisenyi. These two districts are mainly inhabited by very poor people for whom the consumption of cheaper smuggled commodities is more important than for people with higher incomes who can more easily afford to buy the same products at tax-inclusive prices.

To capture the real impact of price decline on the well being of households, questions targeted monthly expenditures, the size of family, the consumption of smuggled goods, and the average share of the household budg*et al*located to the purchase of smuggled commodities. Finally, the monthly cost of consumption of these commodities was calculated both in the presence and in the absence of smuggling.

Impact of smuggling on imported commodities' prices on the markets of Goma and Gisenyi

As argued by Pitt (1981) the most important way in which smuggling positively impacts consumers' welfare appears to be by reducing the domestic prices of imports. Prices on the markets of the two cities can be regarded as smuggling prices, since all commodities considered in this study are exclusively are smuggled. Prices were calculated by visiting shops selling smuggled products and expressed as the average of the shop owners' prices sampled in each city. The formal or tax-inclusive prices were estimated by simulating the prices, which would prevail on the markets if all the commodities in our sample were traded formally with required customs duties paid. These prices[1] were calculated by adding to the purchasing price the transportation and other transaction costs that a formal cross-border trader incurs, including customs duties and other taxes (calculated using the CIF value of the goods), and the average profits that shop owners earn on this type of goods.

A comparison of smuggling prices and tax-inclusive prices shows that smuggling allows a

1. The final formal prices to consumers are considered as minimum because their calculus did not consider the illegal payment (at bribe) done by formal traders at the Congolese side of the border and which can influence the cost price of commodities and therefore their sale prices to final consumers.

	Products	Final smuggling prices for households	Final tax-inclusive price for households	Reduction of prices due to smuggling (in per cen)
GISENY	Salsa tomato paste	33	46.175	-40
	Nido milk powder	42	60.07	-43
	Woven fabrics A	18	24.96	-38.7
	Woven fabrics B	13	17.84	-37.4
	Anny sardines	11.5	15.8	-42
	Mayonnaise	30.5	43.3	-29.5
	Drostdy wine	28.5	36.9	-17
	Duru soap	10	13.9	-39
Average				-38.3
GOMA	Toilet paper	7.5	8.425	-11
	Sonitec radio	16	19.66	-18.6
	Plastic cup	20	27.625	-27.6
	Goat	55	63.1	-12.8
	Paraffin	37	49.44	-25.2
Average				-19

Source: Authors' data (from field work January-June 2011)

Table 1
Estimation of price reduction due to smuggling

substantial price reduction for imported commodities in Goma and Gisenyi. The results indicate, for example, that, on average, the prices at which households currently purchase smuggled commodities are 38.3 per cent (Gisenyi) and 19 per cent (Goma) lower than the tax-inclusive prices. The average decrease in the prices of imported commodities due to smuggling in the two cities, taken together, is about 29 per cent.

It is important to note that the low level of smuggling prices is mainly explained by the capacity of smugglers to reduce risks and thus transaction costs, rendering their business environment more predictable. This makes it easier for them to smuggle large quantities of goods at low cost and sell them at cheaper prices in Goma and Gisenyi. With this finding, it can be expected that smuggling will be beneficial for local consumers, since it generates a consumer surplus as households purchase goods at lower prices. On the other hand, these informal exchanges, when they become widespread, while profitable for the numerous actors involved, can also compromise the capacity of the state to collect tax on international trade (Beard, Paula, & Richard, 1997). The question of how different

		Total monthly expenditure per household	Total expenditure for smuggled commodities	Total expenditure for commodities if taxes were paid	Consumer surplus	Share of consumer surplus in total household expenditure (in per cent)
GISENY	Low income	159	27	37	10	6.2
	High income	500	54	75	21	4.2
GOMA	Low income	185	29	34.5	5.5	3
	High income	543	55	65.5	10.5	2

Source: own data

Table 2
Summary of impact of smuggling on Goma-Gisenyi households' well-being (in USD 6)

All amounts were initially in local currencies, i.e. Congolese francs (Cfr) in Goma and Rwandan francs (Rfw) in Gisenyi and were converted to dollars at the prevailing exchange rates during fieldwork: $ 1 = Rfw 640 and $ 1 = Cfr 950

actors benefit from this activity therefore becomes interesting.

Estimation of the impact of smuggling on households' well-being

The aim of this section is to assess how the living conditions of different actors involved directly or indirectly such as middlemen, consumers (households), soldiers, police and customs agents are affected by smuggling. First, the capacity of smuggling to generate a consumer surplus for local households will be estimated, before measuring the average gains resulting from the business for all these actors.

Are households in Goma and Gisenyi better off with smuggling? Given the facts presented above, one may expect that the well-being of particularly poor households, measured as consumer surplus, will be positively affected. Consumer surplus is the difference between the amount of money that is currently spent by a household and the amount that would be spent in the absence of smuggling. If this difference is negative, i.e. the household's spending with smuggling is lower than that without smuggling, then smuggling generates a gain for the household. The results of this analysis are presented in Table 2.

A family living in the poor suburb of Mudugudu in Gisenyi has an average monthly expenditure of

$157. $26.4 of this amount is spent on smuggled commodities originating from Goma. As we know that these smuggled commodities are purchased at prices 38.3 per cent lower than their tax-inclusive prices in Gisenyi, the households' expenditure in the absence of smuggling for these smuggled commodities could be $36.5. Therefore, due to smuggling, households are able to save up $10 per month. This means that smuggling generates a consumer surplus of $10 per month, which represents 6.2 per cent of the households' total monthly expenditure. However this percentage is low for people with a higher income (whose monthly expenditure is higher than $500 per month). It represents only 4.2 per cent of their monthly expenditure.

With regard to the city of Goma, the survey focused mainly on the poor suburb of Birere. The results show that on average a household spends $185 per month. An average of $29 is allocated to the consumption of smuggled commodities originating from Gisenyi. This expenditure would rise to $34.5 if those commodities were purchased at tax-inclusive prices. This is due to the fact that selling prices to final consumers in Goma would be 19 per cent higher compared to current prices if the goods were imported formally. Smuggling therefore generates a monthly consumer surplus of $7 for the households living in this suburb. This surplus represents 3 per cent of the monthly expenditure of these households. For households with higher incomes, this surplus represents only 2 per cent.

By lowering the prices of imported commodities, smuggling increases the consumer's well-being at the expense of that of the customs administration. Lovely and Nelson (1995) and Baghwati and Hansen (1973) posit that smuggling increases consumers' welfare only when it reduces prices of imported commodities. Smuggling therefore enables people to purchase international goods at prices that are close to international ones. Therefore, the smuggling impact is similar to that of a decrease in tariffs. On the other hand, it is important to mention that smuggling makes available many commodities that are no longer supplied to the markets of Goma and Gisenyi through official channels. In fact, armed conflict in the rural areas, has pushed peasants into Goma and created food shortages in the city. Mots agricultural products are now imported from Gisenyi. Rwandan economic policies, aiming at protecting local production by heavily taxing imported commodities, have also provoked the scarcity of many manufactured products that are now available on local markets only via smuggling.

Gains of smuggling for smugglers, traders, middlemen and state officials

The lack of competitiveness in the African formal sector and its incapacity to create remunerated

Actor	Average revenue earned per day	Average revenue earned per month (26 days)
Smugglers	6.75	175.5
Middlemen	8	208
State agents (soldiers, police officers and customs agents)	11	286

Source: own data

Table 3
Gains for smugglers, middlemen and state officials (in USD)

jobs incite many people to indulge in informal activities (Akinboade, 2005). As stated in a report by the Jubilee-Zambia Debt and Trade Desk (2008), given its capacity to generate incomes and the impact on the availability of goods and on prices, informal cross-border trade, can be a powerful tool for poverty alleviation if the government harnesses it properly.

Thus, incomes generated through smuggling can play a key role in improving the everyday life of people. This business benefits smugglers directly, but also has a multiplier effect on their dependents in different sectors such as education, healthcare and food security (Kiratu & Suryapratim, 2010). Table 3 shows the average revenues generated by the smuggling business for smugglers, middlemen and state agents.

The average daily revenue of a smuggler is estimated to be \$6.75. On a monthly basis, their average revenue is \$175.5. Interviews with middlemen show that smugglers earn up to \$8 per day, (\$208 per month). For soldiers, middlemen and customs agents smuggling generates average monthly revenue of \$286. However, this figure was calculated on the basis of data collected through interviews with only six agents. This is due to the reluctance of these actors to provide information about their involvement in smuggling. On the whole, it appears that with the exception of the customs administrations, smuggling at the Goma-Gisenyi border profits, to different degrees, all other actors involved in it. And it becomes evident that smugglers are not the main beneficiaries. This is clearly illustrated by the analysis of the supply chain of smuggled goods from one city to another. On average, we found that smuggling of an item can generate a total unit gain of \$6.7 This gain is shared among different actors, namely state agents (32%), middlemen (19%), smugglers (18%) and shop owners (31%).

Although revenues generated by smuggling seem to be negligible, they represent a significant means for securing livelihoods in the economic context of the borderland.

These earnings are higher than the monthly salary of a state-employed teacher, for instance. In 2011, the average salary of a secondary school teacher in Rwanda was estimated at \$147 and \$80 in DRC. Furthermore, these incomes are three to four times higher than what an ordinary soldier or police officer can earn in Rwanda (\$47 in 2011) and in DRC (\$59). It is clear, then, that in the context of the state's incapacity to address the problems of poor people, smuggling generates substantial social and economic benefits for these people. As stated byOkuro (2011), smuggling contributes to covering the deficit in household budgets and enables the acquisition of a certain social status in society.

Discussion of results

One of the major reasons for smuggling at the Goma-Gisenyi border is that official channels have failed to make required and desired goods available. Smuggling of commodities into Gisenyi is the effect of economic policies. Imports of many goods are currently discouraged by the Rwandan government's policy of protecting domestic production and imports from countries that are like Rwanda members of the East African Community (EAC). This is the case, for example, of products like tomato paste, metal sheets, liquor and woven fabrics. The consequence of such a policy is an insufficient supply of essential goods at reasonable prices. On the other hand, smuggling of goods into Goma is mainly fuelled by three major factors: the facility with which smuggling can be done with the collusion of different state officials, the high transaction costs in formal trade, and the scarcity of staple commodities as a result of instability and insecurity, particularly in the rural areas.

Our analyses have shown that smuggling generates important gains for smugglers, middlemen and state officials. It is thus a zero sum game where the impoverishment of the government benefits also the other actors. By lowering domestic prices, smuggling at the Goma-Gisenyi border also appears to be a beneficial business for consumers since it redistributes income from governments to consumers and smugglers (Sheikh 1977).

Concerning the Goma-Gisenyi borderland, smuggling contributes to reducing the price of imported goods by approximately 38.3 per cent in Gisenyi and 19 per cent in Goma. As smuggled products are sold below the tax-inclusive prices in Goma and Gisenyi, it is difficult for formal traders to compete in such an environment. Interviews with smugglers and shop owners in the two cities confirmed that affordable commodities are exclusively supplied by smugglers. This is a consequence of the high tariffs and transaction costs, which increase the cost of formal trading. Hence, formal traders have the choice of either shifting from formal to informal trade or withdrawing. This is in line with the argument of Bhagwati and Hansen (1973) who claim that formal cross-border trade can survive only if the prices prevailing on the markets are tax-inclusive prices. However, many other scholars (Thursby & Jensen, 1991; Sheikh, 1974; Pitt, 1981; & Martin & Panagariya, 1984) argue that the coexistence of legal and smuggled goods on the markets is possible, even when the former are sold at a loss, i.e. below the tax-inclusive prices.

This is evident at the Goma-Gisenyi border, where official trade has not completely disappeared, but is negligible in its magnitude. The only justification for a certain level of formal trade, in a context where prices on the markets are lower than formal prices, is its ability to reduce the risks involved in smuggling. This situation is observable for commodities smuggled into Gisenyi. As agents of the RRA make regular inspections in shops, asking shop owners to present clearing documents for the commodities they are selling, the latter usually import legally a small quantity of those commodities. The clearing certificate obtained is then used to cover the smuggled commodities, which are never exhibited in the shop but hidden in their private houses. Any item sold is immediately replaced by another one from the stash until the stock is depleted. Thus, in order to hide smuggled goods, and to protect themselves from the control of customs officers, it is necessary for shop owners to import a small share of their goods legally.

This phenomenon is well analyzed by Pitt (1981) who developed a model showing that the success of smuggling depends on the volume of legal trade. Both Pitt (1981) and Macedo (1987) demonstrate that the coexistence of legal and smuggled goods is possible, when official trade is used to cover unofficial activities. In this case, official and smuggled goods are traded jointly, and the former can be sold on the domestic market at a loss, i.e. at a price inferior to the tax-inclusive price. This loss is largely compensated by the profit earned on the sale of smuggled goods. This "cover effect" is thus a strategy used by smugglers to minimize the risks involved in the smuggling business. It is easier to hide smuggled goods when a certain quantity of legal goods is cleared with the customs authority (Kemp, 1976).

Despite the capacity of actors to easily move across the border, and to reduce risks in their business in a very substantial way, smuggling at the Goma-Gisenyi border is not a completely safe affair. The risk of being arrested and losing goods is real, in particular when goods are smuggled into Gisenyi. Although their collaboration with soldiers prevents them from being easily arrested at the border, smugglers are still exposed to the risk of being arrested and punished by RRA agents or police officers encountered on their way to the markets. Normally, to compensate this risk, smugglers would sell their goods at high prices in order to make a good profit. However, this is not the case. The analysis in the previous section shows that the profits are not as high as one might expect. In fact, shop owners oblige the smugglers to reduce their prices, as they also run the risk of being caught by RRA inspectors.

Both the suppliers of smuggled commodities (smugglers) and the buyers (shop owners) face this risk. Smugglers are rarely retailers of the smuggled commodities to the final consumers (households). They usually sell commodities to shop owners, who resell them to the final consumers. Since the enforcement agencies in Gisenyi make regular and unannounced inspections in shops where smuggled commodities originating from Goma are believed to be sold, shop owners also run a risk of being punished, which in turn effect prices smugglers get for their goods. Aware of such a risk, shop owners force smugglers to sell their commodities below tax-inclusive prices. A shop owner in Gisenyi commented as follows:

"… *We usually oblige them (smugglers) to sell us the commodities at cheaper prices, as we know that they do not pay taxes, and most importantly because we are taking the risk of selling their commodities in our shops. Do you know the risk I am running to sell such commodities in my shop? If they (the RRA authorities) arrive here and find smuggled commodities, they will seize them. I will have to pay a fine, and I may even be imprisoned and lose my business. Therefore, to compensate all those risks, the have to reduce the prices…*"

The risk run by shop owners who sell smuggled products in Gisenyi and other cities in Rwanda is evident. In April 2012, we met Jeanine at the border. Jeanine was a shop owner in Mahoko, a small rural area located 15 km from Gisenyi. At that time, she was just released from prison where she spent six months for selling smuggled products in her shop for the second time in the same month. As RRA confiscated all smuggled products, which represented more than 50 per cent of her business she also lost her entire working capital.

It is therefore understandable that shop owners request a reward from the smugglers. This reward is the reduction of the smugglers' sales prices. In Gisenyi, due to regular inspections by RRA agents, shop owners appear to be the actors who run the highest risk of detection and punishment in the smuggling business. After crossing the border and selling their commodities, smugglers transfer the risk to the shop owners. It is for this transfer of risk that shop owners require a reward from the smugglers.

Since economic agents are naturally averse to risk, shop owners may agree to purchase smuggled commodities at the legal price if they do not face any risk. But if they do face a risk, it is obvious that the smuggling price will be lower than the legal price (Sheik, 1989).

In an empirical study carried out in Pakistan, Sheikh (1974) demonstrated that the price of smuggled televisions was lower in areas situated far away from their border entry points than the price of the same items in areas close to the border entry points. Sheikh argues that the difference between the two prices was due to the high risk faced by consumers in areas far away from the border of being punished if caught purchasing and consuming smuggled commodities. This result suggests that as long as consumers can buy smuggled goods without being punished, they can agree to pay the same price as legally imported goods; otherwise they will require a lower price for the risk taken.

It is important to recall that the ability of smugglers to reduce risk in the smuggling business is one of the major factors explaining their success. In a context where traders are able to mitigate the risk bound to their business, it is not surprising that they are able to smuggle huge quantities of goods needed by the local population. On the other hand, since shop owners are also exposed to risk, they require the traders to sell their commodities at a lower price than the legal price.

However, what is astonishing in the Goma-Gisenyi case is that even the shop owners sell smuggled commodities to households below the legal prices. This situation can be explained by two factors: the low purchasing power of the final consumers, and the competition from goods produced locally or imported at low cost (because exempted from customs duties) from countries that are members of the East African Community. As for the local consumers, the quality of goods originating from Goma is better than that of competing goods, so at an equivalent price they prefer to buy commodities smuggled in from Goma. However, a small difference in price to the advantage of competitive goods could oblige the local population to abandon the consumption of smuggled goods.

Accordingly, given the competition faced by goods imported from Goma and the low purchasing power of the end consumers, shop owners are obliged to sell smuggled goods at prices, which are not above those of the competitive goods, thus allowing local people to buy those commodities at cheaper prices. The combination of elements evoked above (lower transaction costs, competition of goods produced locally or imported from other neighboring countries) explains why smuggling prices are much lower than tax-inclusive prices.

Concluding remarks

In contrast to many studies of the welfare impact of smuggling, we used data collected from small traders and households for a local impact analysis, estimating the gain generated for the different actors involved. This study has brought out the economic importance of smuggling in Africa, and the need for scholars to continue researching this phenomenon given its outstanding welfare impact. As argued in this paper, the lack of interest in this debate is astonishing, given the importance of smuggling in African international trade.

Our aim was to analyze the context and drivers of smuggling, and to contribute to an understanding of the welfare impact of smuggling. A comparison between smuggling prices and tax-inclusive prices reveals that smuggling has reduced the prices of imported commodities significantly both in Goma and in Gisenyi and generates a substantial consumer surplus for households in the two cities. Given the size of the incomes that this business generates, and its capacity to create a consumer surplus for households, policy makers should pay more attention to this phenomenon.

The literature on smuggling predicts that the strengthening of enforcement activities can eliminate or at least reduce smuggling. Fausti (1992) argues for example that the enforcement activities of the government, which increase the probability of smugglers being detected, and the monetary penalty, should normally suffice to reduce smuggling activities. But the case of Rwanda seems to contradict this. According to RRA officers, smuggling has increased rather than decreased since the RRA started its tough policy of fighting smuggling. Thus, enforcement does not seem to be the appropriate response to smuggling at this particular border, since people smuggle because of the lack of other remunerated activities.

A possible solution might be to create an environment, which can facilitate the formalization and legitimatization of smuggling without killing the activity. One way to make this happen is to reduce customs duties or more generally to make sure that transaction costs in formal trade are equal to the smugglers' transaction costs (which include bribes, remuneration of middlemen and transportation costs). Moreover, the Congolese and Rwandan governments should take steps to combat the harassments traders undergo at the border, and lessen the customs bureaucracy that increases traders' non-monetary transaction costs. Traders spend much time to clear their commodities, and combined with other administrative harassments it is an important motivation for smuggling. It can be reduced if the documentary requirements for importing goods are reduced, and the two countries put in place transparent procedures for goods clearance. By doing so, the governments will confer to smuggling a legitimacy which will protect smugglers from the abuses they sometime suffer in the hands of border officials.

Such a formalization of smuggling may be profitable both for the government and for the smugglers.

The government will see its tax revenue increased, because bribes and commissions paid to border officers and middlemen will be used to pay taxes. Furthermore, by formalizing the smuggling business, governments will broaden their tax base and this may enable them to reduce the level of customs duties (Lesser & Moisé-Leeman, 2009). For smugglers, the benefit of this formalization is that it will render more certain the environment in which they operate, while the profitability of their activity will not be affected because transaction costs will not increase. Local consumers should normally continue enjoying imported commodities at cheaper prices despite the formalization of smuggling, since prices would not increase, given that the transaction costs of the smugglers would remain unchanged.

References

Akinboade, O. A. (2005), 'A review of Women, Poverty and informal Trade Issues in East and Southern Africa', *International Social Studies Journal*, Vol. 57, No. 184, June, 255-275.

Ansoms, A. (2008), 'Striving for growth, bypassing the poor ? A critical review of Rwanda's rural sector policies', *Journal of Modern African Studies*, Vol. 46, No. 1, March,1-32.

Azam, J. P. (2007), *Trade, exchange rate and growth in Sub-Saharan Africa*, Cambridge University Press, Cambridge, UK.

Barka, H. B. (2012), *Border Posts, Checkpoints, and Intra-African Trade: Challenges and Solutions*, African Development Bank, Abidjan, Côte d'Ivoire.

Beard. T. R., Paula A. G. and Richard P. S. (1997), 'Border-Crossing Sales, Tax Avoidance, and State Tax Policies: An Application to Alcohol', *Southern Economic Journal*, Vol. 64, No. 1, July, 293-306.

Bhagwati, J. N. and Hansen, B. (1973), 'A theoretical Analysis of Smuggling', *Quarterly journal of economics*, Vol. 87, No. 2, 172-187.

Büscher, K. and Vlassenroot, K. (2010), 'Humanitarian presence and urban development: new opportunities and contrasts in Goma, DRC'. *Disasters*, Vol. 34, No. S2, April, S256-S273.

Connoly, M., Devereux, J. and Cortes, M. (1995), 'The Transshipment Problem: Smuggling and Welfare in Paraguay', *World Development*,Vol. 23, No. 6, June, 975-985.

Deaedorff, A. V. and Stolper, W. F. (1990), 'Effects of Smuggling under African Conditions. A factual, Institutional and analytic Discussion', *Weltwirtschaftliches Archiv*, Vol. 126, No. 1, March, 116-141.

Doevenspeck, M. and Morisho, M. N. (2012), 'Navigating uncertainty: Observations from the Congo-Rwanda border', in *Subverting Borders. doing Research on Smuggling and small-scale Trade*, B. Bruns,and J. Miggelbrink (eds), 85-106, VS, Wiesbaden, Germany.

Economic Commission for Africa (2010), *Assessing Regional Integration in Africa IV. Enhancing Intra-African Trade*, Addis Ababa, Ethiopia.

Falvey, R. (1978), 'A Note on preferential and illegal Trade under quantitative Restriction', *Quarterly journal of economics*, Vol. 92, No. 1, February, 175-178.

Fausti, S.W. (1992), 'Smuggling and parallel Markets for Exports', *The International trade journal*, Vol. 6, No. 4, 443-470.

Golub, S. (2010), *The Role of Transit and Re-export Trade in Togo's Economy*, Paper Prepared for Togo DTIS/CEM, http://www.swarthmore.edu/Documents/academics/economics/Golub/Togo-reexports.pdf (accessed: 03.03.2014)

Henderson, A. (1941), 'Consumer's Surplus and the Compensating variation', *The Review of Economic Studies*,Vol. 8, No. 2, February, 117-121.

Janvry, A. de and Sadoulet, E. (2009), *The impact of rising Food Prices on Households Welfare in India*, Working paper, UC Berkley: Institute for Research on Labor and Employment, Berkley, USA.

Jubilee- Zambia Debt and trade Desk (2008), *A Synthesis of Case Studies on Trade Constraints faced by local Communities*, http//www.jctr.org.zm (accessed: 03.03.2014).

Kemp, M.C. (1976), 'Smuggling and Optimal Commercial Policy'. *Journal of Public Economics,* Vol. 5, No. 3-4, April-May, 381-384.

Kimanuka, C. and Lange, M. (2010), *Petit commerce et amélioration des relations transfrontalières entre Goma (RD Congo), et Gisenyi (Rwanda)*, International Alert, London, UK.

Kiratu, S. and Suryapratim, R. (2010), *Beyond Barriers: The gender Implications of Trade Liberalization in Southern Africa*, International Institute for Sustainable Development, Winnipeg, Canada.

Lesser, C. and Moisé-Leeman, E. (2009), *Informal Cross-Border Trade and Trade Facilitation Reform in Sub-Saharan Africa*, Trade Policy Working Paper No. 86, OECD, Paris, France.

Little, P. (2007), *Unofficial Cross-Border Trade in Eastern Africa*, Paper Presented at the FAO workshop on "Staple Food Trade and Market Policy Options for Promoting Development in Eastern and Southern Africa, March 1-2, 2007, FAO Headquarters, Rome, Italy.

Lovely, M.E (1994), 'Crossing the Border: Does Commodity Tax Evasion Reduce Welfare and Can Enforcement Improve It?'*The Canadian Journal of Economics / Revue Canadienne d'Economique*, Vol. 27, No. 1, February, 157-174.

Lovely, M. E. and Nelson, D. (1995), 'Smuggling and Welfare in a Ricardo-Viner Economy', *Journal of Economic Studies*, Vol. 22, No. 6, October, 26-45.

Macedo, J. B. de (1987), 'Currency Inconvertibility, Trade Taxes and Smuggling', *Journal of Development Economics,* Vol. 27, No. 1-2, October, 109-125.

Martin, L. and Panagariya, A. (1984), 'Smuggling, Trade, and Price Disparity: A crime-theoretic

Approach', *Journal of International Economics*, Vol. 17, No. 3-4, November, 201–217.

National Institute of Statistics of Rwanda (2011), 'The Third Integrated Household Living Conditions Survey', *Main Indicators Report*, Kigali, Rwanda.

Okuro, S. O. (2011), 'Globalization and the Question of Women Smugglers in East Africa: Observations of a Cross Kenya-Uganda Boundary (1980-2002)', in *Global Exchanges and Gender Perspectives in Africa*, J.-B. Ouédraogo and R. M. Achieng' (eds), p. 95-113, Codestria, Dakar, Senegal.

Perloff, J.M. (2003), *Microeconomic*, Prentice Hall, Upper Saddle River, USA.

Pitt, M. (1981), 'Smuggling and Price Disparity', *Journal of International economics*, Vol. 11, No. 4, November, 447-458.

Sheikh, M. A. (1974), 'Smuggling, Production and Welfare', *Journal of international economics*, Vol. 4, No. 4, November, 355-364.

Sheikh, M. A. (1977), 'A Partial Equilibrium Model of Smuggling', *Review of World Economics*, Vol. 113, No. 2, June, 268-283.

Sheikh, M. A. (1989), 'A Theory of Risk, Smuggling and Welfare', *World Development*, Vol. 17, No. 12, December, 1931-1944.

Tegera, A. and Johnson, D. (2007), *Rules For Sale: Formal and informal cross-border trade in Eastern DRC*, Pole Institute, Regards Croisés 19, Goma, Congo.

Thursby, M. and Jensen, R. (1991), 'Smuggling, Camouflaging, and Market Structure', *The Quarterly Journal of Economics*, Vol. 106, No. 3, August, 789-814.

World Bank (2011), *Facilitating Cross-Border Trade between the DRC and Neighbors in the Great Lakes Region of Africa: Improving Conditions for Poor Traders*, World Bank, Washington DC, USA.

L'HARMATTAN ITALIA
Via Degli Artisti 15; 10124 Torino
harmattan.italia@gmail.com

L'HARMATTAN HONGRIE
Könyvesbolt ; Kossuth L. u. 14-16
1053 Budapest

L'HARMATTAN KINSHASA
185, avenue Nyangwe
Commune de Lingwala
Kinshasa, R.D. Congo
(00243) 998697603 ou (00243) 999229662

L'HARMATTAN CONGO
67, av. E. P. Lumumba
Bât. – Congo Pharmacie (Bib. Nat.)
BP2874 Brazzaville
harmattan.congo@yahoo.fr

L'HARMATTAN GUINÉE
Almamya Rue KA 028, en face
du restaurant Le Cèdre
OKB agency BP 3470 Conakry
(00224) 657 20 85 08 / 664 28 91 96
harmattanguinee@yahoo.fr

L'HARMATTAN MALI
Rue 73, Porte 536, Niamakoro,
Cité Unicef, Bamako
Tél. 00 (223) 20205724 / +(223) 76378082
poudiougopaul@yahoo.fr
pp.harmattan@gmail.com

L'HARMATTAN CAMEROUN
BP 11486
Face à la SNI, immeuble Don Bosco
Yaoundé
(00237) 99 76 61 66
harmattancam@yahoo.fr

L'HARMATTAN CÔTE D'IVOIRE
Résidence Karl / cité des arts
Abidjan-Cocody 03 BP 1588 Abidjan 03
(00225) 05 77 87 31
etien_nda@yahoo.fr

L'HARMATTAN BURKINA
Penou Achille Some
Ouagadougou
(+226) 70 26 88 27

L'HARMATTAN SÉNÉGAL
10 VDN en face Mermoz, après le pont de Fann
BP 45034 Dakar Fann
33 825 98 58 / 33 860 9858
senharmattan@gmail.com / senlibraire@gmail.com
www.harmattansenegal.com

L'HARMATTAN BÉNIN
ISOR-BENIN
01 BP 359 COTONOU-RP
Quartier Gbèdjromèdé,
Rue Agbélenco, Lot 1247 I
Tél : 00 229 21 32 53 79
christian_dablaka123@yahoo.fr

Achevé d'imprimer par Corlet Numérique - 14110 Condé-sur-Noireau
N° d'Imprimeur : 134993 - Dépôt légal : janvier 2017 - *Imprimé en France*

www.ingramcontent.com/pod-product-compliance
Lightning Source LLC
LaVergne TN
LVHW010930061026
849535LV00007B/2332
* 9 7 8 2 3 4 3 1 1 2 2 6 8 *